THE

Christian Father's Present

TO HIS CHILDREN

by

John Angell James
Author of "Young Woman's Friend,"
"Christian Duty," "Christian Professor,"
"The Anxious Enquirer," "True Christian,"
"Widow Directed," Etc.

From the Seventeenth London Edition.

Soli Deo Gloria Publications
...for instruction in righteousness...

Soli Deo Gloria Publications
P.O. Box 451, Morgan, PA 15064
(412) 221-1901/FAX 221-1902

*

The Christian Father's Present to His Children
was reprinted in 1853 by Robert Carter and
Brothers, New York. This Soli Deo Gloria
reprint is 1993. The copy from which this
book was photo-lithographed is courtesy
of the Barbour Library at Pittsburgh
Theological Seminary.

*

ISBN 1-877611-70-0

*

Second printing 1995

*

Publisher's Note: Due to defects in the original
copy, it was necessary to reproduce 4 pages on a
computer. We were unable to match the printer's
font from the 1853 edition.

PREFACE.

As a *Christian,* the author of the following volume believes that there is a state of everlasting happiness prepared beyond the grave for those, and those only, who are partakers of pure and undefiled religion ; and, as a *parent,* he will freely confess, his supreme solicitude is, that his children, by a patient continuance in well doing, might seek for glory, honor, immortality ; and finally possess themselves of eternal life. He is not insensible to the worth of temporal advantages ; he is neither cynic nor ascetic ; he appreciates the true value of wealth, learning, science, and reputation, which he desires, in such measure as God shall see fit to bestow, both for himself and his children ; he has conquered the world, but does not despise it ; he resists its yoke as a master, but values its ministrations as a servant. Still, however, he views the present state of sublunary affairs as a splendid pageant, the fashion of which passeth away to give place to the glory

which shall never be moved: " he looketh not at the
things which are seen, but at the things which are
not seen; for things which are seen are temporal,
but things which are not seen are eternal." It is
on this ground that he attaches so much importance
to a *religious* education. To those, if such there
should be, who imagine that he is too anxious about
this matter, and has said too much about it, he has
simply to reply, that " he believes, therefore has he
spoken." The man who does not make the religious character of his children the supreme end of
all his conduct towards them, may profess to believe as a Christian, but certainly acts as an Atheist; besides, if *this* end be secured, the most likely
step is taken for accomplishing every other; as
" godliness is profitable for all things, having the
promise of the life that now is, as well as that which
is to come."

With these views, the Author has embodied in
the following volume his own parental wishes, objects, and pursuits. Much that is here written, has
been the subject of his personal converse with his
children, and should God spare his life, will still
continue to be the topics of his instruction.

What is beneficial to his own family, the Author

thought might be no less useful to others; and this was another reason which induced him to publish. The multiplication of books of this kind, even if they make small pretensions to classic elegance of composition, is to be looked upon as a benefit, provided they contain sound scriptural sentiments, and an obvious tendency to produce right moral impressions. Books are sometimes read merely because they are new; it is desirable therefore, to gratify this appetite for novelty, when at the same time we can strengthen and build up the moral character by a supply of wholesome and nutritious food. Nor is it always necessary that new books should contain new topics, or new modes of illustration, any more than it is necessary that there should be a perpetual change in the kinds of food, in order to attain to bodily strength. Whatever varieties may be introduced by the wisdom that is sensual, bread will still remain the staff of life. So there are some primitive truths and subjects, which, whatever novelties and curiosities may be introduced for the gratification of religious taste, must still be repeated, as essential to the formation of religious character.

The Author has not selected the sermonic form of discussion, because some of his subjects did not admit of it; and also because sermons are perhaps the least inviting species of reading to young people. Letters would not have been liable to these objections; but, upon the whole, he preferred the form of chapters, in which the style of direct address is preserved. The advantage of this style is obvious; it not only keeps up the reader's interest, but, as every parent who presents this volume to his children adopts the advice as his own, such young persons, by an easy effort of the imagination, lose sight of the Author, and read the language of their own father. If anything is necessary to secure this effect, beyond the simple act of presenting this book, it might be immediately obtained by an inscription to the child, written by the parents own hand upon the fly-leaf.

The Author scarcely need say that his work is not intended for young people below the age of fourteen. In the composition of the book, a seeming tautology sometimes occurs; what is just touched upon in one place, is more expanded in others; and some subjects are intentionally repeated. To give additional interest to the volume, numerous extracts, and some anecdotes are introduced, which tend to relieve the dulness of didactic composition, and prevent the tedium of unvarying monotony.

In the references which the author has given to books, both in the chapter on that subject and in marginal notes, he does not wish to be considered as laying down, much less limiting, for young people a perfect course of reading; but as simply directing them to *some* works, which, among others, ought by no means to be neglected.

Once more let it be stated, and stated with all possible emphasis, that the chief design of this work is to form the religious character of its readers, and to implant those virtues which shall live, and flourish, and dignify, and delight, infinite ages, after every object that is dear to avarice or pride, to learning or science, to taste or ambition, shall have perished in the conflagration of the universe.

Contents.

V.

VI.

VII.

VIII.

IX.

X.

XI.

XII.

XIII.

XIV.

XV.

XVI.

XVII.

XVIII.

XIX.

XX.

XXI.

XXII.

XXIII.

XXIV.

XXV.

An Address to Christian Parents.

MY DEAR FRIENDS,—

IT is a situation of tremendous responsibility to be a parent: for the manner in which you discharge the duties of this relation, you must give an account in that awful day when the secrets of all hearts shall be judged by Jesus Christ. With every babe that God entrusts to your care, he in effect sends the solemn injunction—" Take this child, and bring it up for me;" and at the final audit, will inquire in what manner you have obeyed the command. It will not then be sufficient to plead the strength of your affection, nor the ceaseless efforts to which it gave rise; for if these efforts were not directed to a right end, if all your solicitude was lavished upon inferior objects, you will receive the rebuke of Him that sitteth upon the throne.

It is of infinite importance that you should contemplate your children in their true character. They are *animal* beings, and therefore it is highly proper that you should use every effort to provide them with suitable food, clothing, habitations, and everything else that can conduce to the comfort of their present existence. They are *social* beings, and it is important that you should qualify them to enjoy the comforts, and discharge the duties of social life. They are *rational* beings, and it is your duty to furnish them with every possible advantage for the culture of their minds. But if you look no further than this, you leave out of sight the grandest and most interesting relations in which they can be seen, and will of course neglect the most important of your duties towards them: for they are IMMORTAL beings; the stamp of eternity is upon them; everlasting ages are before them. They are like the rest of the human race—depraved, guilty, and condemned creatures; and consequently in danger of eternal misery. Yet are they, through the mercy of God, and the mediation of Christ, creatures capable of attaining to glory, honor, immortality, and eternal life. Looking upon them in this light (and this is the light in which you profess to contemplate them), say what *should* be your chief anxiety concerning them, and what your conduct towards them?

Recognizing in your children beings placed in this world in a state of probation, and hastening to eternal happiness or torment, will you be contented to seek for them anything short of ETERNAL SALVATION? Even a Deist, who has any belief of a future state of reward and punishment, does not act consistently, unless he is supremely desirous of the *everlasting* welfare of his children. None but an avowed Atheist can, with the least propriety, fix his aim lower for his children than the possession of a happy immortality. But, in the case of a *Christian parent*, it is in the highest degree inconsistent, absurd, cruel, and wicked ever to lose sight of this in the arrangements which he makes for his family, or in the manner of conducting himself towards them. Do you really believe in the ruin of the human race by sin, and their recovery by Christ? in the existence of such states as heaven and hell? in the necessity of a life of faith and holiness, in order to escape the one and secure the other? Then act up to these solemn convictions, not only in reference to your own salvation, but to the salvation of your children. Let a supreme concern for their immortal interests be at the bottom of all your conduct, and be interwoven with all your parental habits. Let them have, in the fullest sense of the term, a CHRISTIAN EDUCATION. Act so towards them and for them, as that you shall be able to say to them, however they may turn out—" I take you to record that *I* am clear of your blood."

But my principal object in this address is to *point out what appear to me to be the most prevailing obstacles to success in the religious education of children.*

That, in many cases, the means employed by Christian parents for their children's spiritual welfare are unsuccessful, is a melancholy fact, established by abundant, and, I fear, accumulating evidence. I am not now speaking of those families (and are there indeed such ?) where scarcely the semblance of domestic piety or instruction is to be found, where no family altar is seen, no family prayer is heard, no parental admonition is delivered! What! this cruel, wicked, ruinous neglect of their children's immortal interests in the families of *professors!* Monstrous inconsistency! shocking dereliction of principle! No wonder that *their* children go astray. This is easily accounted for. Some of the most profligate young people that I know, have issued from such households. Their prejudices against religion, and their enmity to its forms, are greater than those of the children of avowed worldlings. Inconsistent, hypocritical, negligent professors of religion, frequently excite in their sons and daughters an unconquerable aversion and disgust against piety, which seems to produce in them a determination to place themselves at the furthest possible remove from its influence.

But I am now speaking of the failure of a religious education, where it has been, in some measure, carried on ; instances of which are by no means unfrequent. Too often do we hear the echo of David's sorrowful complaint, uttered by the distressed and disappointed Christian father, "Although my house be not so with God." Too often do we see the child of many prayers and many hopes forgetting the instructions he has received, and running with the multitude to do evil. Far be it from me to add affliction to affliction, by saying that this is to be traced, in every case, to parental neglect. I would not thus, as it were, pour nitre and vinegar upon the bleeding wounds with which filial impiety has lacerated many a father's mind. I would not thus cause the wretched parent to exclaim—" Reproach hath broken my heart, already *half-broken* by my child's misconduct." I know that in many cases no blame whatever could be thrown on the parent; and that it was the depravity of the child alone, which nothing could subdue but the power of the Holy Ghost, that led to the melancholy result. The best possible scheme of Christian education, most judiciously directed, and most perseveringly maintained, has, in some cases, totally failed. God is a sovereign, and He hath mercy on whom He will have mercy. Still, however, there is in the order of means a tendency in a religious education to secure the desired result; and God usually does bless, with His saving influence, such efforts. " Train up a child in the way he should go, and when he is old he will not depart from it." This is certainly true, as a general rule, though there are many exceptions to it.

I shall now lay before you the principal obstacles to the success of religious education, as they strike *my* mind.

First—*It is frequently too negligently and capriciously maintained, even where it is not totally omitted.*

It is obvious, that, if at all attended to, it should be attended to with anxious earnestness, systematic order, and perpetual regularity. It should not be maintained as a dull form, an unpleasant drudgery, but as a matter of deep and delightful interest. The heart of the parent should be entirely and obviously engaged. A part of every returning Sabbath should be spent by him in the instruction of his filial charge; and his concern should be embodied, more or less, with the whole habit of parental conduct. The father may lead the usual devotions at the family altar; the mother may join with him in teaching their children catechism, hymns, and scripture; but, if this be unattended by serious admonition, visible anxiety, and strenuous effort to lead their children to think seriously on religion, as a matter of infinite importance, little good can be expected. A cold, formal, capricious system of religious instruction, is rather likely to create prejudice against religion, than prepossession in its favor.

Then again, a religious education should be *consistent*—it should extend to *everything* that is likely to assist in the formation of character. It should not be a mere abstract tuition, but a complete whole. It should select the schools, the companions, the amusements, the books of youth; for if it do nothing more than merely teach a form of sound words to the understanding and to the memory, while the impression of the heart and the formation of the character are neglected, very little is to be expected from such efforts. A handful of seed, scattered now and then upon the ground, without order or perseverance, might as rationally be expected to produce a good crop, as that a mere lukewarm, capricious, religious education, should be followed by true piety. If the parent be not *visibly in earnest*, it cannot be expected that the child will be so. Religion, by every Christian parent, is theoretically acknowledged to be the most important thing in the world; but if in practice the father appears a thousand times more anxious for the son to be a good scholar than a real Christian, and the mother more solicitous for the daughter to be a good dancer or musician than a child of God, they may teach what they like in the way of good doctrine, but they are not to look for genuine piety as the result: this can only be expected where it is really taught and inculcated as the *one thing needful*.

Secondly—*The relaxation of domestic discipline* is another obstacle in the way of a successful religious education.

A parent is invested by God with a degree of authority over his children, which he cannot neglect to use, without being guilty of trampling under foot the institutions of heaven. Every family is a community, the government of which is strictly despotic, though not tyrannical. Every father is a sovereign, though not an oppressor; he is a legislator, and not merely a counsellor; and his will should be law, not merely advice. He is to command, to restrain, to punish; and children are required to obey: he is, if necessary, to threaten, to rebuke, to chastise ; and they are to submit with reverence. He is to decide what books shall be read, what companions invited, what engagements formed, and how time is to be spent. If he sees anything wrong, he is not to interpose merely with the timid, feeble, ineffectual protest of Eli—"Why do ye thus, my sons ?" but with the firm though mild prohibition. He must *rule* his own house ; and by the whole of his conduct make his children feel that obedience is his due and his demand.

The want of discipline, wherever it exists, is supplied by confusion and domestic anarchy. Every thing goes wrong in the absence of this. A gardener may sow the choicest seeds ; but if he neglect to pluck up weeds, and prune wild luxuriances, he must not expect to see his flowers grow, or his garden flourish ; and so a parent may deliver the best instructions ; but if he do not, by discipline, eradicate evil tempers, correct bad habits, repress rank corruptions, nothing excellent can be looked for. He may be a good prophet and a good priest ; but if he be not also a good KING, all else is vain. When once a man breaks his sceptre, or lends it to his children as a plaything, he may give up his hopes of success from a religious education.

I have seen the evil resulting from a want of discipline in innumerable families, both amongst my brethren in the ministry and others. Frightful instances of disorder and immorality are now present to my mind, which I could almost wish to forget. The misfortune, in many families is, that discipline is unsteady and capricious, sometimes carried even to tyranny itself, at others relaxed into a total suspension of law ; so that the children are at one time trembling like slaves, at others revolting like rebels ; at one time groaning beneath an iron yoke, at others rioting in a state of lawless liberty. This is a most mischievous system, and its effects are generally, just what might be expected.

In some cases discipline commences too late, in others it ceases too early. A father's magisterial office is nearly coëval with his parental relation. A child, as soon as he can reason, should be made to feel that obedience is due to parents ; for if he grow up to boyhood before he is subject to the mild rule of paternal authority, he will, very probably, like an untamed bullock, resist the yoke. On the other hand, as long as children continue beneath the parental roof, they are to be subject to the rules of domestic discipline. Many parents greatly err in abdicating the throne in favor of a son or daughter, because the child is *becoming* a man or a woman. It is truly pitiable to see a boy or girl of fifteen, just returned from school, allowed to sow the seeds of revolt in the domestic community, and to act in opposition to parental authority, till the too compliant father gives the reins of government into filial hands, or else by his conduct declares his children to be in a state of independence. There need not be any contest for power : for where a child has been accustomed to obey, even from an infant, the yoke of obedience will gen·rally be light and easy ;

if not, and a rebellious temper should begin to show itself early, a judicious father should be on his guard, and suffer no encroachments on his prerogative; while, at the same time, the increased power of his authority, like the increased pressure of the atmosphere, should be felt without being seen, and this will make it irresistible.

Thirdly, *Undue severity,* in the other extreme, is as injurious as unlimited indulgence.

If injudicious fondness has slain its tens of thousands, unnecessary harshness has destroyed its thousands. By an authority which cannot err, we are told that the cords of *love* are the bands of a man. There is a plastic power in love. The human mind is so constituted as to yield readily to the influence of kindness. Men are more easily led to their duty than driven to it. A child, says an eastern proverb, may lead the elephant by a single hair. You remember, and perhaps have often seen verified, the old story of the Sun, the Wind, and the Traveler. Love seems so essential an element of parental character that there is something shockingly revolting not only in a cruel, not only in an unkind or severe, but even in a coldhearted father. Study the parental character as it is exhibited in that most exquisitely touching moral picture, the parable of the Prodigal Son. When a father governs entirely by cold, bare, uncovered authority; by mere commands, prohibitions and threats, by frowns, untempered with smiles; when the friend is never blended with the legislator, nor authority modified with love; when his conduct produces only a servile fear in the hearts of his children instead of a generous affection; when he is served from a dread of the effects of disobedience rather than from a sense of the pleasure of obedience; when he is rather dreaded in the family circle as a frowning spectre than hailed as the guardian angel of its joys; when even accidents raise a storm, or faults produce a hurricane of passion in his bosom; when offenders are driven to equivocation or lying, with the hope of averting by concealment those severe corrections which disclosure always entails; when unnecessary interruptions are made to innocent enjoyments; when, in fact, nothing of the father, but everything of the tyrant is seen: can we expect religion to grow in such a soil as this? Yes, as rationally as we may look for the tenderest hot-house plant to thrive amidst the rigors of eternal frost.

It is useless for such a father to teach *religion;* he chills the soul of his pupils; he hardens their hearts against impression; he prepares them to rush with eager haste to their ruin as soon as they have thrown off the yoke of their bondage; and to employ their liberty, as affording the means of unbridled gratification. Like a company of African slaves, they are at first tortured by their thraldom, and by that very bondage, trained up to convert their sudden emancipation into a means of destruction.

Let parents, then, in all their conduct, blend the lawgiver and the friend, temper authority with kindness, and realize in their measure that representation of Deity which Dr. Watts has given us, where he says,

> " Sweet majesty and awful love
> Sit smiling on his brow."

In short, let them so act, that their children shall be convinced that their law is holy, and their commandment is holy, and just, and good ; and that to be so governed it to be blessed.

Fourthly.—*The inconsistent conduct of parents* themselves is a frequent and powerful obstacle to success in religious education.

Example has been affirmed to be omnipotent, and its power, like that of gravitation, to be in proportion to the nearness of the attracting body : what, then, must be the influence of *parental* example ? Now, as I am speaking of *religious* parents it is of course assumed that they do exhibit, in some measure, the reality of religion ; but may not the reality often be seen, where much of the beauty of true godliness is obscured, just as the sun is beheld when his effulgence is quenched in a mist ; or as a lovely prospect is seen through the haze, which veils the beauty of the scene, though it does not altogether conceal its extent. Religion may be seen in dim outline by the children in their parents' conduct, but it is attended with so many minor inconsistencies, such a mist of imperfections, that it presents little to conciliate their regard, or raise their esteem. There is so much worldly-mindedness, so much conformity to fashionable follies, so much irregularity of domestic piety, such frequent sallies of unchristian temper, such inconsolable grief and querulous complaint under the trials of life, such frequent animosities towards their fellow Christians, observable in the conduct of some Christians, that their children see religion to the greatest possible disadvantage, and the consequence is, that it either lowers their standard of piety, or inspires a disgust towards it altogether. Parents, as you would wish your instructions and admonitions to your family to be successful, enforce them by the power of a holy example, It is not enough for you to be pious on the whole, but you should be wholly pious ; not only to be real disciples, but eminent ones ; not only sincere Christians, but consistent ones. Your standard of religion should be very high. To some parents I would give this advice, " *Say* less about religion to your children, or else *manifest* more of its influence. Leave off family prayer, or else leave off family sins." Beware how you act, for all your actions are seen at home. Never talk of religion but with reverence, be not forward to speak of the faults of your fellow Christians, and when the subject is introduced, let it be in a spirit of charity towards the offender, and of decided abhorrence of the fault. Many parents have done irreparable injury to their children's minds by a proneness to find out, to talk of, and almost to rejoice over the inconsistencies of professing Christians. Never cavil at, nor find fault with the religious exercises of the minister you attend; but rather commend his discourses, in order that your children may listen to them with greater attention. Direct their views to the most eminent Christians, and point out to them the loveliness of exemplary piety. In short, seeing that your example may be expected so much to aid or to frustrate your efforts for the conversion of your children, consider " what manner of persons ought ye to be in all holy conversation and godliness."

Fifthly.—Another obstacle to the success of religious instruction is sometimes found *in the wild conduct of an elder branch of the family, especially in the case of a dissipated son.*

The elder branches of a family are found, in general, to have considerable influence over the rest, and oftentimes to give the tone of morals to the others; they are looked up to by their younger brothers and sisters; they bring companions, books, amusements into the house; and thus form the character of their juniors. It is of great consequence therefore that parents should pay particular attention to their elder children; and if unhappily the habits of these should be decidedly unfriendly to the religious improvement of the rest, they should be removed, if possible, from the family. One profligate son may lead all his brothers astray. I have seen this, in some cases, most painfully verified. A parent may feel unwilling to send from home an unpromising child, under the apprehension that he will grow worse and worse ; but kindness to him in this way is cruelty to the others. Wickedness is contagious, especially when the diseased person is a brother.

Sixthly.—*Bad companions* out of the house counteract all the influence of religious instruction delivered at home.

A Christian parent should ever be on the alert to watch the associations which his children are inclined to form. On this subject I have said much to the young themselves in the following work ; but it is a subject which equally concerns the parent. One ill-chosen friend of your children's may undo all the good you are the means of doing at home. It is impossible for you to be sufficiently vigilant on this point. From their very infancy encourage them to look up to you as the selectors of their companions ; impress them with the necessity of this, and form in them a habit of consulting you at all times. Never encourage an association which is not likely to have a decidedly friendly influence on their religious character. This caution was never more necessary than in the present age. Young people are brought very much together by the religious institutions which are now formed, and altogether there is a great probability that in such a circle suitable companions will be found, yet it is too much even for charity to believe that all the active young friends of Sunday Schools, Juvenile Missionary Societies, &c., are fit companions for our sons and our daughters.

Seventhly.—*The schisms which sometimes arise in our churches, and imbitter the minds of Christians against each other*, have a very unfriendly influence upon the minds of the young.

They see so much that is opposite to the spirit and genius of Christianity in both parties, and enter so deeply into the views and feelings of one of them, that either their attention is drawn off from the essentials of religion, or their prejudices raised against them. I look upon this as one of the most painful and mischievous consequences of ecclesiastical contentions.

Eightly.—*The neglect of young persons by our churches and their pastors*, is another impediment to the success of domestic religious instruction.

This, however, does not so much appertain to parents in their separate capacity, as in their relation as members of a Christian society, and even in this relation it belongs less to them, than to their pastors. There is a blank yet to be filled up in reference to the treatment of the young who are not in church communion. As a Dissenter, I object of course to the rite of Confirmation as practised in the Established Church; but we want something, I will not say like it, but in lieu of it. We want something that shall recognize the young, interest them, attract them, guard them.

Ninthly.—*The spirit of filial independence*, which is sanctioned by the habits, if not by the opinions of the age, is another hinderance, and the last which

I shall mention, to the good effect contemplated and desired by a religious education.

The disposition, which is but too apparent in this age to enlarge the privileges of the children by diminishing the prerogative of their parents, is neither for the comfort of the latter, nor for the well-being of the former. Rebellion against a justly constituted authority can never be in any case a blessing, and all wise parents, together with all wise youth, will unite in supporting that just parental authority, which, however the precocious manhood of some might feel it to be an oppression, the more natural and slowly approaching maturity of others will acknowledge to be a blessing. Children who find the parental yoke a burden, are not very likely to look upon that of Christ as a benefit.

Such, my dear friends, as they appear to my mind, are the principal obstacles to the success of those efforts which are carried on by many for the religious education of their children. Seriously consider them; and, having looked at them, endeavor to avoid them. Survey them as the mariner does the flame of the light-house, for the purpose of avoiding the rock on which it is placed. Recognize your children, as every Christian parent should do, not only as animal, rational, social beings; but as immortal creatures, lost sinners, being invited to eternal life through the mediation of Christ; and while you neglect not any one means that can promote their comfort, reputation, and usefulness in this world, concentrate your chief solicitude, and employ your noblest energies, in a scriptural, judicious, persevering scheme of RELIGIOUS education. " Ye fathers, provoke not your children to wrath, but bring them up in the nurture and admonition of the Lord."

I.

The Anxiety of a Christian Parent for the Spiritual Welfare of his Children.

My Dear Children,—

NEVER did I pass a more truly solemn or interesting moment than that in which my first-born child was put into my arms, and when I felt that I was a father. A new solicitude was then produced in my bosom, which every succeeding day has tended to confirm and strengthen. I looked up to heaven and breathed over my babe the petition of Abraham for his son—" O! that Ishmael might live before thee !" Recognizing, in the little helpless being which had been so lately introduced into our world, a creature born for eternity, and who, when the sun shall be extinguished, would be still soaring in heaven or sinking in hell, I returned to the closet of private devotion, and solemnly dedicated the child to the God who had given me the precious boon ; and earnestly prayed that whatever might be his lot in this world, he might be a partaker of true piety, and numbered with the saints in glory everlasting.

During the days of your infancy I watched you, together with your sainted mother, with all the fondness of a parent's heart. We have smiled upon you when you were slumbering in healthful repose; we have wept over you when tossed with feverish restlessness and pain; we have been the delighted spectators of your childish sports; we have witnessed with pleasure the development of your intellectual powers, and have often listened, with somewhat of pride, to the commendations bestowed upon your persons and attainments. But amidst all, one deep solicitude took hold of our minds, which nothing could either divert or abate; and that was, *a deep anxiety for your spiritual welfare—for your religious character.*

You cannot doubt, my children, that your parents love you. In all your recollections, we have a witness to this. We have, as you know, done everything to promote your welfare; and, so far as was compatible with this object, your pleasure also. We have never denied you a gratification which our duty and ability allowed us to impart; and if at any time we have been severe in reproof, even *this* was an awful form of love. We have spared no expense in your education : in short, love, an intense love, of which you can at present form no adequate conception, has been the secret spring of all our conduct towards you; and, as the strongest proof and purest effort of our affection, we wish you to be partakers of true piety. Did we not cherish this anxiety, we should feel that amidst every other

expression of regard, we were acting towards you a
most cruel and unnatural part. Genuine love desires and seeks for the objects on which it is fixed
the greatest benefits of which they are capable; and
as you have a capacity to serve, and enjoy, and
glorify God by true religion, how can we love you
in reality, if we do not covet for you this high and
holy distinction? We should feel that our love
had exhausted itself upon trifles, and had let go
objects of immense, infinite, eternal consequence, if
it were not to concentrate all its prayers, desires,
and efforts in your personal religion.

Almost every parent has some one object, which
he desires, above all others, on behalf of his children.
Some are anxious that their offspring may shine as
warriors; others, that theirs may be surrounded
with the milder radiance of literary, scientific, and
commercial fame. Our supreme ambition for you
is, that whatever situation you occupy, you may
adorn it with the beauties of holiness, and discharge
its duties under the influence of Christian principles.
Much as we desire your respectability in life (and
we will not conceal our hope that you will occupy
no mean place in society), yet we would rather see
you in the most obscure, and even menial situation,
provided you were partakers of true piety, than
behold you on the loftiest pinnacle of the temple
of fame, the objects of universal admiration, if, at
the same time, your hearts were destitute of the
fear of God. We might, indeed, in the latter case,
be tempted to watch your ascending progress, and

hear the plaudits with which your elevation was followed, with something of a parent's vanity; but, when we retired from the dazzling scene to the seat of serious reflection, the spell would be instantly broken, and we should sorrowfully exclaim—"Alas! my son, what is all this, in the absence of religion, but soaring high, to have the greater fall!"

You must be aware, my dear children, that all our conduct towards you has been conducted upon these principles. Before you were capable of receiving instruction, we presented ceaseless prayer to God for your personal piety. As soon as reason dawned, we poured the light of religious instruction upon your mind, by the aid of familiar poetry, catechisms, and conversation. You cannot remember the time when these efforts commenced. How often have you retired with us, to become the subjects of our earnest supplications at the throne of grace! You have been the witnesses of our agony for your eternal welfare. Have we not instructed, warned, admonished, encouraged you, as we laid open to your view the narrow path which leadeth to eternal life? Have we not been guided by this object in the selection of schools for your education, companions for your amusement, books for your perusal? Has not this been so interwoven with all our conduct, that, if at any time you had been asked the question—" What is the chief object of your parents' solicitude on your account?" you must have said, at at once—" For my being truly pious." Yes, my children, this is most strictly true. At home, abroad, in sickness and in health, in prosperity and in adversity, this is the ruling solicitude of our bosoms.

How intently have we marked the development of your character, to see if our fondest wishes were likely to be gratified. We have observed your deportment under the sound of the gospel, and when you have appeared listless and uninterested, it has been as wormwood in our cup: while, on the other hand, when we have seen you listening with attention, quietly wiping away the tear of emotion, or retiring pensive and serious to your closet, we have rejoiced more than they which find great spoil. When we have looked on the conduct of any pious youth, we have uttered the wish, " O that my child were like him !" and have directed your attention to his character, as that which we wished you to make the model of your own. When, on the other hand, we have witnessed the behavior of some prodigal son, who has been the grief of his parents, the thought has been like a dagger to our heart, " What if my child should turn out thus !"

1. Now, we cherish all this solicitude on *our own account.* We candidly assure you that nothing short of this will make us happy. Your piety is the only thing that will make us rejoice that we are parents. How can we endure to see our children choosing any other ways than those of wisdom, and any other path than that of life ? How could we bear the sight, to behold you travelling along the broad road which leadeth to destruction, and running with the multitude to do evil ? " O God, hide

us from this sad spectacle, in the grave, and ere that time comes, take us to our rest." But how would it imbitter our last moments, and plant our dying pillow with thorns, to leave you on earth in an unconverted state ; following us to the grave, but not to heaven. Or should you be called to die before us, and take possession of the tomb in our names, how could we stand at " the dreadful post of observation, darker every hour," without one ray of hope for you, to cheer our wretched spirits ? How could we sustain the dreadful thought, which in spite of ourselves would sometimes steal across the bosom, that the very next moment after you had passed beyond our kind attentions, you would be received to the torments which know neither end nor mitigation ? And when you had departed under such circumstances, what could heal our wounds, or dry our tears ?

Should you become truly pious, this circumstance will impart to our bosoms a felicity which no language could enable me to describe. It will sweeten all our intercourse with you, establish our confidence, allay our fears, awaken our hopes. If we are prosperous, it will delight us to think that we are not acquiring wealth for those who will squander it on their lusts, but who will employ it for the glory of God when we are in dust. Or if we are poor, it will cheer us to reflect, that though we cannot leave you the riches of this world, we see you in possession of the favor of God, a portion which, after comforting you on earth, will enrich you through eternity. My dear children, if you are anxious to comfort the hearts of your parents, if you would fulfil our joy, if you would repay all our labor, anxiety, affection, if you would most effectually discharge all the obligations which you cannot deny you owe us, *Fear God, and choose the ways of religion :* this, this only will make us happy.

2. We cherish this solicitude on behalf of the *church*, and the cause of God.

We see every year conveyed to the tombs of their fathers, some valued and valuable members of the Christian church. We are perpetually called to witness the desolations of the last enemy in the garden of the Lord. How often do we exclaim over the corpse of some eminent Christian and benefactor, " Departed saint, how heavy the loss we have sustained by thy removal to a better state ! Who now shall fill up thy vacant seat, and bless like thee both the church and the world ?" My children, under these bereavements, to whom should we look but to you ? To whom should we turn but to the *children* of the kingdom, for *subjects* of the kingdom ? You are the property of the church. It has a claim upon you. Will ye not own it, and discharge it ? Must we see the walls of the spiritual house mouldering away, and you, the rightful materials with which it should be repaired, withheld ? We love the church, we long for its prosperity, we pray for its increase, and it cannot but be deeply distressing to us to witness the ravages of death, and, at the same time, to see the want of religion in those young persons whose parents during their life filled places of honor and usefulness in the fellowship of the faithful.

We are anxious for your being pious that you might be the instruments of blessing the *world* by the propagation of religion. The moral condition of the world is too bad for description. If it be ever improved, this must be done by Christians. True piety is the only reformer of mankind. A spirit of active benevolence has happily risen up, rich in purposes and means, for the benefit of the human race. But the men, in whose bosoms it now lives and moves, are not immortal upon earth ; they too must sleep in dust, and who then shall succeed them at their post and enter into their labors? Who will catch their falling mantle, and carry on their glorious undertaking for the salvation of millions? If it ever be done, it must be done of course by those who are now rising into life. The propagation of religion to the next generation, and to distant nations, depends on you, and on others of your age. While I write, the groans of creation are ascending, and future ages are rising up to plead with you, that you would bow to the influence of religion, as the only way of extending it to them.

3. But we are chiefly anxious, after all, on *your* account.

My children, the anxiety which we feel on this head, is far too intense for language. Here I may truly say, " poor is thought, and poor expression." If piety were to be obtained for you only by purchase, and I were rich in the possession of worlds, I would beggar myself to the last farthing to render you a Christian, and think the purchase cheap. " Godliness is profitable for all things, having the promise of the life that now is, as well as that which is to come." As I shall have more than one chapter on the advantages of piety, it will not be necessary to enlarge upon them here, any further than to say, that true godliness will save you from much present danger and inconvenience, promote your temporal interests, prepare you for the darkest scenes of adversity, comfort you on a dying bed, and finally conduct you to everlasting glory. The want of it will ensure the reverse of all this. Sooner or later such a destitution will bring misery on earth, and be followed with eternal torments in hell.

What then, my children, are all worldly acquirements and possessions, without piety? What are the accomplishments of taste, the elegancies of wealth, the wreaths of fame, but as the fragrant and many-colored garland which adorns the miserable victim about to be sacrificed at the shrine of this world? Original genius, a vigorous understanding, a well-stored mind, and all this adorned by the most amiable temper and most insinuating address, will neither comfort under the trials of life, nor save their lovely possessor from the worm that never dies and the fire that is never quenched. O ! no : they may qualify for earth, but not for heaven. Alas! alas ! that such estimable qualities should all perish for want of that piety which alone can give immortality and perfection to the excellences of the human character!

Can you wonder, then, at the solicitude we feel for your personal religion, when such interests are involved in this momentous concern?

II.

The Dispositions necessary for an Inquiry into the Nature of Religion.

RELIGION is a subject of a spiritual and moral nature, and, therefore, requires a different frame of mind to that which we carry to a topic purely intellectual.

1. The first disposition essentially necessary is *a deep seriousness.*

Religion is the very last thing in the universe with which we should allow ourselves to trifle. Nothing can be more shocking and incongruous than that flippancy and inconsiderateness with which some people treat this dread theme. When Uzzah put forth his hand, *in haste,* to support the ark, his life paid the forfeit of his temerity; and if the man, who takes up his Bible to inquire into the meaning of its contents, with a frivolous and volatile temper, do not suffer the same penalty, it is not because the action is less criminal or less dangerous, but because God has now removed the punishment to a greater distance from the sin. I cannot conceive of anything more likely to provoke God to give a person up to the bewildering influence of his own inherent depravity, and, consequently, to a confused and erroneous perception of religious truth, than this temper. To see a person approaching the Oracle of God with the same levity as a votary of fashion and folly enters a place of amusement, is, indeed, revolting to taste, to say nothing of more sacred feelings. Religion, enthroned behind the veil in the temple of truth, and dwelling amidst the brightness which the merely curious eye cannot bear to look upon, refuses to unfold her glories or discover her secrets to the volatile mind; and delivers to every one who draws near to her abode the admonition of Jehovah to Moses—" Put off thy shoes, for the place whereon thou standest is holy ground."

The subjects treated of by religion are of the most awfully important nature. Everything about it is serious. The Eternal God, in every view of His nature and operations; the Lord Jesus Christ, in His sufferings and death; the soul of man, in its ruin and salvation; the solemnities of judgment, the mysteries of eternity, the felicities of heaven, the torments of hell, are all involved in the mighty comprehension of religion. Should *such* themes be ever touched with irreverence? My dear children, I warn you against the too common practice of reducing, to the level of mere intellectual theories, and of treating with the same unconcern as the systems of philosophy, that sacred volume, which, to use the words of Locke, "has God for its author, salvation for its end, and truth, without any mixture of error, for its contents. Do not forget, then, that the very first requisite, not only in religion itself, but also in that frame of mind which enables us to understand its nature, is SERIOUSNESS.

2. *A great solicitude to be guided aright* is the next disposition, and nearly allied to the former.

Eternal consequences hang upon this question. According as we mistake it or understand it, we shall travel onward to heaven or to hell. An inquiry of such importance should, of course, be urged with the deepest anxiety. It might be rationally expected that events so awfully tremendous as death and judgment—a subject so deeply interesting as whether we shall spend eternal ages in torments or in bliss, could in no possible case, and in no constitution of mind whatever, fail of exciting the most serious apprehension and concern.   And yet there are multitudes who have talked a thousand times about religion, but yet have never had, in all their lives, one hour's *real solicitude*, to know whether their views of its nature are correct.   Is it to be wondered at, then, that so many remain in ignorance, or plunge into error ?

3. *Docility*, or a teachable disposition, is of great consequence.

Our Lord laid great emphasis on this, when he said—" Except ye be converted, and *become as little children*, ye shall not enter into the kingdom of heaven." Children, when they first go to school, have a sense of their own ignorance ; they have neither prepossessions nor prejudices ; they present their unfurnished minds to their teachers, to receive, with implicit confidence, all that they are taught. Docility is essential to improvement in everything; for, if a child go to school puffed up with high notions of his own attainments, imagining that he knows as much as his master can teach him, and with a disposition to cavil at everything that is communicated : in this case, improvement is out of the question ; the avenues of knowledge are closed. In nothing is docility more necessary than in religion, where the subject is altogether beyond the cognizance of the senses and the discoveries of reason. Christianity is purely and exclusively matter of revelation. Of course, all our knowledge on this topic must be derived from the·Bible ; to the right understanding of which, we must carry the same consciousness of our ignorance, the same destitution of prejudice and prepossession, the same implicit submission of the understanding, as the child, on his first going to school, does to his instructor. We must go to the word of God with these convictions in our mind : " This is the Master, from whom I, who know nothing, am most implicitly to receive all things. My Teacher is infallible, and I am not to cavil at his instructions, however, in some things, they may transcend my ability to comprehend them."

Yes, the Bible, the Bible alone, is the infallible teacher in religious matters, from whose authority there does and can lie no appeal ; before whose solemn dicta reason must bow in humble silence, to learn and to obey. This is docility, by which I mean, not a supple disposition to believe what others believe, or to adopt the creed which they would impose upon us. No: this is the surrendering our understanding to be enslaved by human authority; but teachableness means going direct to the Master, with this determination—whatever he teaches I will believe; be it so sublime, so humiliating, so novel, and, to my present limited capacities, so incomprehensible as it may.

Are we, then, to exclude reason from the business of religion? By no means. It would be as absurd to attempt it as it would be impossible to accomplish it. The whole affair of piety is a process of reason; but then it is reason submitting itself to the guidance of revelation. Reason bears the same relation to religion, and performs the same office, as it does in the system of jurisprudence; it examines the evidence by which a law is proved to be an enactment of the legislature; interprets, according to the known use of terms and phrases, its right meaning, and then submits to its authority. Thus, in matters of religion, its province is to examine the evidences by which the Bible is proved to be a revelation from God; having done this, it is to ascertain, according to the fixed use of language, its true meaning, and then to submit to its authority, by believing whatever it reveals, and obeying whatever it enjoins. This is what we mean by prostrating our reason before the tribunal of revelation—than which surely nothing can more accord with the design of the Bible or the ignorance of the human mind.

But, suppose that reason should meet with palpable contradictions in the word of God, is she to believe them? This is putting a case which cannot happen, since it is supposing that God will give His sanction to a lie. There can be no contradictions in the word of God; the thing is impossible. But still, it will be replied—Is not one kind of evidence for the divine authority of revelation derived from its contents? and, if so, may not reason make the nature of a doctrine a test of its truth? At best, this is but a secondary species of evidence, and cannot oppose the primary kind of proof. If it cannot be proved that a doctrine is really an interpolation, and if there be, at the same time, all the evidence that the case admits of that it is a part of divine revelation, no difficulty in the way of understanding its meaning, no seeming mystery in its nature, should lead us to reject it: we must receive it, and wait for further light to understand it.

Revelation is the sun, reason the eye which receives its beams, and applies them to all the purposes of life, for which, in ceaseless succession, they flow in upon us; and it can no more be said that revelation destroys or degrades reason, by guiding it, than it can be said the solar orb renders the faculty of vision useless, by directing its efforts.

Docility, then, my dear children—by which I mean a submission of the human understanding, in matters of religion, to the word of God—is essential to all true piety. I insist upon this with more earnestness, because it is easy to perceive the tendency of the present age is in an opposite direction. A haughty and flippant spirit has arisen, which, under the pretext of freedom of inquiry, has discovered a restless propensity to throw off the authority of divine truth; a spirit more disposed to teach the Bible than to be taught by it; to speculate upon what it should be, than to receive it as it is; a spirit which would receive the morality of the word of God as it finds it, but which is perpetually employed in mending its theology; which, in fact, would subvert the true order of things, and, instead of subjecting reason to revelation, would make reason the teacher and revelation the pupil. Beware, my children, of this dangerous spirit, which, while it pays flattering compliments to your understanding, is injecting the deadliest poison into your soul.

4. A *prayerful spirit* is essential to a right disposition for inquiring into the nature of true piety.

Religion is an affair so spiritual in its nature, so tremendously important in its consequences, and so frequently misunderstood; and, on the other hand, we ourselves are so liable to be misled in our judgments by the bewildering influence of internal depravity and external temptation, that it betrays the most criminal indifference, or the most absurd self-confidence, to enter on this subject without constant, earnest supplication for direction, to the Father and Fountain of lights.

The religious world is like an immense forest,

through which lies the right road to truth and happiness ; but besides this, there are innumerable paths running in all directions : every way has its travellers, each traveller thinks he is right, and attempts to prove it by referring to the map which he carries in his hand. In such circumstances, who that values his soul or her eternal salvation, would not seek for guidance to Him who has promised to disclose to us, by His Spirit, the path of life? When young people trust to the efforts of their own unaided reason, and neglect to ask for the guiding influence of the eternal God, it is matter of little surprise that they are found walking in the paths of error. There is a degree of pride and independence in this, which God often punishes by leaving them to the seductions of sophistry and falsehood. In addition, then, to the greatest seriousness of mind and the most intense desire after truth, and the most unprejudiced approach to the oracle of scripture, pray constantly to God to reveal to you the nature of true piety, and to dispose you to embrace it. This is the way appointed by God to obtain it. "If any man lack wisdom, let him ask of God, who giveth to all men liberally, and upbraideth not; and it shall be given him." "If ye, being evil, know how to give good gifts unto them which are your children, how much more shall your heavenly Father give His Holy Spirit to them that ask Him." "I will instruct thee, and teach thee in the way thou shalt go ; I will guide thee with mine eye."

These, surely, with a thousand other passages of

similar import, are sufficient to enjoin and encourage the temper I now recommend.   I have no hope of those who neglect habitual prayer for divine illumination.   I expect to see them left to embrace error for truth, or to content themselves with the mere forms of godliness, instead of its power.

III.

Right Sentiments in Religion.

TRUTH and error, my children, are essentially distinct, and diametrically opposed to each other. It is important to perceive in every case this difference, that we may embrace the one, and reject the other. To have the judgment misled in its decisions on any subject, is an evil, which, as rational creatures, we should ever deprecate; but to be mistaken on that subject, where "he that believeth shall be saved, and he that believeth not shall be damned," is most fearful, most fatal. To be in error on the topics of literature, science, commerce, history, is a mere inconvenience, at worst a derogation from our mental reputation or our worldly comfort; but to be fundamentally wrong in religion, is an evil which commences its chief mischief from the day of our death, and perpetuates it through all the ages of eternity.

I need not inform you, that there prevails an endless variety of opinions on the subject of religion. This circumstance, however with pious minds it might be matter of regret, with philosophic ones is no cause of surprise.   Infidels who profess to study theology in the book of nature, are divided into many sects.   Scarcely a subject exists, however plain and apparently incapable of producing a diversity of opinion, but what is viewed by different men in various lights.   What clashing opinions exist amongst lawyers, concerning the precise meaning of the words of a statute, which was drawn up with the most anxious care to exclude all litigation.   That different opinions should exist on the meaning of the scriptures, is less to be wondered at, when we consider how deeply we are all interested in the matter of revelation, and how apt we are in cases of personal interest to have our judgments biassed by our feelings.   The Bible, if read in heaven by holy angels and spirits made perfect, produces no discordant opinions there.   It is to the depravity of human nature that all religious error is to be traced.

Diversity of sentiment, although confessedly an evil, has been productive of some benefits.   It has afforded opportunity for the more vigorous exercise and conspicuous display of Christian charity and forbearance between the various sects ; while it is a constant pledge for the purity of the sacred text. As they all profess to draw their opinions from the Bible, they of course maintain a constant and sleepless jealousy over each other's treatment of the word of God.   Their opposition to each other, converts them all into vigilant guardians of the source of their faith ; so that although they have corrupted the *streams* of truth, they have jointly guarded the purity of the *fountain*. The suspicion of any liberties having been taken with the word of God, would be an evil more to be deplored than the existence of a diversity of opinion on the sacred text. While the genuineness of the statute is admitted, and the incorruptiblity of the judge is maintained, the wranglings of counsellors, about the meaning of terms and phrases, cannot subvert the foundations of justice.

Still, however, these opposite sentiments cannot of course be *all* right. Although error is multiform, truth is uniform; and it is of infinite consequence, that we should embrace the one, and reject the other.

1. Some errors unquestionably exclude a man from salvation. " He that believeth shall be saved, and he that believeth not shall be damned." Now, certainly from this language, it is evident that salvation is suspended on a belief of the gospel; and of course upon a belief of the true gospel, not on the belief of a false one. If, therefore, what we believe is not the same as that which the word of God reveals, it is not the gospel; and such a faith will not save us. To ascertain with precision what truths are essential to the hope of eternal life, is a very difficult task: to say how far a person may go in error, and yet after all be saved, is what no mortal should presume to do. When a man, however, disbelieves the Bible to be the word of God; or rejects the doctrine of the atonement; or the justification of the soul by faith; or the necessity of divine influence to renew and sanctify the heart; or the ob-

ligation of true holiness ; I do not see how such an individual can be saved. He subverts the very foundations of the gospel. *Something* must be believed, as our Lord himself tells us, in order to the possession of everlasting happiness; and if *these* things may be disbelieved, and yet a sinner be saved, it is difficult to find out what there is left for him to believe. If some sentiments then are essential to a saving faith, we should be most tremblingly afraid of error; and as it is not for us to say how far an individual may go in error in order to be excluded from the blessings of the gospel, we should certainly be alarmed at the least deviation from the truth, as there is no doubt that one wrong notion prepares the mind for the reception of another. This leads me to observe,

2. That all error has a tendency to pollute the mind to the degree in which it exists, and therefore must be so far sinful.

" Sanctify them by thy truth," saith our Lord, " thy word is truth." Now if truth sanctifies, error must corrupt the mind ; except two causes so diametrically opposite to each other, as these are, can be supposed to produce the same effects ; which is absurd. Whatever is not truth must be error. Whatever opinion we profess to have received from the word of God, must be classed under one or other of these heads, and must have some influence or other upon our religious character as it appears in the sight of God. Wrong sentiments may not produce immorality in the life ; but if they corrupt our secret motives; if they render us spiritually proud, and lead us to glory before God; if they make us self-confident and self-dependent; if they cause us to lean to our own understanding; if they lead us to look with contempt upon others; if they keep us from using any means of grace instituted by God, they pollute and injure the mind in the sight of its Omniscient Creator. The least disease in the body, although it be unobserved by others, and be yet unfelt by the subject of it, is an injury to the health. It may never come to a fatal attack, or bring on death, but still it is injurious to the frame; and it is precisely thus with error in the mind.

All religion is founded upon knowledge. It begins in the reception of truth into the understanding; if therefore the whole truth *is not* received, some part of the moral means appointed for our spiritual improvement is not applied; and if anything contrary to the truth *is* received, a cause is in operation upon our minds, opposite to the right one. The order of piety is the order of nature; first, we receive an opinion, then our feelings are excited by the opinion, and then the will acts under the influence of the feelings; as is the opinion, such are the resolutions and the actions. If the opinion therefore be wrong, all that follows must be wrong as to its moral character in the sight of God.

I am aware that a difficulty presents itself here to many young persons, which does not a little perplex them. They see individuals who have embraced the widest extremes of opinion, equally exemplary for

the discharge of all the relative and social obligations. They see those who have embraced error, as
useful, peaceful, ornamental members of society as
those who have received the truth. This is undoubt-
edly a fact. I know very many who have rejected
almost all that is peculiar to Christianity, who are
yet amongst the most truly respectable inhabitants
of the places in which they live. But this does not
disprove my statements, nor in any degree prove
that error is innocent and harmless. There are two
lights in which the human character is to be viewed;
its aspect towards men, and that which it bears towards God. Now I do not mean to say that religious error may, in any material, or visible degree,
alter the former. A man may be a good subject,
neighbor, husband, father, tradesman, master, with
any or with *no* religious opinions at all. A few infidels have been exemplary in their attention to all
the duties of social life. This, however, only proves
that error does not always disfigure the character in
the sight of man; but we are now more particularly
speaking of its aspect towards God. In this view
of it there may be degree of obliquity truly awful,
while all is correct towards man. Pride of intellect
and of heart; self-sufficiency and self-dependence; a
stout and pertinacious resistance of Jehovah's authority; a peremptory refusal to submit to his schemes
and will, may all be rife in the soul, where everything is fair in the exterior. God looketh to the
heart; and in his eye the character is decided by the
state of the mind. Religion, properly speaking, has

to do with God and heaven ; it is a right disposition towards God, and a spiritual preparation for a celestial state, which, as is perfectly evident, may be wanting, where there are the most splendid social virtues.   What I affirm then is, that error, according to the degree in which it exists, must vitiate the character, and deprave the heart in the sight of God ; must obstruct the growth and exercise of the religious principle, must unfit a person for divine fellowship here, and for eternal glory hereafter.

Error on religious subjects is not a mere intellectual defect ; it is not the result of mere weakness of understanding ; its seat is in the heart ; it springs from carelessness, prejudice, pride, or some other operation of our depravity, which exerts a bewildering influence on the judgment.   We are as certainly accountable to God for it as for evil conduct.   It is not to be conceived for a moment that we are responsible for the exercises of every other faculty of the soul, yet not for the understanding, which is the noblest of them all.   If a man may *believe* error and yet be innocent, he may *preach* it without guilt ; and, if this be the case, may employ all his faculties, his talents, his time, his influence, in a direct opposition to the counsels of heaven, and to all the revelation of God, and yet be without blame.

If this statement be correct, then error is certainly criminal.   How can there be a doubt of this ? If a man may disbelieve the less important truth and yet be innocent in that act of his disbelief, then he may reject a more important one, and be equally faultless.   If he may discredit one truth without guilt, then he may discredit two; if two, ten; if ten, half the Bible; if half the Bible, the whole; and yet be innocent, even though he be a Deist or Atheist, provided he be not immoral, and profess, at the same time, to be inquiring after truth.   And then, why is it said to all the world—" He that believeth not shall be damned?"   And what saith the scripture in other places?   " For this cause God shall send them strong delusions, that they should believe a lie, that they all might be damned who believe not the truth."   " But though we, or an angel from heaven, preach any other gospel unto you than that which we have preached unto you, let him be accursed.   As we said before, so I say now again, if any man preach any other gospel unto you than that ye have received, let him be accursed."   " Whosoever transgresseth, and abideth not in the doctrine of Christ, hath not God.   If there come any unto you, and bring not this doctrine, receive him not into your house, neither bid him Godspeed; for he that biddeth him Godspeed is a partaker of his evil deeds."   " Henceforth be no more children tossed to and fro, and carried about with every wind of doctrine, by the sleight of men, and cunning craftiness, whereby they lie in wait to deceive."   " Be not carried about with divers and strange doctrines, for it is a good thing that the heart be established with grace."   " For the time will come when they will not endure sound doctrine; but after their own lusts shall they heap to themselves teachers, having itching ears; and they shall turn away their ears from the truth, and shall be turned into fables." " There were false prophets, also, among the people, even as there shall be false teachers among you who privily shall bring in damnable heresies, even denying the Lord who bought them, and bring upon them swift destruction; and many shall follow their pernicious ways, by reason of whom the way of truth shall be evil spoken of; whose judgment now of a long time lingereth not, and their damnation slumbereth not."*

These, and many more similar texts, decide the point that errors are blamable and destructive; that they spring from the depravity of our nature, and demonstrate a heart, in so far as they prevail, not yet brought into subjection to Christ.

Beware, then, my dear children, of that spurious candor which looks with an equal eye on all opinions; which talks of the innocence of error, and thus diffuses a baneful indifference to the truth. The adage of Pope, who was a free-thinking Roman Catholic, has been circulated round society by innumerable echoes:

> " For modes of faith let graceless zealots fight;
>   His can't be wrong whose life is in the right."

This, you will perceive, is an equivocal expression.

* 2 Thess. ii. 11, 12. Gal. i. 8, 9. 2 John, ix. 10, 11. Ephes. iv. 14. Heb. xiii. 9. 2 Tim. iv. 3. 2 Peter, ii. 1, 2.

In one view of it, nothing can be more correct; for in every case, a right life—*i. e.*, right in the scriptural sense of the term, must proceed from a right creed : if, therefore, the life *be* right, so must also the creed.   But the design of the author was to teach that a right life may stand connected with any creed, or with no creed; and that, therefore, religious opinions are of no consequence whatever. This, you will perceive, is the popular and dreadful dogma of infidelity.   " This bantling of scepticism has been foisted into the Christian world, and profanely baptized by the name of charity. But though it may wear the smiling countenance of this heavenly virtue, it has an infidel heart.   If this counterfeit, hollow thing, which dares to take to itself the sacred name of charity, had not renounced the Bible, it would have certainly known that errors in faith are the offspring of a heart wholly or partially unrenewed, and as decisive a proof, so far as they prevail, of a want of religion, as an unsanctified life."

Contend earnestly, then, for the faith once delivered to the saints.   I would not have you bigots. This, however, is a vague and plastic term, which in the slang of modern infidelity has been generally applied to every one who attaches importance to religious opinions.   If by a bigot is meant an overweening attachment to sentiments confessedly of lesser importance than many others, or a blind zeal for opinions adopted rather from custom than from conviction ; or a spirit of intolerance, contempt, and persecution towards those who differ from us in the

articles of their belief: if this be bigotry, be you
no bigots; abhor and avoid a disposition of this
kind. Adopt all your sentiments after a close
examination, and upon a full conviction of their
truth. Apportion your zeal for their diffusion, upon
the scale of their relative importance. Exercise
the greatest forbearance and candor towards those
who differ from you; but, at the same time, contend
for the articles of your faith as matters of infinite
consequence. Defend your opinions with an enlightened, dispassionate, but, at the same time,
ardent zeal. Insist upon the connection of right
sentiments with right feelings; that the former,
when really held, lead to the latter, and that the
latter can never exist without the former. If *this*
is what is meant by bigotry, then may you possess
it more and more. Shrink not from the charge, if
this be its meaning in the lips of those who use it.
If you partake of true faith and genuine holiness,
you must expect that the one will be called enthusiasm, and the other bigotry. Disregard both the
accusations, and be not deterred by opprobrious
names from the pursuit of eternal life.

Do you ask me what are right sentiments? I
reply—search the scriptures for yourselves, with
docility, with prayer, with earnestness. No language
can express the infinite importance of entering,
without delay, on a deep and solemn examination
into these matters.* Call no man master, but consult

---

* Without pledging myself to approve of every express-

the oracle of heaven. One evil, never enough to be deplored, is, that many people do not and will not distinguish. They are pleased with different preachers, who bring as different gospels as the Koran is different from the Bible. They are as ready to put themselves in the way of hearing error as truth, and swallow down whatever comes, provided only it is gracefully administered. Elegant language, good elocution, theatrical attitudes, fascinating imagery, are to them of far more importance than the truth. They are like children rushing into the shop of an apothecary, tasting at random of every phial, and selecting the most imposing in appearance, without the power of distinguishing medicines from poisons. And even where there is some general attachment to right sentiments, in how few cases is this attended with an enlightened ability to defend and enforce them! Our young people do not sufficiently store their minds with the proofs and arguments of the opinions they have adopted. They are satisfied with believing without proof. This is not the case with the advocates of error. They are instructed in the whole system of attack and defence. They are skilful in all the manœuvres

ion contained in the answers of the Assembly's Shorter Catechism, I know not where to find a summary of Christian doctrines expressed with so much brevity and so much precision. And although I do not approve of the practice of teaching this Catechism to children below the age of twelve, yet all our youth above that age should be acquainted with it, as a synopsis of right sentiments in religion.

of controversy: sophisms, assertions, interrogatories, arguments, are all at their command.   The friends of truth are, in these respects, often behind them. Reposing an unlimited confidence in the invulnerable security and the impregnable strength of their cause, they do not exercise themselves in the use of their arms, and appear sometimes to a disadvantage in skirmishing with their opponents.   Be you not behind them in ability to defend your principles. The truth is of infinite value; may you clearly and comprehensively understand it; cordially and practically believe it; sincerely and ardently love it; and be able both to state it with precision and to support it with argument.

I cannot conclude this chapter without recommending to you the perusal of an excellent sermon by Dr. Pye Smith, "On the Best Means of Obtaining Satisfaction with regard to the Truth of Religious Sentiments."

After a suitable introduction, he points out, as the common and principal sources of error with regard to divine things—1. The weakness of our faculties; 2. Our taking up wrong subjects of investigation; 3. And our being affected by the secret influence of sinful dispositions and habits.   Under the last particular, we find the following impressive observations:

"'A sinner,' says the wise King of Israel, 'seeketh wisdom, and findeth it not.'   The entire want, or the great deficiency of love, of reverence, and devotedness to God, cannot but give a fatal obliquity to our professed researches after truth. Such a state of mind is also invariably connected with wrong affections in relation to ourselves. Instead of an humble, adoring, and delightful admiration of the universal perfection of the Most High, there will be pride, self-confidence, and a determination to think, at all events, favorably of our own dispositions and practices. The judgment of God will be little regarded, and its impression felt very slightly. His supremacy will be the object of secret murmur, or of virtual denial. The heart will rise in dislike against His glorious and unchangeable rectitude, and the necessary obligation of His rational creatures to love Him with a perfect heart. His sole and sovereign competency to determine whether at all, to what extent, and in what way and manner He may be pleased to pardon and bless sinners, will be met by a strong, though perhaps disguised repugnance. And the duty of a cheerful and implicit reliance on the unsullied purity, righteousness, and benevolence of Jehovah, notwithstanding the perplexity of present appearances, may, indeed, be faintly acknowledged in words; but as to practical effect, it will be treated with neglect, or even with disgust. These, and all other movements of the heart which is under the power of revolt from God, will most certainly darken the understanding and mislead the judgment; 'evil will be put for good,' and good will be treated as evil."—pp. 14, 15.

6*

" The remedies of the erroneous tendencies of the human heart are stated to be—1. The maintenance of *right affections* towards the great Author and Revealer of religious truth. 2. A habit of entire *subjection* to the authority of the Holy Scriptures. 3. The use of all proper methods of acquiring and improving the art of *just reasoning.* 4. Establishment in the evidence and influence of *primary truths.* 5. *Living under the benign and purifying influence of divine truth.* 6. Cautious observations of the *effect of particular sentiments* upon ourselves or others. 7. Keeping in mind that what has been adopted on impartial inquiry and sufficient evidence, *is not to be lightly given up on the mere occurrence of some new objection.* 8. *Fervent prayer.*

" The constant, serious, and affectionate practice of this great and necessary duty, will have the most happy effect in obtaining and preserving the rational and scriptural satisfaction of the truth of our sentiments, if they be indeed true ; and, if otherwise, of leading us to the timely and beneficial discovery of our errors. Prayer elevates the soul above the mists and darkness of this revolted world, and places us under the very shining of the Everlasting Light. It tends to exterminate the greatest obstruction to the entrance of that light, the prepossessions of sin in the heart. It gives vigor and delicacy to the sanctified perceptions. It guides that holy, mental sense which is the characteristic of the real Christian, to the quick discrimination and the delightful reception of truth and goodness. Through prayer, the hallowed medium of intercourse with heaven, the devout mind ascends to its closest enjoyment of communion with the Lord God of truth; and from Him descend the returns of prayer, 'every good gift, and every perfect gift.' "—pp. 29, 30.

IV.

The Nature of True Religion.

ALL other questions, compared with this, are "trifles light as air," or but as the dust of the balance. Philosophy, literature, commerce, the arts and the sciences, have, it is true, a relative importance; they soften the manners, alleviate the evils, multiply the comforts of life; yet it is impossible to forget that they are the mere embellishments of a scene which we "must shortly quit; the decorations of a theatre, from which the actors and spectators must soon retire together." But RELIGION is of infinite and eternal moment, and *then* develops, most perfectly, its consequence, in that very moment when the importance of all other subjects terminates forever. A mistake in this affair, persisted in till death, is followed by effects infinitely dreadful, and of eternal duration. You should bring to this inquiry, therefore, my children, a trembling solicitude to be led in the right way.

Some consider religion as a mere notional assent to certain theological opinions; others, as a bare attendance on religious ordinances; others, as the performance of moral duties. They are all equally wrong: for, instead of being any one of these separately and apart from the rest, it is the union of them all. Religion admits of many definitions in scripture language. It is "repentance towards God, and faith in our Lord Jesus Christ;" or it is "faith working by love;" or it is receiving "that grace which bringeth salvation, and teacheth us to deny ungodliness and worldly lusts, and to live soberly, righteously, and godly, in this present evil world; or it is "denying ourselves, taking up our cross and following after Christ;" or it is being born again of the Spirit, and sanctified by the truth; or it is the supreme love of Christ, or the habitual fear of God. Each one of these phrases is a definition of true piety; but I shall now adopt another, and represent it as *"A right disposition of mind towards God, implanted in our nature by the influence of the Holy Ghost, and exercising itself according to the circumstances in which we are placed."*

Religion is the same in substance in all rational creatures, whether innocent or fallen. In angels it is still a right disposition towards God, exercising itself in a way of adoration, love, gratitude, and obedience; but not of faith, hope, and repentance, because their circumstances preclude the possibility of these acts. Religion, in reference to fallen man, is a right disposition of mind; but inasmuch as he is a sinful and ruined creature, yet a creature capable of salvation, through the mediation of Christ, it must necessarily include in it, in addition to the feelings of angelic piety, all those mental exercises and habits which are suitable to a state of guilt and a dispensation of mercy.

Let us take each part of the definition by itself.

I. *God* is the *primary object* of religion.

It is not enough that we perform our duties towards our fellow-creatures; but to be truly pious we must perform our duty towards God. We may be exemplary and even punctilious in discharging every social obligation; we may be moral in the usual acceptation of the term—honorable, amiable; and yet may be all this, without one single spark of true piety; because in all this there may be no reference whatever to God. An atheist may be all this. Until the mind is rightly affected towards God, there is no religion because *He* is the direct and primary object of it. It is something perfectly independent, as to its essence, of all the social relations. If a man were wrecked, like Alexander Selkirk, on an uninhabited island, where there would be no room, of course, for loyalty, honesty, kindness, mercy, justice, truth, or any of the *relative* virtues, the claims of piety would still follow him to this dreary and desolate abode; and even there, where he should never hear the sweet music of speech, nor look on the human face divine, he would still be under the obligations of piety; even there one voice would be heard breaking the silence around him, with the solemn injunction of scripture, " Thou shalt love the Lord thy God." Bear in recollection, then, my dear children, that God, as he is revealed in his word, is the direct and primary object of all true piety; and that the most exemplary discharge of the social duties can be no substitute for that reverence, and love, and gratitude, and obedience, which we owe to him.

Most strange it is, and yet most lamentably prevalent, for mankind to make the discharge of their duties towards each other, a substitute for those, and an excuse for neglecting them, which they owe to God; as if the Divine Being were the only one in the universe, who could, with propriety, be forgotten; and as if He, without any criminality on our part, might be utterly neglected. He is our Creator, Preserver, and Benefactor; in Him we live, and move, and have our being. His nature includes everything that can entitle him to our esteem and adoration; His goodness, everything that can claim our gratitude and love; how then can it be thought that the practical remembrance of our duty to man can be any reason for not loving and serving HIM! Our first and most important relation is that of creatures dependent on the Creator; and, therefore, our first and most indispensable duty is a right disposition towards God. Hence, the scriptures resolve all crime into forgetfulness of God. "The wicked shall be turned into hell, and all the nations that forget God." To be a wicked man, and to forget God, are one and the same thing. To be destitute of right affections towards God, is the very essence of sin; and to possess these affections the essence of religion.

II.   Religion is *a right disposition of mind* towards God.   It is not merely a thing of outward
forms and ceremonies, but of the *heart*.   It is more
than an external action, it is a disposition ; not only
a performance, but a taste ; not an involuntary or
compulsory pursuit, but a voluntary and agreeable
one.   That religion must be an internal principle,
an affair of the soul, is evident from the nature of
its object, of whom it is said, " God is a spirit, and
they that worship him must worship him in *spirit*
and in truth."   As the heart lies all open to him,
unless there be religion there, he scorns the uplifted
hand and bended knee.   It is evident from *reason*,
that piety must have its seat in the breast; for what
spiritual excellence can there be in an action, which
is either performed from a bad motive, or from none
at all?   It is evident from *revelation*.   Read such
injunctions as these.   " My son, give me thine *heart*."
" Get thee a new *heart*."   " Thy *heart* is not right
in the sight of God."   " Be renewed in *the spirit of
your mind*."   " Ye must be born again."   Equally
in point are all those passages which command us to
love God, to fear him, to trust in him, to glorify
him ; duties which of course imply the exercise, and
the vigorous exercise of the affections of the mind.
Notions however clear, morality however exemplary,
are not enough till the current of *feeling* is turned
towards God.   A mere cold correctness of deportment, but which leaves the heart in a state of alienation and estrangement from God, is not the piety of
the word of truth.

Now, in consequence of our natural descent from Adam since his fall, we come into the world totally destitute of this right disposition towards God and grow up under the influence of a contrary temper. " The carnal mind is enmity against God." This is what we mean by the total depravity of human nature ; not that there is an absence of all amiable and praiseworthy feeling towards our fellow-creatures ; not that there is the predominance of criminal and vicious appetite ; but that there is a total destitution of all right feeling towards God. Much loose and incorrect representation has been given, by injudicious writers, to the public, on the subject of human depravity. It would seem, from their statements, as if mankind were all like, as bad as vice could make them. Now, by the total depravity of the whole race of man, we simply mean, that since the fall, every man comes into the world totally destitute of holiness, or in other words, of the love of God, and in consequence of this destitution will, and does live without God, till renewed by divine grace. Some will go further astray in sin than others, according to the circumstances in which they are placed ; but so far as the state of the heart is concerned all are equally destitute of the principles of holiness, as long as they are unrenewed by the Divine Spirit. Before true religion can be possessed by one human being, there must of consequence be an entire change of mind, a complete alteration in the disposition. The scriptures inform us that all are inherently depraved, for " that which is born of

the flesh is flesh ;" and, therefore, with equal ex-
plicitness they inform us, that all must be changed
before they can partake of true piety.   This change
is so great that our Lord himself calls it a second
birth.   " Verily, verily, I say unto you, Except a
man be born again, he cannot see the kingdom of
heaven."

Until this change takes place, there cannot be
even the commencement of true religion.   Whatever
is avoided, or whatever is done that bears the semblance of piety, is carried on without a right disposition of mind ; and we cannot suppose that God,
who sees the heart, is pleased with such service,
any more than *we* should be with compliments from
a person whose bosom we knew to be destitute of all
right feeling toward us.   The mistake which many
make in religion is, they do not begin with the
beginning.   They attempt to carry up the superstructure without seeking to have the foundation
laid in the renewal of the nature.   They profess to
serve God outwardly before they have surrendered
their *heart* to His renewing grace.   Their religion
is a new dress, but not a new nature.   It is the
mechanical performance of an automaton, not the
voluntary actions of a living man.   It wants that
which alone constitutes piety—a " *right disposition
towards God.*"

III. This disposition is implanted in the soul *by
the power of the Holy Ghost.*

The operations of Deity, in the formation of the
material world, are frequently alluded to by the

sacred writers, as illustrating the work of Jehovah in renewing the human mind and bringing forth the beauties of holiness in the human character. The soul of man, as to all spiritual excellence, is in its natural state a chaos; and the same Divine Spirit which brooded on the materials of the formless void, which moved on the face of the deep, and brought order out of confusion, and beauty out of deformity; which said—Let there be light, and there was light; now operates on the dark mind, the irregular affections, the hard heart of the sinner, giving true light to the understanding, a right disposition to the soul, submission to the will; and, in short, creating the whole man anew in Christ Jesus, unto good works. This is declared in many passages of the scriptures. "A new heart also will *I* give you," said God to the Jews, "and a new spirit will *I* put within you; and *I* will take away the stony heart out of your flesh, and *I* will give you a heart of flesh. And *I* will put my spirit within you, and cause you to walk in my statutes."* To the same effect are our Lord's words to Nicodemus: "Except a man be born of water and the Spirit, he shall not see the kingdom of heaven." This same truth is often repeated by the apostles. "You hath *he* quickened," "Who hath saved us by washing of regeneration, and renewing of the Holy Ghost." "It is God who worketh in us to will and to do." That it must be some power out of a man, and

* Ezekiel, xxxvi. 26, 27.

beyond himself to effect the change, is evident from
the circumstance that it is not merely the conduct,
but the *disposition* itself, which requires to be
changed; and who can reach the *mind*, and regulate the springs of action, but God? Not that we
are to lie down in indolent neglect, and say—" If,
then, it is the Holy Ghost who must change the
mind, I may give up all concern about the matter,
and wait before I attempt to perform the duties of
religion, till I feel that I am changed." No: as
rational creatures, we must use our faculties, consider our case, examine our hearts, tremble at our
situation, call upon God in prayer, and give Him no
rest till He pour out His spirit upon us. The very
circumstance that we are thus dependent on God,
should make us more tremblingly anxious, more
importunate in prayer for divine help. If you were
entirely dependent upon the assistance of a fellow-
creature for help to recover your property, liberty,
or life, would not that very conviction impel you to
the door and presence of the person, in all the eloquence and urgency of importunate entreaty? Would
you not pour out your very soul in the language of
wrestling supplication? Would you not press your
suit by every argument, so long as a ray of hope
fell upon your spirits? In *this* case, the idea that
help must come from another, would not render you
indolent, and why should it do so in the business of
conversion?

The only circumstance which renders the influence of the Holy Spirit necessary for the conversion

of the soul, is the want of inclination or disposition
to love and serve God. That is what we call *moral
inability*, in distinction from *natural* inability. A
man is morally unable when he has no inclination ;
he is naturally unable when he has no opportunity.
When a master commands a servant to go and fetch
him something, and the servant hears the command
and at the same time has the use of his limbs, but
refuses to obey, he is morally unable—that is, he
has no inclination, no disposition ; but if the master
were to command the servant to go to another room,
or to another street, and the servant at that time
were deprived of the use of his limbs, he is, in that
case, naturally unable: in the former case, he could
go if he would ; in the latter, he would if he could :
the former is guilty of rebellion, for all he wanted
was disposition ; the latter is innocent, for he has
no opportunity. One wants will, the other wants
power. This illustrates the case of the sinner : he
is morally unable to obey and love God ; he has
enough natural power, he has reason, will, affections,
and he has eyes to read God's commands, and ears
to hear them. Why, then, does he not obey them ?
Because he has no disposition. If he were a lunatic or an idiot, from his birth, his inability to serve
God would be a natural inability. Now, moral
inability, or want of disposition, so far from being
an excuse for neglecting God and religion, is the
very essence of sin. The less disposition a man has
to that which is good, and the more disposition he
has to that which is evil, the more wicked he is ;

7*

just as a person addicted to dishonesty, cruelty, or injustice, is the more guilty the stronger his propensities are to his wickedness. The more natural inability we have, the more we are excused from not doing what is right; but the greater our moral inability is, the more guilty we are.

Now, this moral inability is what our Lord speaks of us when he says—" No man *can* come unto me except the Father who hath sent me draw him." He *cannot*, because he will not; and he will not, because he has no disposition. Hence he says, in another place—" Ye *will* not come unto me, that ye may have life." The inability which the Spirit of God removes, then, in conversion, is the want of inclination; the ability which he gives is a right disposition. In conversion, no violence is done to the will, because the will always follows the disposition.

If this be correct, we are to take pains with ourselves, to think, to resolve, to act, though in dependence upon the grace of God.

IV. I shall now state how a right disposition of mind towards God *will exercise itself in our circumstances as sinners ;* and this will bring us more immediately to a consideration of the nature of real religion.

First—*Reverence, veneration, and awe,* are due from us to that great and glorious Being who is the author of our existence, the fountain of our comforts, the witness of our actions, and the arbiter of our eternal destiny. How sublimely grand and

awful is the character of God, as it is revealed in
His word! Acknowledging, as you do, my children, His existence, you should make Him the object of your habitual fear and dread. You should
maintain a constant veneration for Him, a trembling
deprecation of His wrath. A consciousness of His
existence and of His immediate presence should
never, for any length of time, be absent from your
mind. The idea of an ever-present, omniscient,
omnipotent Spirit, should not only be sometimes
before your understanding, as an article of faith,
but impressed upon your heart as an awful and
practical reality. Your very spirits should ever
be laboring to apprehend and to apply the representation which the scriptures give us of the Deity.
A desire to know Him, to feel and act towards Him
with propriety, should be interwoven with the entire
habit of your reflections and conduct.

Secondly—*Penitence* is indispensably necessary.

In order to this, there must be *deep conviction of
sin;* for none can mourn over a fault, which he is
not convinced that he has committed. A deep consciousness of guilt is one of the first feelings of a
renewed mind, and is one of the first operations of
the Holy Spirit. "When he is come, he shall
convince the world of sin." We come to a knowledge of our sinful state by an acquaintance with
the spirituality, purity, and extent of the moral
law; "for sin is the transgression of the law."
Until we know the law, which is the rule of duty,
we cannot know in what way, and to what extent,

we have offended against it.   The exposition which
our Lord has given us of the law, in his sermon on
the mount, informs us that it is not only the overt
act of iniquity which makes man a sinner, but the
inward feeling, the imagination, the desire.   An
unchaste look is a breach of the seventh commandment ; a feeling of immoderate anger is a violation
of the sixth.   Viewing ourselves in such a mirror,
and trying ourselves by such a standard, we must
all confess ourselves to be guilty of ten thousand
sins.   And then, again, we are not only sinful for
what we *do that is wrong*, but for what we *leave
undone that is right*, and ought to be done.   If,
therefore, we have a right disposition towards God,
we must have a deep feeling of depravity and guilt,
an impressive sense of moral obliquity, a humbling
consciousness of vileness.   To the charges of the
law, we must cry guilty! guilty!   We must not
only admit, upon the testimony of *others*, that we
are sinful, but, from a perception of the holiness of
God's nature, and the purity of His law, we must
discern the number, aggravations, and enormity of
our offences.   We must do homage to infinite
holiness, by acknowledging ourselves altogether
sinful.

Sorrow is essential to penitence.   We cannot
have been made partakers of penitence if we do not
feel inward grief on the review of our transgressions.   We read of "godly *sorrow*, which worketh
repentance unto salvation."   If we have injured a
fellow-creature, the first indication of a right sense

of the aggression is a sincere *regret* that we should have acted so. How much more necessary is it that we should be unfeignedly sorry for our innumerable offences against *God.* Sorrow for sin is not, however, to be estimated only by violent emotions and copious tears. The passions are much stronger in themselves, and much more excitable in some than in others ; and, therefore, the same degree of inward emotion, or of outward grief, is not to be expected from all. The degrees of sorrow, as well as the outward modes of expressing it, will vary, as belonging more to the sensitive nature than to the rational ; and for avoiding all scruple and doubtfulness on this head, it may be laid down for certain, that the least degree of sorrow is sufficient, if it produce reformation ; the greatest insufficient, if it do not.

The next step in penitence is *confession.* Real sorrow for sin is always frank and impartial, while false or partial sorrow is prone to concealment, palliation, and apology. There is a wretched proneness in many persons when convinced of sin, to offer excuses and to endeavor to think the best of their case. They cannot be brought to admit the charge in all its length and breadth, but they attempt to hide its magnitude from their own eyes. This is a dangerous disposition, and has often come between a man's soul and his salvation. All the great and precious promises of pardon are suspended upon the condition of confession. " If we *confess* our sins, God is faithful and just to forgive us our sins."

Confession must be in detail, not in generals only ; it must be free and impartial.

Abhorrence of sin is also included in penitence. There can be no real grief for an action, which is not accompanied by dislike of it.   We shall unquestionably *hate* sin, if we partake of godly sorrow. This, indeed, is the true meaning of the term *repentance*, which does not signify *grief* merely, but an entire change of mind towards sin.   Abhorrence of sin is as necessary a part of repentance, as grief. Our hatred of transgression must be grounded not merely on viewing it as *an injury to ourselves*, but as *an insult to God*.   For penitence, on account of sin, is altogether a different feeling to that which we experience over a fire, a shipwreck, or a disease which has diminished our comforts.   Our tears, then, are not enough, if not followed by abhorrence.   " If we are sincere in our grief, we shall detest and fly the viper which has stung us, and not cherish and caress the beast, whilst with false tears we bathe the wound we have received."

Thirdly.—*Faith in Jesus Christ* is no less necessary.

Faith is a very important, and most essential part of true religion.   Faith in Christ is a firm *practical belief* of the gospel testimony concerning Christ, a *full persuasion* of the truth of what is declared, and a *confident expectation* of what is promised.   The testimony is this :—" It is a faithful saying, and worthy of all acceptation, that Jesus Christ came into the world to save sinners."   " God so loved

the world as to give his only begotten Son, that
whosoever believeth in him should not perish, but
have everlasting life." Hence, then, faith is a belief that Jesus Christ died as a sacrifice of atonement to divine justice for human guilt, accompanied
by an exclusive dependence on that atonement for
acceptance with God, and a confident expectation of
pardon and eternal life according to the promises of
the gospel. Mere assent does not amount to the
scriptural idea of faith. There must be dependence
and expectation. The subject of the divine testimony is not like a problem in mathematics, which
appeals exclusively to the understanding ; in this
case mere assent, or a perception of the truth of the
proposition, is all that belief contains ; but the gospel is a report that interests our hearts, and which
is, in fact, proposed to us not only as a promise to
be believed but a rule to be obeyed. Faith, then,
certainly includes in it an exercise of the will, or
else there can be nothing moral in its nature. We
cannot affirm of anything merely intellectual, that it
is matter of duty. Exclude an exercise of volition,
or disposition from faith, and then, it is no longer
obligatory upon the conscience. Besides, if belief
be merely an intellectual exercise, so is unbelief ;
for they are opposites. A scriptural faith, then, includes dependence and expectation.

Faith is, most obviously, as much a part of a right
disposition towards God, as penitence. God having
given Jesus Christ for the salvation of sinners, and
promised to save those who depend upon the atone-

ment, and commanded all to ask for pardon and eternal life; it is manifest, that not to believe, is to dispute the divine veracity, as well as to rebel against the divine authority. To believe the gospel, and to expect salvation through Christ, is to honor all the attributes of Deity at once, is to praise that mercy which prompted the scheme of redemption, that wisdom which devised it, that power which accomplished it, that justice which is satisfied by it, and that truth which engages to bestow its benefits on all that seek them. Not to believe is an act of contempt which insults Jehovah in every view of his character at once. Until we are brought, therefore, actually to depend on Christ so as to expect salvation, we have no real religion.

Fourthly.—A *willingness in all things to obey God*, completes the view which ought to be given of a right disposition towards him.

There must be a distinct acknowledgment of His right to govern us, and an unreserved surrender of our heart and life to his authority; an habitual desire to do what he has enjoined, to avoid what He has forbidden. Where there is this desire to please, this reluctance to offend God, the individual will read with constancy and attention the sacred volume, which is written for the express purpose of teaching us how to obey and please the Lord. Finding these innumerable injunctions against all kinds of immorality and sin, and as many commands to practise every personal, relative, and social duty, the true

Christian will be zealous for all good works. Remembering that Jesus Christ is proposed there as our example, no less than our atonement, he will strive to be like him in purity, spirituality, submission to the will of God, and devotedness to the divine glory. Nor will he forget to imitate the beautiful meekness, lowliness, and kindness of his deportment; so that the love which a right view of his atonement never fails to produce, transforms the soul of the believer into his image. Finding in the word of God many commands to cultivate the spirit and attend on the exercises of devotion; the true Christian will remember the sabbath-day to keep it holy, will maintain daily prayer in his closet, and unite himself in the fellowship of some Christian church, to live in communion with believers, and with them to celebrate the sacred supper.

During the trials of life, he will console himself with the promises of grace and the prospects of glory. He will soften his earthly cares by the influence of his heavenly hopes. He will endeavor to. keep himself pure from the vices of the world, and shine as a spiritual light amidst surrounding darkness. His great business in this world will be to prepare for a better; and when the times arrives for him to quit the visible for the invisible state, he will bow in meek submission to the will of God, and retire from earth, cheered with the prospect and the expectation of eternal glory.

Such appears to me to be the nature of true religion. Its possessor, daily conscious of his defects,

will habitually humble himself before God ; and
while he seeks forgiveness for past offences, through
the blood of Jesus Christ, will as earnestly implore
the gracious aid of the Holy Spirit to sanctify him
more perfectly for the future.

V.

The Advantages and Responsibility of a Pious Education.

THE advantage of any system of means, must, of course, as to their value, be estimated by the importance of the end to be obtained, which, in the present case, is the possession of real religion in this world, and eternal happiness in that which is to come. The end to be obtained includes not only a profession of piety in our present state of being, but all that infinite and everlasting felicity which piety brings in its train: of what vast consequence, then, must be the most suitable means for attaining to this sublime purpose!

The value of a thing, my dear children, is sometimes learnt by the want of it: consider, therefore, the situation of those young persons whose parents, careless of their own souls, take no pains for the salvation of their children. In what a helpless situation are such young people placed! They are taught, perhaps, everything but religion. They are instructed in all the elegant accomplishments of fashionable life; but how to serve God and obtain eternal salvation, is no part of their education. In *their* abode, wisdom, in the form of parental piety, is never heard saying—" Hearken, ye children, and I will teach you the fear of the Lord." They see cards and other amusements often introduced to the domestic circle, but no Bible; they hear singing, but it is not the songs of Zion; there is feasting and conviviality, but no devotion; there is no domestic altar, no family prayer. The Sabbath is marked with the same levity as other days. They go to church, perhaps, but hear anything rather than the true gospel of Christ. They are taken to every gay party in the neighborhood, and are studiously trained up for pleasure. They scarcely ever see the lovely form of religion in the circles which they frequent, except when, like its divine Author, it is brought there to be despised and rejected of men. How are such young people to be pitied! Who can wonder that *they* do not fear the Lord!

How different has been your lot!—the very contrast of this. From your earliest childhood, you have been taught the nature and the necessity of true religion. *Instruction* on this subject has been coëval with the dawn of reason. Every topic of piety has been explained to you, as you could bear it. The doctrines of Christianity have been stated and proved, its duties unfolded and enforced. The nature and attributes of God, the extent and obligation of His law, the design and grace of the gospel, have been explained; your sinful state has been clearly set before you, the object of Christ's death

pointed out, the necessity of regeneration, justification, and sanctification impressed upon your
heart. If you perish, will it be for lack of knowledge? If you miss the path of life, will it be from
not having it pointed out?

To instruction has been united *admonition*. With
all the tenderness of parental affection, and all the
seriousness which the nature of the subject demanded,
you have been warned, entreated, and even besought
to fear God and seek the salvation of your souls.
You have seen the tear glistening in a father's eye,
while his tongue addressed to you the fondest wishes
of his heart for your eternal happiness.

You have enjoyed the advantage of a system of
mild and appropriate *discipline*. Remember you
not the time when your budding corruptions were
nipped by the kind hand of parental care, and the
blossoms of youthful excellence were sheltered and
fostered by a mother's watchful solicitude? Have
they not often reproved you for what was wrong,
and commended you for what was right? Have
they not, by praise and by dispraise, judiciously administered, endeavored to train you up to hate that
which is evil, and to cleave to that which is good?
Have they not kept you from improper company,
and warned you against associates that were likely
to injure you? Have they not, with weeping eyes
and bleeding hearts, administered that correction
which your faults deserved?

You have also seen all this enforced by the
power of *a holy example*—imperfect, it is true, yet

8*

sufficient, like the sun, even when partially covered by a mist, to be your guide. You have seen them walking with God, and in fellowship with Christ. You have seen them retiring for prayer, and marked what an impression of devout seriousness they have brought from the presence of God. You cannot doubt that religion was the governing principle of their hearts. The happiness as well as holiness of true piety has appeared in their conduct. You have seen the cloud of sorrow which affliction brought upon their brow, irradiated with the sunbeams of Christian faith and hope. Thus, the whole weight of parental example has been employed to give impression in favor of religion on your heart.

But the advantage of a pious education rests not here; for you well know that it has procured for you all other religious benefits which conduce, in the order of means, to the salvation of the soul. You have been taken, from childhood, *to hear the gospel preached* by those who were anxious to save themselves, and them that hear them. You have been associated with religious people, and joined the circles of the righteous, where the claims of religion are respected, and her holy image has been welcomed with affection, and treated with respect. Religious books have been put into your hands. Schools have been selected for your education, which would aid the work of your parents, and everything kept out of your way which would be likely to be an impediment to the formation of your religious character, and your pursuits of eternal salvation. Thus, so far as means go, the very avenues of perdition have been blocked up, the way to destruction has been filled with mounds and barriers; while the path of life has been carefully laid open to your view, and everything done to facilitate your entrance to the road to immortality. You have been born, cradled, and instructed in an element of religion; you have trod the ground, and breathed the atmosphere of piety. What advantages! Who shall count their number, or calculate their value!

And now think of the *responsibility* which all these privileges entail upon you. This thought fills me with trembling for you, if you do not tremble for yourselves. Man is an accountable being, and his accountability to God is in exact proportion to his opportunities for knowing and doing the will of his Creator. No talents of this kind, that are entrusted to man, are so precious as those of a religious education; and with no persons will God be so awfully strict in judgment, as with those who have possessed them. A law of *proportion* will be the rule of the final judgment. Ten talents will not be required from those to whom only five were delivered; nor will only five be demanded from those with whom ten were intrusted. This is plainly stated by Christ, in that most impressive passage— "That servant which knew his Lord's will, and prepared not himself, neither did according to his will, shall be beaten with many stripes. But he that knew not, and did commit things worthy of

stripes, shall be beaten with few stripes. For unto
whomsoever much is given, of him shall be much
required; and to whom men have committed much,
of him they will ask the more." *   Who, upon this
scale, shall measure the height and depth of your
responsibility? The poor pagan who hews down a
tree, makes a god of its wood, and worships the
deity which he has thus fashioned, who lives in all
kind of lust, and cruelty, and falsehood,—the Mahometan, who turns his face to the rising sun, and
calls upon his prophet,—the rustic, who revels in
the village, where his father rioted before him, and
where neither of them ever heard one parental admonition, nor one gospel sermon; nay, even the
infidel, who derides the scripture, and was taught to
do it by his sire, will not have so much to account
for in the day of scrutiny as you, who have enjoyed
the advantages of a pious education. Think, I
beseech you, upon all your privileges, the instructions, the warnings, the admonitions, the reproofs,
you have received, even from your infancy—your
father's earnest prayers, and your mother's monitory
tears—domestic teaching and ministerial advice—
Sabbaths spent, and sermons heard—all, all must be
accounted for at the last day : all will be demanded
in judgment. You may now think lightly of these
things, but God does not. *You* may forget them as
they pass, but God does not. They are dealt out
to you as precious things; the number of them is

* Luke, xii. 47, 48.

written down amongst the records of Omniscience; and in that day, when the throne shall be set and the books shall be opened, the improvement of each will be demanded, by a voice at which the universe shall tremble. You will not be tried as one that had only the feeble glimmering of natural reason to guide his perceptions and his conduct, but as one that walked amidst the noontide splendor of divine revelation—as one that occupied just that station in the moral world, where the light of heaven fell with the clearest and the steadiest brightness.

Do fancy yourself called into judgment to answer for your religious privileges; summoned by a voice which it is impossible to resist, from the throng of trembling spirits waiting for their doom; fancy you hear the voice that commanded the universe into being, saying to you, " Child of the righteous, son of many prayers and much anxiety, give an account of thyself; exhibit the fruits and improvement of all thy rich and innumerable advantages for a life of piety. Ye parents who taught him, bear witness. I intrusted him to your care. Did ye bring him up in the fear, and nurture, and admonition of the Lord? resign your trust; deliver your testimony; clear yourselves." Impressive and awful spectacle. There you stand before the tribunal of God, confronted by the mother that bore you, and the father that loved you. If you shall then be found to have neglected your advantages, and lived without piety, what a testimony will they bear. " Thou art our witness, O God, and that unhappy individual in whom we once delighted as our child, but whom we now renounce forever, with what affectionate solicitude, and unwearied perseverance ; with how many tears and prayers we labored for his salvation. But all was useless. This is not the season of mercy, or we would still pour over his guilty head one more fervent prayer for his salvation ; but forbidden to commend him to thy mercy, we can now do nothing but leave him to thy justice." Miserable man, what can he say? He is speechless. Conscious guilt leaves him without excuse, and despair seals up his lips in silence. One piercing, agonizing look is directed to his parents, one deep groan escapes his bosom, as the ghosts of murdered opportunities rise upon his vision, and crowd the regions of his fancy. As his distracted eye ranges over the millions who stand on the left hand of the Judge, there is not one whose situation he does not envy. The Pagan, the Mahometan, the poor peasant, who sinned away his life in a benighted village, even the infidel going up to receive his doom for blaspheming the God of revelation, appears less guilty, less miserable than he.

But where my pen dipped in the gall of celestial displeasure, I could not describe the weight of the *sentence*, nor the misery which it includes, that will fall upon the ungodly child of righteous parents. Who shall portray the hell of such a fallen spirit, or set forth the torments with which it will be followed to the regions of eternal night ? We all know that no sufferings are so dreadful as those which are self-procured ; and that self reproach infuses a bitterness into the cup of woe, which exasperates the anguish of despair. Disappointment of long and fondly-cherished hopes is dreadful ; but if there be no reason for self-reproach, even this is tolerable ; but to suffer through eternal ages, in the bottomless pit, with no prospect but of misery, no employment but that of numbering over the advantages we once possessed for escaping from the wrath to come —*this* is hell. My children, my children ! my heart agonizes as I write. I groan over these lines of my book—these pictures of my fancy. Do take warning. Hearken to these sentiments. Let them have their due weight with your souls. Treasure up this conviction in your minds—that of all lands on the earth, it is the most dreadful to travel to the bottomless pit from a Christian country ; and of all the situations in that country, it is the most awful to reach the bottomless pit from the house of godly parents. *Let me be anything in the day of judgment, and in eternal misery*, RATHER THAN THE IRRELIGIOUS CHILD OF RELIGIOUS PARENTS.*

* There is a little repetition in this chapter of some of the sentiments in the first, but as the subject led to it the Author was not anxious to avoid it.

VI.

The Prevailing Obstacles which prevent Young People from entering on a Religious Life.

OUR Lord has most explicitly taught us, my dear children, that the entrance to the path of life is not unattended with difficulty, and is not to be accomplished without effort. Into that road, we are not borne by the pressure of the thronging multitude, nor the force of natural inclination. No broad and flowery avenue attracts the eye ; no syren songs of worldly pleasure allure the ear ; "but strait is the gate, and narrow is the way, that leadeth to life, and few there be that find it." Hence the admonition— "Strive to enter in at the strait gate ; for many shall seek to enter in, and shall not be able." This implies that there are obstructions to be removed, and difficulties to be surmounted.

The fundamental and universal obstruction with which every one has to contend, and which can be removed only by the power of the Holy Spirit, is the darkness and depravity brought upon human nature by the fall ; and the indulged sensuality, prejudice and enmity of the carnal mind. But this prevailing depravity manifests itself in various specific forms, according to the different circumstances, constitutions, ages, and tempers of its subjects. It is an inward and universal evil, exhibiting its opposition to religion in an immense variety of ways.

1. *Self-conceit* is not uncommonly to be met with in the character of the young, and is very much opposed to the spirit of true piety.

This is a sort of ·epidemic disease, which finds a peculiar susceptibility in persons of your age to receive it. Young in years and experience, they are very apt, nevertheless, to form high notions of themselves, and to fancy that they are competent judges of all truth and conduct. They decide, where wiser minds deliberate; speak, where experience is silent; rush forward with impetuosity, where their sires scarcely creep; and think themselves quite as competent to determine and to act, as those who have witnessed the events of threescore years and ten. This disposition shows itself oftentimes in reference to business; and the bankrupt list has, a thousand times, revealed the consequences. But it is seen in more important matters than business. In the gaiety of their spirits, and in the efflorescence of youthful energy, *they* see no great need of religion to make them happy; or if *some* religion be necessary they do not think it requires all that solicitude and caution with which older Christians attend to its concerns; *they* are not so much in danger as some would represent; *they* shall not take up with the humbling, self-abasing, penitential religion of their fathers, but adopt a more rational piety; *they* have reason to guide them, strength to do all that is necessary, and therefore, cannot see the need of so much fear, caution, and dependence.

My children, be humble; pride and self conceit will otherwise be your ruin. Think of your age and inexperience. How often already have you been misled, by the ardor of youth, in cases where you were most confident that you were right. When the Athenian orator was asked, what is the first grace in oratory? he replied, Pronunciation; the second? Pronunciation; the third? still he replied, Pronunciation; so, if I am asked what is this first grace in religion? I reply, Humility; the second? Humility; the third? still Humility; and self-conceit is the first, and the second, and the third obstruction.

2. *Love of worldly pleasure* is a great impediment to piety. It has been most profanely said, " Youth is the time for pleasure, manhood for business, old age for religion." It is painful to observe, that if the two latter allotments of human life are neglected, the first is not. Young people too often answer the description given by the apostle, " Lovers of pleasure more than lovers of God." In youth, there are many temptations to the gratification of this propensity; the senses are vigorous, the spirits lively, the imagination ardent, the passions warm, and the anxieties of life but few and feeble. Hence many give themselves up to the impulses of their corrupt nature, and are held in alienation from a life

of piety by a love of pleasure. Some are carried away by a vain and frivolous love of dress and show; others by a delight in convivality and parties; others by routs, balls, and theatrical representations; others by the sports of the field; others by intemperance and debauchery.

It is admitted that all these gratifications are not equally degrading in themselves, nor equally destructive of reputation and health; but if indulged as the chief good, they may all prevent the mind from attending to the concerns of religion. A predominant love of worldly pleasure, of any kind, is destructive in every point of view. It unfits you for the pursuits, and disinclines you for the toils of business, and thus is the enemy of your worldly interests; it often leads on from gratifications which, in the opinion of the world, are decent and moral, to those which are vicious and immoral; it is incompatible with the duties and comforts of domestic life; it hinders the improvement of the understanding, and keeps the mind barren and empty; it prevents us from becoming the benefactors of our species; but its greatest mischief is, that it totally indisposes the mind for religion, and thus extends its mischief to eternity; in short, if cherished and persisted in, it ruins and damns the soul forever.

My children, beware of this most dangerous propensity; consider whither it leads; check it to the uttermost; and ask grace from heaven to acquire a better taste. "What a hideous case is this, to be so debased in the temper of your minds, as to lose

all the laudable appetites and advantages of an intellectual nature ; and to be sunk into the deformity
of a devil, and into the meanness of a brute ! To
be so drenched in malignant delights, and in sensual,
fading, and surfeiting pleasures, as to forego all real
and eternal satisfactions for them, and to entail in-
supportable and endless miseries upon yourselves by
them !" Yes, if you live for worldly pleasure, and
neglect religion, you are giving up an exceeding
great and eternal weight of glory, for light and frivolous gratifications, which are but for a moment.
You are, for the sake of a few years' empty mirth,
entailing everlasting ages of unmitigated torments.

Besides, though worldly pleasure gratifies, it does
not satisfy ! When the honey is all sucked, does it
leave no sting behind? And then, what are the
pleasures of the world, compared with those of religion, but the shadow to the substance ; the stag-
nant pool to the fresh and running fountain ; the
smoking taper to the mid-day sun ? Shall worldly
pleasure cheat you of salvation ?

3. *Prejudice against the ways of religion as
gloomy*, keeps many from yielding to its claims.

Many young people seem to compare religion to
a dark subterranean cavern, in descending to which,
you quit all that is joyous in life; which is imper-
vious to the light of heaven, and inaccessible to the
melodies of creation ; where nothing meets the eye
but tears, nor the ear but sighs ; where the inhabitants, arrayed in sackcloth, converse only in groans ;
where, in short, a smile is an offence against the su-

perstition that reigns there, and a note of delight would be avenged by the awful genius of the place, with an expulsion of the individual who had dared to be cheerful. *This* religion? No, my children, I will give you another figurative view of it. " Wisdom hath builded her house, she hath hewn out her seven pillars; she hath killed her beasts; she hath mingled her wine; she hath also furnished her table; she hath sent forth her maidens; she crieth upon the highest places of the city, come, eat of my bread, and drink of the wine which I have mingled."* This is a metaphorical description of religion under the name of wisdom, and the figure of a feast. It is declared in revelation, and all the saints in the universe will confirm the truth of the assertion, that " Wisdom's ways are ways of pleasantness, and all her paths peace."†

4. *An inconsiderate heedless temper* is with many an obstruction to piety.

There is frequently, in persons of your age and circumstances, a peculiar thoughtlessness of mind; a want of calm consideration and steady reflection. They do not deliberate and ponder. Their minds seem as light as thistle-down, and as volatile as the butterfly. They are always walking, talking, smiling; but rarely thinking. The meditative mood, the contemplative attitude, is never theirs. If you want them, never look for them at home, but watch

* Proverbs, ix. 1, 5.

† See this proved at large in the chapter on the Pleasures of Religion.

for them abroad. Their extreme volatility prevents them from giving due heed even to the concerns of the world; and as for *religion*, though they are immortal creatures, lost sinners invited to salvation, destined to eternity, and hastening to heaven or hell, they have scarcely ever had a serious thought upon the subject: even *these* momentous topics are treated with the utmost lightness of mind. If the eye of any one of this class should range over these pages let me beseech her to look at her picture, and ask herself if she can admire it. O! my young friend, cannot the high themes of eternity make you serious? Placed as you are, on this earth, between the torments of the damned and the felicities of the redeemed—with the preparations for judgment going on, and the scenes of eternity opening before you; will you laugh out your little share of existence, and flutter through life, till, like a bird dropping into a volcano, you fall into the bottomless pit! Let these things soberize your thoughts, and bring you to the subject of religion, with something like an appropriate seriousness of mind.

5. *Evil companions* have often proved an obstruction to young people in the ways of piety.

Young people are generally inclined to company, and too often it proves a snare to them. Many a hopeful youth, that seemed at one time setting out in the ways of piety, has been arrested in his career by some unsuitable associate, with whom he has joined himself in the bonds of friendship; and thus he who seemed beginning in the spirit has ended in the flesh, leaving his pious friends to. exclaim, in the tone of grief and disappointment—"You did run well; who did hinder you?" How difficult is it, when a young person is first brought under the influence of genuine piety, to break from his former gay companions! and yet, if he would persevere in his new course, it *must* be done. In such cases the bonds of association *must* be broken. You must give up your society or your salvation; and can you hesitate?

6. *The misconduct of professing Christians, especially if they be our parents*, proves to many young persons a stone of stumbling at the entrance of the path of godliness.

They have seen the open immorality or the secret hypocrisy of those who profess to be partakers of true piety, and, under the influence of disgust and disappointment, are ready to conclude that all are alike, and that there is no reality in religion, no truth in revelation. I know that these things must often prove an obstruction in their way, and have produced, in some instances, an unconquerable antipathy to the ways of godliness. Yet is it rational to have our minds thus prejudiced against Christianity by the apostasies of those who were only its *pretended* disciples. But can that system be divine, you exclaim, amongst whose followers there are so many hypocrites? Can that system, I reply, be otherwise than divine, which has outlived them all, and triumphs alike over the apostasies of its seeming friends, and the opposition of its real foes?

Considering the numberless instances of this kind which have occurred, even from the beginning, I am persuaded that had not Christianity been supported by Omnipotence, nothing more than its name, as an ancient delusion, would have reached the nineteenth century. Nothing but that which is sustained by a principle of divine life, could have outlived so much internal decay, and so much external violence. Besides, does not the perpetual effort to counterfeit, prove its real excellence? For who imitates that which is worthless? Look at the bright as well as at the dark side. Against the troops of deserters and renegades, muster the thronging millions, who have endured temptation, and continued faithful unto death; call up the noble army of martyrs, whom neither dungeons nor fetters, scaffolds nor stakes could intimidate; who held fast their principles, amidst unheard-of tortures, and suffered not the king of terrors to rescue from their grasp the doctrines of their faith.

Judge of religion, as it demands to be tried, by its own evidences, and not by the conduct of its professors. Look at it in its own light, and there you will derive a conviction of its truth and importance, which would make you cling to it in a crisis, when even all men should forsake it. Religion an imposture, because some of its professors are false! As rationally may you conclude that there is no real orb of day, because, by an optical illusion, mock suns are sometimes seen in the atmosphere.

Remember, your neglect of religion will not be

excused, on the ground that your prejudices were shocked by the misconduct of professing Christians. Your obligations are in no degree dependent on the manner in which others discharge theirs.

7. *A spirit of procrastination* has considerable influence in preventing the young from attending to the claims of religion.

This has been the ruin of multitudes now in hell. How many amongst the lost souls in prison are now rueing the cheat which was practised upon their judgment, when they were persuaded to put off the affairs of eternity till another time! Perhaps there is not one in perdition but intended to be religious, at some future period. It is recorded of Archius, a Grecian magistrate, that a conspiracy was formed against his life. A friend, who knew the plot, despatched a courier with the intelligence, who, on being admitted to the presence of the magistrate, delivered to him a packet, with this message: " My lord, the person who writes you this letter conjures you to read it immediately—it contains serious matters." Archius, who was then at a feast, replied, smiling: " Serious affairs to-morrow," put the packet aside, and continued to revel. On that night the plot was executed, the magistrate slain, and Archius, on the morrow when he intended to read the letters, a mutilated corpse, leaving to the world a fearful example of the effects of procrastination. My children, when God and the preacher say *to-day*, give your attention to religion; do not reply *to-*

morrow; for, alas! on that morrow you may be in—
ETERNITY!

Young people are very apt to presume on long
life; but on what ground? Have they an assurance? No, not for an hour. Is it a rare thing for
young people to die? Go into any churchyard in
the kingdom, and learn the contrary from the records of the tombs. Have you any security in the
vigor of your constitution, from the melancholy
change produced by decay and death? "So have
I seen a rose, newly springing from the clefts of its
hood; and at first it was as fair as the morning,
and full with the dew of heaven as a lamb's fleece;
but when a ruder breath had forced open its virgin
modesty, and dismantled its too youthful and unripe
retirements, it began to put on darkness, and to
decline to softness, and the symptoms of a sickly
age; it bowed the head, and broke its stalk; and at
night, having lost some of its leaves, and all its
beauty, it fell into the portion of weeds and worn-
out faces." *

But, besides, admitting that you should live, is
not your inclination likely, if possible, to be less
and less towards religion? Your acts of sin will be
confirmed into habits; your heart will become
harder and harder, for it is the nature of depravity
to increase. If you wished to extinguish a fire,
would you wait till it was a conflagration? if to
cure a cold, would you wait till it was a fever?

* Jeremy Taylor's Holy Dying, p. 8.

What if God should withdraw His Spirit, and give you up to total insensibility! For, consider His grace is necessary to salvation. Religion is the work of God in the soul of man. Despised and rejected to-day, is He not likely to abandon you to-morrow? and then what a situation are you in! Like a barren rock, insensible both to the beams of the sun and the showers of heaven! You may felicitate yourselves in these circumstances, on the protraction of life; but it is your curse and not your blessing. You would tremble with indescribable horror at the thought of going the next hour to the flame which is never to be quenched! You would account it the climax of ruin. No, it is not. I can tell you something worse than even this. What! worse than going immediately to the bottomless pit! Yes. To live longer abandoned by God, given up to the deceitfulness of sin and hardness of heart, left to fill up still more to the brim the measure of iniquity: this, this is worse than instant damnation. Horrible as it seems, yet it is true, that many now in torment, wish they had been there before, and that they had not been permitted to live and commit those sins which are the sources of their bitterest sufferings.

These are amongst the most prevailing obstacles which often prevent young people from entering on a life of piety. Happy are they who, by the grace of God, are enabled to surmount them, and press through these impediments into the kingdom of God!

VII.

The Deceitfulness of the Heart.

THE detection of deceit, if not a pleasant employment, is certainly a profitable one; and that man
deserves well of society who puts them upon their
guard against a dangerous impostor. The object of
this section of my book is to expose the greatest
deceiver in the world, whose design is to cheat you,
my dear children, not of your property, nor of your
liberty, nor of your life; but of what is infinitely
dearer than all these—*the salvation of your immortal soul.* His success has been frightful, beyond
description. Earth is full of his operations—hell
of his spoils. Millions of lost souls bewail his
success in the bottomless pit, as the smoke of their
torment ascendeth up forever and ever. Who is
this impostor, and what is his name? Is it the false
prophet of Mecca? No. The spirit of paganism?
No. The genius of infidelity? No. It is the
human heart. It is to this that the prophet's description belongs—" deceitful above all things, and
desperately wicked." You will perceive that to the
wiles of this deceiver *you* are exposed. Let me,

then, request your very serious attention, whilst I lay open to you some of his deep devices and endless machinations.

By the deceitfulness of the heart, we are to understand the liability of our judgment to be perverted and misled by the depravity of our nature. And the following are the proofs of the fact:

1. *The astonishing ignorance in which many persons remain of their character and motives.*

It is with the mind, as with the countenance, every one seems to know it better than its possessor. Now, is not this somewhat singular? With the power of introspection, with access to our spirits every moment, is it not remarkable that any one should remain in ignorance of himself? Yet, is it not the case of myriads? How often do we hear persons condemning others for those very faults of which every one perceives that they themselves are guilty. We have a striking instance of this in David, when the prophet related to him the parable of the little ewe lamb. It is astonishing with what dexterity some persons will ward off the arrows of conviction which are aimed at *their* hearts, and give them a direction towards others. When in preaching or in conversation a speaker is endeavoring, in a covert way, to make them feel that *they* are intended as the objects of his censure, they are most busily employed in fastening it upon others, and admire the skill and applaud the severity with which it is administered. And when at length it becomes necessary to throw off the disguise, and to declare to them—" Thou art the man," it is quite amusing to see what surprise and incredulity they will manifest, and how they will either smile at the ignorance or frown on the malice which could impute to them faults, of which, however guilty they may be in other respects, they are totally innocent.

This self-deception prevails to a most alarming extent in the business of personal religion. The road to destruction is crowded with travellers, who vainly suppose that they are walking in the path of life, and whose dreams of happiness nothing will disturb, but the dreadful reality of eternal misery. How can this mistake arise ? The scripture most explicitly states the difference between a good man and a wicked one: the line of distinction between conversion and impenitence is broad, and deep, and plain. It can only be accounted for on the ground of the deceitfulness of the heart.

Then, when conviction forces itself upon the mind, and the real character begins to appear, what a degree of evidence will be resisted, and on what mere shadows of proof will men draw a conclusion in their own favor. How they mistake motives which are apparent to every bystander ; and, in some instances, even commend themselves for virtues, when the corresponding vices are rife in their bosoms.

2. Another proof of the deceitfulness of the heart lies in *the disguises which it throws over its* vices.

It calls evil good, and good evil. How common is it for men to change the names of their faults, and endeavor to reconcile themselves to sins, which, under their own proper designations, would be regarded as subjects of condemnation. Thus, intemperance and excess are called social disposition and good fellowship; pride is dignity of mind; revenge is spirit; vain pomp, luxury, and extravagance, are taste, elegance, and refinement; covetousness is prudence; levity, folly, obscenity, are innocent liberty, cheerfulness, and humor. But will a new name alter the nature of a vice? No; you may clothe a swine in purple and gold, and dress a demon in the robes of an angel of light; and the one is a beast, and the other a devil still.

The same operation of deceit which would *strip vice of its deformity*, would *rob holiness of its beauty*. Tenderness of conscience is called ridiculous precision; zeal against sin is moroseness and ill-nature; seriousness of mind, repulsive melancholy; superior sanctity, disgusting hypocrisy—in short, all spiritual religion is nauseating cant, whining methodism, wild enthusiasm. It is, however, the climax of this deceitfulness, when *vice is committed under the notion that it is a virtue;* and this has been done in innumerable instances. Saul of Tarsus thought he was doing God service while he was destroying the church. The bigots of Rome have persuaded themselves they were doing right while they were shedding the blood of the saints. O! the depth of deceit in the human heart!

3. What a proneness is there, in most persons, *to frame excuses for their sins;* and by what shallow pretexts are they often led to commit iniquity.

Ever since that fatal moment when our first parents endeavored to shift the blame of their crime from each other upon the serpent, a disposition to apologize for sin, rather than to confess it, has been the hereditary disease of their offspring. It discovers itself early in the human character; and it is truly affecting to see how much adroitness is manifested by very young children in excusing their faults; and this disposition grows with their growth and strengthens with their strength. Some excuse their sins on the ground of custom; others plead the smallness of their sins; others endeavor to persuade themselves that the suddenness and strength of temptation will be admitted as a justification of their conduct; while some plead the power of example; it is the first offence, say some; it is force of habit, exclaim others. Some attempt to find excuse for their actual sins in the inherent depravity of their nature; others in the peculiarity of their temper and constitution; a few go so far as to lay all their sins upon the Author of their nature. These are but some amongst the many excuses by which men are first led on to sin; by which they afterwards defend themselves against the accusations of conscience; and which most convincingly demonstrate the deep deceitfulness of the human heart.

4. It is proved also by *the gradual and almost*

insensible manner in which it leads men on to the
commission of sin.

No man becomes wicked all at once. The way
of a sinner in his career has been compared to the
course of a stone down a steep hill, the velocity of
which is accelerated by every revolution. The heart
does not offend and shock the judgment by asking
for too much at first; it conceals the end of the
career, and lets only so much be seen as is required
for the immediate occasion. When the prophet of
the Lord disclosed to Hazael his future enormities,
he exclaimed, " Is thy servant a dog, that he should
do this?" The exclamation was perfectly honest.
At that time, no doubt, he was incapable of such
wickedness, and it was a sincere revulsion of nature
which prompted the expression of his abhorrence.
But he knew not his heart. Little by little, he was
led forward in the course of iniquity, and, at length,
exceeded by his wickedness the prophet's prediction.
Habit renders all things easy, not excepting the most
atrocious crimes. Men have often done that without reluctance or remorse, which, at one period of
their lives, they would have shuddered to contemplate. Many have committed forgery, who at one
time could have been persuaded by no arguments,
nor induced by any motives to wrong an individual
of a farthing; and the murderer whose hands are
stained with blood, would, probably a few years or
months before, have trembled at the idea of destroying an animal. " When the heart of man is bound
by the grace of God, and tied in the golden bands

10*

of religion, and watched by angels, and tended by ministers, those nurse-keepers of the soul, it is not easy for a man to wander, and the evil of his heart is like the fierceness of lions' whelps ; but when he has once broken the hedge, and got into the strength of youth, and licentiousness of ungoverned age, it is wonderful to observe what a great inundation of mischief, in a very short time, will overflow all the banks of reason and religion.   Vice is first pleasing —then it grows easy—then it is delightful—then it is frequent—then habitual—then confirmed—then the man is independent—then he is obstinate—then he resolves never to repent—then he dies—then he is damned."*

I have somewhere read of one of the early Christians, who, on being asked by a friend to accompany him to the amphitheatre, to witness the gladiatorial combats with wild beasts, expressed his utmost abhorrence of the sport, and refused to witness a scene condemned alike by humanity and Christianity. Overcome, at length, by the continued and pressing solicitations of his friend, whom he did not wish to disoblige, he consented to go ; but determined that he would close his eyes as soon as he had taken his seat, and keep them closed during the whole time that he was in the amphitheatre.   At some particular display of strength and skill, by one of the combatants, a loud shout of applause was raised by the spectators, when the Christian almost involuntarily

* Jeremy Taylor's Sermons.

opened his eyes; being once open he found it difficult to close them again; he became interested in
the fate of the gladiator, who was then engaged with
a lion.   He returned home, professing to dislike, as
his principles required him to do, these cruel games;
but still his imagination ever and and anon reverted
to the scenes he had unintentionally witnessed.   He
was again solicited by his friend, who perceived the
conquest that had been made, to see the sport.   He
found less difficulty now than before in consenting.
He went, sat with his eyes open, and enjoyed the
spectacle.   Again and again he took his seat with
the pagan crowd, till at length he became a constant
attendant at the amphitheatre, abandoned his Christian principles, relapsed to idolatry, died a heathen,
and left a fatal proof of the deceitfulness of sin.

When a young man who has received a pious
education, begins to be solicited to break through
the restraints imposed upon him by conscience, he
can venture only on *lesser sins;* he perhaps only
takes a walk on the Sabbath with a friend, or goes
to see a play, or joins in one midnight revel; but
even this is not done with ease; he hears the voice
of an internal monitor, starts, and hesitates, but
complies.   A little remorse follows, but it is soon
worn off.   The next time temptation presents itself,
his reluctance is diminished, and he *repeats the
offence* with less previous hesitation, and less subsequent compunction.   What he did once, he now
without scruple does *frequently.*   His courage is so
far increased, and his fear of sin is so far abated,

that he is soon emboldened to commit a *greater sin*, and the tavern and the horse-race are frequented with as little reluctance as the theatre. Conscience now and then remonstrates, but he has acquired the ability to *disregard its warnings*, if not to silence them. In process of time, the society of all who make the least pretensions to piety is avoided as troublesome and distressing, and the heedless youth joins himself to companions better suited to his taste. Now his sins grow with vigor under the fostering influence of *evil company*, just like trees which are set in a plantation. By this time the Bible is put out of sight, all prayer neglected, and the sabbath constantly profaned. At length he feels *the force of custom*, and becomes enslaved by inveterate habit. The admonitions of a father, and the tears of a pious mother, produce no impressions, but such as are like the " morning cloud, or early dew, which soon passeth away." He returns to the society of his evil associates, where parental admonitions are converted into matter of wicked sport. The sinner is *settled now in an evil way ;* and the sapling of iniquity has struck his roots deep into the soil of depravity. The voice of conscience is now but rarely heard, and even then only in the feeble whisper of a dying friend. His next stage is *to lose the sense of shame.* He no longer wears a mask, or seeks the shade, but sins openly, and without disguise. *Conscience now is quiet ;* and without sceptre to warn, or angel to deliver, he pursues without a check the career of sin. He can meet a saint without a blush, and hear the voice of warning with a sneer. Would you believe it? he *glories in his shame*, and attempts to justify his conduct. Not content with being wicked, *he attempts to make others as bad as himself*, puts on the character of an apostle of Satan, and, like his master, goeth about as a roaring lion, seeking whom he may devour. As he is condemned in all his ways by the Bible, he endeavors to get rid of this troublesome judge, and persuades himself that religion is a cheat. With *infidel principles*, and immoral practices, he now hurries to destruction, polluted and polluting. His parents, whose gray hairs he brought in sorrow to the grave, have entered on their rest, and in mercy are not permitted to live to witness his shame. His vices lead him to extravagance; his extravagance is beyond his resources, and in an evil hour, under the pressure of claims which he is unable to meet, he commits an act which forfeits his life. He is arrested, tried, convicted, condemned, executed.

This is no fancy picture; it has often occurred. My dear children, see the deceitfulness of sin. Meditate, and tremble, and pray. Be alarmed at little sins, for they lead on to great ones; at acts of sin, for they tend to habits; at common ones, for they issue in those that are uncommon. I have read of a servant who went into a closet, with an intention only to gratify his palate with some sweetmeats, but perceiving some silver articles, he relinquished the meaner prey for these, purloined them, became a confirmed thief, and died at the gallows. Many a prostitute, who has perished in a garret upon straw, commenced her miserable and loathsome course with mere love of dress. Sin is like a fire, which should be extinguished in the first spark, for if it be left to itself, it will soon rage like a conflagration.

5. The last proof of the deceitfulness of the heart which I shall advance is, *the delusive prospects which it presents to the judgment.*

Sometimes it pleads for the commission of sin on the ground of *the pleasure which it affords.* But while it speaks of the honey of gratification, does it also tell of the venom of reflection and punishment ?

At other times it suggests *that retreat is easy in the career of sin,* and may be resorted to if its progress be inconvenient. Is it so ? The very contrary is true. Every step we advance renders it more and more difficult to return.

Then it urges us forward with the delusive idea that *it is time enough to repent in old age.* But does it say, what indeed is true, that for aught you know, you may die to-morrow ? No ; and herein is its deceit.

It dwells upon the mercy of God ; but is silent upon the subject of his justice.

What think you now of the human heart ? Can you question its deceitfulness, or that it is deceitful above all things ? How then will you treat it ?

Think meanly of it. Surely with such a picture before you, you will not talk of the moral dignity of human nature ; because this would be to talk of the dignity of falsehood and imposition.

Seek to have it renewed by the Holy Ghost.   It is a first principle of religion, that the heart must be renewed, and here you see the need of it.   It is not only the conduct which is bad, but the *heart*, and therefore it is not only necessary for the conduct to be reformed, but the very *nature* must be regenerated.   It is the heart which imposes upon the judgment, and the judgment which misleads the conduct ; and therefore the root of the evil is not touched until the disposition is changed.

Suspect the heart and search it.   Treat it as you would a man who had deceived you in every possible way, and in innumerable instances had been proved to be false.   Continually suspect it.   Always act under the supposition that it is concealing something that is wrong.   Perpetually examine it. Enter the house within you ; break open every door ; go into every apartment; search every corner ; sweep every room.   Take with you the lamp of revelation, and throw a light on every hiding-place.

Watch the heart with all diligence, knowing that out of it are the issues of life.   You would observe every attitude, every movement, every look of an impostor who had fixed his eye upon your person and property.   Thus treat your hearts.   Let every thought, every imagination, every desire, be placed under the most vigilant and ceaseless inspection.

Place it in the hand of God to keep it. " My son, give me thine heart," is his own demand.   Give it to him that it may be filled with his love, and kept by his power.   Let it be your daily prayer, " Lord, hold thou me up and I shall be safe ; keep me by thy power through faith unto salvation."

VIII.

Transient Devotions.

" THE church," said Saurin, " had seldom seen
happier days, than those described in the nineteenth
chapter of Exodus. God had never diffused his
benedictions on a people in a richer abundance.
Never had a people gratitude more lively, piety more
fervent. The Red Sea had been passed ; Pharaoh
and his insolent court were buried in the waves ;
access to the land of promise was opened ; Moses
had been admitted to the holy mountain to derive
felicity from God the source, and sent to distribute
it amongst his countrymen ; to these choice favors,
promises of new and greater blessings yet were added ; and God said, ' Ye have seen what I have done
unto the Egyptians, and how I bare you on eagles'
wings, and brought you unto myself. Now therefore, if you will obey my voice indeed, and keep my
covenant, then ye shall be a peculiar treasure unto
me above all people, although all the earth be mine.'
The people were deeply affected with this collection
of miracles. Each individual entered into the same
views, and seemed animated with the same passion ;

11

all hearts were united, and one voice expressed the sense of all the tribes of Israel;—'all that the Lord hath spoken we will do.' But this devotion had one great defect—*it lasted only forty days.* In forty days the deliverance out of Egypt, the catastrophe of Pharaoh, the passage of the Red Sea, the articles of the covenant; in forty days, promises, vows, oaths, all were effaced from the heart, and forgotten. Moses was absent, the lightning did not glitter, the thunder claps did not roar, and ' the Jews made a calf in Horeb, worshipped that molten image, and changed their glorious God into the similitude of an ox that eateth grass.' "

Here, my children, was a most melancholy instance of transient devotion. Alas! that such instances should be so common! Alas! that Jehovah should so frequently have to repeat the ancient reproach, and his ministers have to echo, in sorrowful accents, the painful complaint—" O Ephraim! what shall I do unto thee? O Judah! what shall I do unto thee? For your goodness is as a morning cloud, and as the early dew it passeth away." Nothing, however, is more common than such fugitive impressions. Disappointment of the bitterest kind is very frequently experienced, both by parents and ministers, in consequence of the sudden turning aside of those young persons, who, for awhile, seemed to run the race that is set before us in the word of God. At one time, they appeared to be inflamed with a holy ambition to win the prize of glory, honor, and immortality; we saw them start with eagerness, and run with speed; but after awhile, we met them returning to the barrier, leaving us, in the bitterness of our spirits, to exclaim—"Ye did run well; what did hinder you?"

" The religion I am now describing is not the hypocrisy of the pretending Christian, nor is it the backsliding of the real one; it goes further than the first, but does not go so far as the last. It is sincere of its kind, and in that it goes further than hypocrisy; but it is unfruitful, and in that it is inferior to the piety of the weak and revolting Christian. It is sufficient to discover sin, but not to correct it; sufficient to produce good resolutions, but not to keep them; it softens the heart, but does not renew it; it excites grief, but does not eradicate evil dispositions. It is a piety of times, opportunities, and circumstances, diversified a thousand ways, the effect of innumerable causes, but it expires as soon as the causes are removed."

Inconstans was a youth who had enjoyed a pious education; he discovered many amiable qualities, and was often impressed by the religious admonitions he received; but his impressions soon wore off, and he became as careless about his eternal concerns as before. He left the parental roof, and was apprenticed; and his parents having taken care to place him in a pious family, and under the faithful preaching of the word, he still enjoyed all the external means of grace, and still, at times, continued to feel their influence. His attention was oftentimes fixed when hearing the word, and he was sometimes observed to weep. On one occasion in particular, when a funeral sermon had been preached for a young person, a more than ordinary effect was produced upon his mind. He returned from the house of God pensive and dejected, retired to his closet, and with much earnestness prayed to God, resolved to attend more to the claims of religion, and to become a real Christian. The next morning he read the Bible, and prayed before he left his chamber. This practice he continued day after day. A visible change was produced in his deportment. His seriousness attracted the attention and excited the hopes of his friends. But, by degrees, he relapsed into his former state, gave up reading the scriptures, then prayer; then he reunited himself with some companions from whom, for a season, he had withdrawn himself, till at length he was as unconcerned about salvation as ever. Some time after this, *Inconstans* was seized with a fever. The disease resisted the power of the medicine, and baffled the skill of the physician; he grew worse and worse. His alarm became excessive. He sent for his minister and his parents, confessed and bewailed his fickleness. What tears he shed! What sighs he uttered! What vows he made! "O, if God would but spare me this once! if he would but grant me one more trial; if He would but indulge me with one more opportunity of salvation, how would I improve it to His glory, and my soul's eternal interest!" His prayers were answered; he recovered. What became of his vows, resolutions,

and promises? The degree of his piety was reg-
ulated by the degree of his malady. Devotion rose
and fell with his pulse. His zeal kept pace with his
fever; as one decreased, the other died away, and
the recovery of his health was the resurrection of
his sins. *Inconstans* is at this moment, what he
always was, a melancholy specimen of the nature of
mere transient religion.

What is wanting in this religion? You will, of
course, reply—"Continuance." This is true. But
why did it not continue? I answer—*There was no
real change of the heart*. The passions were moved,
the feelings were excited; but the disposition remained unaltered. In the affairs of this life, men are
often led by the operation of strong causes to act
in opposition to their real character. The cruel
tyrant, by some sudden and most affecting appeal
to his clemency, may have the spark of pity smitten
from his flinty heart; but the flint remaining, the
wretch returns again to his practices of blood. The
covetous man may, by a vivid description of want
and misery, be for a season melted to liberality;
but, like the surface thawed for an hour by the sun,
and frozen again immediately after the source of
heat has retired, his benevolence is immediately
chilled by the prevailing frost of his nature. In
these cases, as in that of religion, there is a suspension of the natural disposition, not a renewal of it.
All religion must be transient, by whatever cause
it is produced, and with whatever ardor it should,
for a season, be practised. that does not spring from

11*

a regenerated mind. It may, like the grass upon the house-top, or the grain that is scattered in unprepared soil, spring up and flourish for a season, but for want of root it will speedily wither away. Do not then, my dear children, be satisfied with a mere excitement of the feelings, however strong it may happen to prove; but seek to have the general bias of the mind renewed.

You cannot, if you consider only for a moment, suppose that these fugitive impressions will answer the ends of religion, either in this world or in that which is to come. They will not honor God—they will not sanctify the heart—they will not comfort the mind—they will not save the soul—they will not raise you to heaven—they will not save you from hell. Instead of preparing you at some future time to receive the gospel, such a state of mind, if persisted in, has a most direct and dangerous tendency to harden the heart. What God, in His sovereign grace, *may* be pleased to effect, it is not for me to say; but as to natural influence, nothing can be more clear than that this fitful piety is gradually putting the soul further and further from true religion. Iron, by being frequently heated, is hardened into steel; water that has been boiled becomes the colder for its previous warmth; soil that has been moistened with the showers of heaven becomes, when hardened by the sun, less susceptible of impression than before; and that heart which is frequently impressed by religion, without being renewed by it, becomes more and more insensible to its sacred influence. They who have trembled at the terrors of the Lord without being subdued by them, who have outlived their fears without being sanctified by them, will soon come to that degree of insensibility which will enable them to hear, without being appalled, the most awful denunciations of divine wrath. They who have been melted, from time to time, by the exhibitions of divine love, but have not been converted by it, will come at length to hear of it with the coldest indifference. It is a dreadful state of mind to be given up to a spirit of slumber and a callous heart; and nothing is more likely to accelerate the process than occasional, yet ineffectual religious impressions. Can we conceive of anything more likely to induce Jehovah to give us up to judicial blindness and insensibility, than this tampering with conviction, this trifling with devotional impressions? These pious emotions which are occasionally excited, are kind and gentle admonitions that He has come near to the soul, with all the energies of his Spirit; they are the work of mercy knocking at the door of our hearts, and saying—" Open to me, that I may enter with salvation in my train." If they are from time to time neglected, what can be looked for but that the celestial visitor should withdraw, and pronounce, as he retires, the fearful sentence—" Woe unto you when my Spirit departeth from you."

There is something inexpressibly *wicked* in remaining in this state of mind. Such persons are in some respects more sinful than they whose minds

have never been in any degree enlightened ; whose
fears have never been in any degree excited ; who
have paid no attention whatever to religion, but
whose minds are sealed up in ignorance and insensibility.   When persons who have taken some steps
in religion return again ; when they who have come
near the kingdom of God, recede from it ; and they
who have sipped, as it were, of the cup of salvation, withdraw their lips from the water of life,
the interpretation of their conduct is this—" We
have tried the influence of religion, and do not find
it so worthy of our cordial reception as we expected ;
we have seen something of its glory, and are disappointed ; we have tasted something of its sweetness, and, upon the whole, we prefer to remain
without it.   Thus they are like the spies who
brought a false report of the land of promise, and
discouraged the people.   They defame the character
of true piety, and prejudice men's minds against it.
They libel the Bible, and persuade others to have
nothing to do with religion.   My children, can you
endure the thought of this ?

Mere transient devotions *have a great tendency
to strengthen the principle of unbelief* in our nature.
It is not only very possible, but very common for
men to sin themselves into a state of despair of
God's mercy ; and none are so likely to do this, as
those who have repeatedly gone back to the world
after a season of religious impression.   In our intercourse with society, if we have greatly offended
and insulted a man after professions of decided

friendship and warm attachment, we can hardly persuade ourselves to approach him again, or be persuaded to think he will admit us again to the number of his friends. And, as we are prone to argue from ourselves to God, if we have frequently repented, and as frequently returned again to sin, we shall be in great danger of coming to the conclusion that we have sinned past forgiveness, and abandon ourselves to guilt and despair. I have read of a gentleman who lived without any regard to religion till he was taken alarmingly ill, when his conscience was roused from its slumber, and he saw the wickedness of his conduct. A minister was sent for, to whom he acknowledged his guilt, and begged an interest in his prayers, at the same time vowing that if God would spare his life, he would alter the course of his behavior. He was restored to health, and for awhile was as good as his word. He set up family worship, maintained private prayer, and frequented the house of God; in short, appeared to be a new man in Christ Jesus. At length he began to relax, and step by step went back to his former state of careless indifference. The hand of affliction again arrested him. His conscience again ascended her tribunal, and in terrible accents arraigned and condemned him. The state of his mind was horrible. The arrows of the Lord pierced him through, the poison whereof drank up his spirits. His friends entreated him to send for the minister, as above. "No!" he exclaimed, "I who have trifled with the

mercy of God once, cannot expect it now!" No
persuasion could shake his resolution; no representation of divine grace could remove his despair;
and, without asking for pardon, he died

The same despair has, in many other instances,
resulted from the sin of trifling with religious impressions.

These pages will probably be read by some, whose
minds are under religious concern. Your situation
is more critical and important than any language
which I could employ would enable me to represent. If your present anxiety subsides into your
former carelessness, you are in the most imminent
danger of being left to the depravity of your nature.
God is now approaching you in the exercise of his
love, and waiting that he may be gracious. Seek
him while he is to be found, call upon him while he
is near. The soft breezes of celestial influence are
passing over you, seize the auspicious season, and
hoist every sail to catch the breath of heaven.
Tremble at the thought of losing your present feelings. Be much and earnest in prayer to God, that
he would not suffer you to relapse into unconcern
and neglect. Take every possible means to preserve
and deepen your present convictions. Read the
Scriptures with renewed diligence. Go with increased earnestness, and interest, and prayer, to the
house of God. Endeavor to gain clearer views of
the truth as it is in Jesus, and labor to have your
mind instructed as well as your heart impressed.

Be satisfied with nothing short of a renewed mind—the new birth. Be upon your guard against self-dependence. Watch against this, as much as against grosser sins. Consider yourself as a little child, who can do nothing without God. Study your own sinfulness in the glass of God's holy law. Grow in humility ; it is not well for a plant to shoot upwards quickly, before it has taken deep root; if there be no fibres in the earth, and no moisture at the root, whatever blossoms or fruit there may be in the branches, they will soon fall off; and in the same way, if your religion do not strike root in humility, and be not moistened with the tears of penitential grief, whatever blossoms of joy or fruits of zeal there may be on the mind or conduct, they will soon drop off under the next gust or heat of temptation. Take heed of secret sinning. A single lust unmortified, will be like a worm at the root of the newly-planted piety of your soul. Continually remember that it is yet but the beginning of religion with you. Do not rest here ; believe in the Lord Jesus Christ; nothing short of this will save you ; without faith, all you have felt, or can feel, will do you no good ; you must come to Christ, and be anxious to grow in grace, and in the knowledge of God our Saviour.

Some, it is probable, will read these lines, who have had religious impressions, and lost them. Your goodness has vanished like the cloud of the morning ; and, like the early dew, has sparkled and ex-

haled.   Sometimes you exclaim, with an emphasis
of deep melancholy,

> " What peaceful hours I once enjoyed ?
> How sweet their mem'ry still !
> But they have left an aching void
> The world can never fill."

You *are* not, you *cannot* be happy.   Oh no ; the
din of pleasure or of business cannot drown the
voice of conscience ; a pause now and then occurs,
when its thunders are heard, and heard with indescribable alarm.   Sometimes, in the midst of your
pleasures, when all around you is jollity and mirth,
you see a spectacle which others do not see, and are
terrified by a mystic hand which writes your doom
upon the wall.   From that moment there is no more
joy for you.   Sometimes you almost curse the hour
when the voice of a faithful preacher lodged conviction in your bosom, and half-spoiled you for a man
of pleasure and the world.   You look with almost
envy on those who, by never having been taught to
fear God, are wrapt in total darkness, and see not
the dim spectres, the half-discovered shapes of mischief, which, in the twilight of your soul, present
themselves to *your* affrighted vision.   At other
times, a little relenting, you exclaim, " O that it
were with me as in months past, when the candle of
the Lord shined on my tabernacle.   What would I
give to recall the views and feelings of those days !
Happy seasons ! ye are fled like visions of spiritual
beauty.   And are ye fled forever ?   Can no power

recall you to this troubled mind?" Yes, my young
friend, they are all within reach, lingering to return.
Fly to God in prayer, beseech him to have mercy
upon you. Implore him to rouse you from the
slumber into which you have fallen. Beware of the
chilling influence of despondency. There is no room
for despair. Covet the possession of true religion.
Search for the cause which destroyed your impress
ions in the time that is past. Was it some improper companion? Abandon him forever, as you would
a viper. Was it some situation unfriendly to godliness which you voluntarily chose, as Lot did Sodom, on account of its worldly advantages? Re-
linquish it without delay. Escape for thy life, and
tarry not in all the plain. Was it some besetting
sin, dear as a right eye, or useful as a right hand?
Pluck it out, tear it off without hesitation or regret; for is it not better to make this sacrifice, than
to lose eternal salvation, and endure everlasting
torments? Was it self-dependence, self-confidence?
Now put your case into the hand of Omnipotence,
and call upon God. Ask for the Holy Spirit to renew, to sanctify, and to keep your soul. Learn
from your past failure what to do, and what to avoid
for the future. Believe the gospel, which declares
that the blood of Christ cleanseth from all sin. It
was faith that was wanting, in the first instance, to
give permanence to your religious impressions.
There was no belief, no full persuasion, no practical
conviction, of the truth of the gospel. Your religious feelings were like the stream raised by external

and adventitious causes, but there was no spring. You stopped short of believing, you made no surrender of the soul to Christ, nor committed yourselves to him, to be justified by his righteousness, and to be sanctified by his Spirit. This do and live.

IX.

Decision of Character in Religion.

How deep, and how just a reproach did the prophet cast upon the tribes of Israel, when he addressed to the assembled multitudes on Mount Carmel, that memorable interrogation, "How long halt ye between two opinions? if the Lord be God, follow him; but if Baal, follow him." From this it appears they were in a state of indecision, in reference to the most momentous question in the universe, not wholly satisfied that they were doing right in worshipping Baal, yet not sufficiently resolute to abandon his service. What a criminal, what a degrading, what a wretched state of mind! Not decided whom they would acknowledge to be their God! to whom they would pay divine homage! But is this state of mind, my dear children uncommon? By no means. To how many of the youth who attend our places of devotional resort, could we address, with propriety, the same question, "How long halt ye between two opinions?" How many are there who can go no further than Agrippa, when he said to Paul, "*Almost* thou persuadest me to be a Christian." Almost! Only almost persuaded to be a Christian! What a melancholy thought!

In the last chapter you saw in the character of *Inconstans*, an instance of this indecision. Did you admire it? Impossible. What was wanting?— DECISION. But what do I mean by decision? "A fixed purpose, not made in haste, but with much deliberation; not in our own strength, but in reliance on the grace of God; without delay, and at all risks, to seek the salvation of the soul through faith in Christ, and to live soberly, righteously, and godly in this present evil world." It includes an inflexible severity of conviction, that this is the one great thing we have in this world to do, and such a concentration of all the energies of our soul in this mighty business, as, to idle spectators, shall put on the appearance of enthusiasm. It is such a purpose as subordinates everything to itself. In opposition to transient devotion, it is permanent; in opposition to fluctuating opinions, it is a fixed, abiding resolution; in opposition to mere occasional acts, it is an indelible character, an indestructible habit. In short, it is faith in opposition to mere opinion and speculation : it is actually receiving Christ instead of talking about him. It is not like the vapor, which, after attracting every eye by its meteoric splendor, vanisheth away while yet the surprised and delighted spectator beholds its luminous course; but it is like the shining light which holds on its way in the heavens, and shineth more and more unto the perfect day. It is attended with a relinquishment of former associations, former pursuits and pleasures, and the embracing of all such as are on the side of religion. We have a fine instance of this decision in the heroic leader of the hosts of the Lord, when looking round upon the wavering tribes of Israel, he exclaimed, " Let others do what they will, as for me and my house, we will serve the Lord." Another example, equally splendid, was presented by the great apostle of the Gentiles, when with the perspective of his suffering career before his eyes, he gave utterance to that burst of sublime heroism, " None of these things move me, neither count I my life dear unto me, so that I might fulfil the ministry I have received of the Lord, and finish my course with joy." Similar to this is the language of a decided Christian, " Self-denial, ridicule, rage, mortification, loss, all are nothing to me, so that I may believe the gospel, live in the fear of God, die in his favor, and, through the merits of Christ, be received to everlasting glory."

It will be proper to state here the reasons why so many that have strong impressions occasionally made upon their minds, are not thoroughly and decidedly engaged in the practice of religion. Some of these will be found in the chapter " On the Obstacles of Piety," but there are others which are still more specific in reference to the case before us.

There is in many *a want of deep serious consideration.* They do not follow up the subject of religion, even when it has been impressed with some degree of force upon their hearts. When emotions have been excited, they do not cherish them; but go to their usual conversation, company, or business, instead of entering into their closets to examine their hearts, and to apply the subjects they have heard. An officer in the army, when about to embark for the continent, came to a Christian friend, and told him that he had a great many serious thoughts about the state of his soul, and was resolved to lead a new life; "but," said he, " there is such a company I must be with to-night; I wish I could disengage myself from them." His friend of course attempted to dissuade him from joining the party. He, notwithstanding, went to them, forgot all his serious thoughts when there; was drawn into the revelry of the night; the following day went abroad; and the next news his friends heard of him was, that he was killed in action. Thus his vain companions extinguished his serious thoughts, diverted his good resolutions, and by his own consent, robbed him of his eternal salvation.

Another cause of irresolution is, *the feeble and uncertain perceptions which many persons have of divine and spiritual things.* They have a dim view of the truths of revelation, but they appear like objects in a mist, too indistinct to be made the matter of pursuit. Hence it is of tremendous consequence, that when a young person becomes in any degree serious about religion, he should instantly betake himself to all proper means for informing

his judgment on the nature of true religion.   He
should read the scriptures with intense application
of mind, listen to the preaching of the word with
great fixedness of attention, and peruse good books
with much seriousness of mind.*

The dominion of some one prevailing sin, if cherished and indulged, has a most fatal influence in
preventing decision.   Herod would do many things,
but would not part from Herodias.   Felix was moved
by Paul's preaching, but he would not give up covetousness.   Thus it is with many : they admit the
claims of religion, admire its beauty, are moved by
its force, resolve to submit to its influence; but
then there is some besetting sin, which, when they
come to the point, they cannot be induced to sacrifice.   Every plant has some leading root which
connects it with the soil in which it grows, on which,
more than any of the rest, it is dependent for support and nourishment.   So it is in the human heart :
there is in most persons some prevailing corruptions
of nature, which, more than any of the rest, holds
the heart to an unregenerate state, and to which
very particular attention must be paid in the business of religion.   This sin may be different in different persons ; but whatever it be, it must be
destroyed, or it will destroy us.

Fear of persecution operates in many to prevent
decision.   You are deterred, probably, my children,

---

* Doddridge's " Rise and Progress of Religion in the Soul,"
is a standard treatise.

from giving up yourselves to the influence of piety, by the apprehensions that you shall be called to endure the ridicule of those with whom you have been accustomed to associate, and who, being unfriendly to religion, will vent their scorn and contempt on those who submit to its claims. It is impossible that I can be so ignorant of the irreconcilable enmity existing, and destined ever to exist, between religion and the depravity of human nature ; or of the usual practice of those who hate religion as to promise you an exemption from the sneers of the scorner, if you walk in the paths of wisdom. The only weapons which many are able to wield against Christianity, are sneers ; for there is no mind so imbecile, no fool *so* foolish, as not to be able to laugh ; the individual who could no more argue than an infant, could use the sword or brandish the spear of a Goliath, can shoot out the lip, and cry methodist, puritan, and fanatic. The power to argue is comparatively rare ; but almost every village in the kingdom will furnish a mob of little minds, to follow after religion as it passes by, and, like the children of Bethel persecuting the prophet of the Lord, to ridicule its venerable form.*   A

---

* Never did Satan invent a more successful weapon against religion than ridicule. This apparently mean and contemptible engine, like the pike-head of modern warfare, may be circulated widely, and put into ten thousand hands, which could make nothing of a more dignified kind of instrument. By this means he can arm the *levy en masse* of his dominions, who could do nothing in the ranks of the regular troops, or with the artillery of infidelity.

morbid sensibility to shame, I am perfectly convinced, has kept not a few young people from piety.
They cannot bear the broad, loud laugh, the con-
temptuous sneer, the witty jest.   They cannot endure the attack of the profane, nor the raillery of
the impious.   They blush, and conceal their secret
attachment to piety, directly it is assailed.   But,
my children, where is the dignity or the courage of
your mind?   Are you indeed convinced of the truth
of Christianity and the justice of its claims, and yet
suffer yourselves to be vanquished by the laugh of
folly?   What! flee from the enemy of your souls,
and surrender your salvation, when he only hisses
at you in the skin of a fool!   What though the
world were to unite in scorn, shall this deter you
from acting, when God, truth, heaven, the Bible,
conscience, salvation, saints, angels, are all on your
side?   What! when your spirit has plumed her
wings of faith and hope for flight to heaven, shall
she give up the dazzling object of her high ambition,
and cower down on earth, because she is watched
and ridiculed by the witling?   Or shall her eagle
pinions be blown from their lofty course by the
scoff of the scorner?   Be DECIDED, and all this
mean and feeble kind of persecution will soon
cease. Before that sublime and unbending decision
which dares to be singular, which nothing can divert from its purpose, which nothing can diminish
in its ardor, which clings the closer to its object for
all the efforts that are employed to detach it from
the pursuit; I say before that inflexible spirit, it

is astonishing to see how the space clears away, and how soon she is left to pursue her course, while all the tribe of little, pecking, cavilling, noisy minds, drop down into their hedges, and leave the eagle to her course.

"This invincibility of temper," says the profoundest and most elegant essayist in the English language, "will often make the scoffers themselves tired of the sport. They begin to feel that against such a man it is a poor kind of hostility to laugh. There is nothing that people are more mortified to spend in vain than their scorn. A man of the right kind would say, upon an intimation that he is opposed by scorn—'They will laugh, will they? I have something else to do than to trouble myself about their mirth. I do not care if the whole neighborhood were to laugh in a chorus. I should indeed be sorry to see or hear such a number of fools, but pleased enough to find that they do not consider me one of their stamp. The good to result from my project will not be less, because vain and shallow minds, that cannot understand it, are diverted at it, and at me. What should I think of my pursuits, if every trivial, thoughtless being could comprehend, or would applaud them; and of myself, if my courage needed levity and ignorance for their allies, or could shrink at their sneers?' " *

* See Foster's "Essay on Decision of Character." I should deem it an insult to my readers, to suppose they have not read these essays; and not less so their author, to suppose that they needed my recommendation. I cannot

My children, think of the importance of the matter to be decided upon—the service of God, the pursuit of immortality, the salvation of the soul—and shall a false shame deter you from the pursuit? Think of the example of Jesus Christ, who, for the joy that was set before him, endured the cross, despising the shame.   Look at this divine sufferer, as he is presented to us in the hall of Pilate, when he was made the object of every species of scorn and indignity; and will you shrink from a few sneers and scoffs for Him?   Remember our Lord's most alarming language—" Whosoever shall be ashamed of me, and of my words, in this adulterous and sinful generation, of him also shall the Son of man be ashamed, when he cometh in the glory of his Father, and with the holy angels."   Anticipate, if you can, the shame, the disgrace, the mortification, the torment, of being disowned, rejected, and abandoned by Christ, before assembled worlds; and let that be a preservative against being ashamed of Him now.

It is time now to set before you *the evil of indecision*, as a motive to induce you to seek after the opposite temper.

Such a temper is most *unreasonable*, if you consider both the importance of the subject and the means you possess of coming to speedy and right

help, however, enjoining on my readers to read the essay from which the above extract is made, with the resolution to seek, and the prayer to obtain all that decision which is there so eloquently described, not only in reference to every good work in general, but to religion in particular decision.   Is it a matter of trifling moment? Yes, if God, and eternity, and salvation, and heaven, and hell, are trifles.   If religion be a trifle, where, in all the universe, shall we find anything that is important.   Irresolution here, is to be undetermined whether you will be the friend or the enemy of God; whether you will live in this world under the favor or the curse of Jehovah, and in the world to come, in the torments of the bottomless pit, or amidst the felicities of the heavenly city; whether you will choose condemnation or salvation.   There is no language which can describe, there is no allusion which can illustrate, the folly of indecision in religion. The irresolution of a slave, whether he should continue to groan in fetters or be free; of the leper, whether he should still be covered with the most loathsome disease, or enjoy the glow of health; of the condemned criminal, whether he should choose an honorable life, or the most torturing and ignominious death; is not marked with such desperate folly as an undecided state of mind about personal religion.   *The scripture demands decision,* and it demands it in these striking words—" See, I have set before thee this day life and good, death and evil; therefore choose."   Yet some are undecided whether they will serve God, their Creator, Preserver, and Benefactor, and inherit eternal life; or yield themselves to Satan, their destroyer, and suffer the bitter pains of eternal death.   If the matter were involved in obscurity, as to what was your duty or your interest, there would be some apology;

but when both are as clear as the day, the folly of indecision is so palpably manifest, as to entail a most fearful degree of guilt upon the conscience of the irresolute.

Indecision is *contemptible*. " Unstable as water thou shalt not excel," is a character which no one ever pretended to admire.   In the ordinary affairs of life, indecision renders a man an object of pity or contempt.   " It is a poor disgraceful thing not to be able to answer with some degree of firmness to the questions, What will you be ?   What will you do ?   It is a pitiable thing to see a creature with all the faculties of a rational being about him, so irresolute and undecided, as almost to wish that he could exchange reason for instinct, in order that he might be spared the trouble of thinking, and the pain of choosing ; a poor, dependent, powerless crea- ture, that floats like a feather or a ship along the stream of time, belonging to whatever can seize him ; and without one effort of resistance, whirled in every little eddy, and intercepted by every little twig." But how much more disgraceful is this irresolute- ness of mind in the affairs of religion, where there are so many means, and so many motives for com- ing to a just conclusion.   To be blown about like thistle-down by every wind of doctrine, and carried just wherever the gust or the current impels, is as dishonorable to our understanding as it is detrimen- tal to our salvation.

Indecision is *uncomfortable*.   Suspense is always painful.   Hesitation as to the steps we shall take, and the conduct we shall pursue, is a most undesirable state of mind; and this uneasiness will be in exact proportion to the importance of the business to be decided and to the degree of compunction we feel for not deciding upon a course, which, we cannot help thinking, upon the whole, is the right one. The undecided cannot be altogether easy in their present fluctuating state of mind. No; directed one way by conviction, and dragged another by inclination: determining at one time to serve God fully, and at another smarting under the guilt of broken vows; resolved on the Sabbath, and irresolute on the Monday; sometimes advancing with courage, and then again retreating with fear and shame: no, *this* is not the way to be happy. You may as well expect peace on the field of battle, as in the bosom where such a conflict is carried on. Look up to God, and ask for grace to terminate by decided piety the dreadful strife, if indeed it be carried on in your breast.

Indecision is *dangerous.* Consider the uncertainty of life. How soon and how suddenly the King of Terrors may arrest you, and bear you to his dark domain. Some acute, inflammatory disease, in a few days may extinguish life; or a fatal accident, which leaves you no leisure even to bid adieu to those you love on earth, may hurry you into eternity. *And then what becomes of you?* In a state of indecision you are unprepared for death, for judgment, for heaven. You are within the flood-mark of Divine vengeance. God accounts all

those to be decidedly against him who are not decidedly for him.   There is, properly speaking, no middle ground between regeneracy and unregeneracy,
between conversion and unconversion, and therefore
he that does not occupy the one, is found within the
limits of the other.   You are a child or an enemy of
God.   Whatever may be your occasional relentings,
your transient emotions, your ineffectual desires, if
you do not become decidedly pious, God will take no
account of these things, but treat you, if you die in
this state, as one that had decided against him.
Can you then linger, when death and hell do not
linger ?   Can you halt, hesitate, and fluctuate, when
death may the very next hour decide the business
for you ?   And, oh ! if you *should* die without decision, what will be *your* reflections and what will
be *ours.*   How bitterly will you exclaim, " Fool
that I was, to let anything interfere with my eternal salvation, to let any thing interpose between my
soul and her everlasting welfare.   Why, why did I
hesitate ?   I saw the excellence, I coveted the possession of religion.   Often I felt my heart rising to
go and surrender unreservedly to God ; I wept, I
prayed, I resolved ; but that accursed lust in which
I took pleasure, held me fast, and rather than tear
myself from it, I let go the hope of eternal life.   I
was afraid of a little ridicule, which I ought to
have disregarded or despised, and when I seemed
near the kingdom, was ruined by indecision.   While
I hesitated, death seized me, and now I shall be exhibited, by the light of this flame in which I burn

forever, an awful proof of the folly and the danger of indecision.   Woe, eternal woe upon my
wretched spirit !"

Spare yourselves, my dear children, these dreadful reflections, this inconceivable torment.   Without an hour's delay, resign yourselves to God and
the influence of true religion.   Decide the doubtful point.   Believe and obey.

X.

The Pleasures of a Religious Life.

A DESIRE after happiness, my dear children, is inseparable from the human mind. It is the natural and healthy craving of our spirit; an appetite which we have neither the will nor the power to destroy, and for which all mankind are busily employed in making provision. This is as natural, as for birds to fly, or fishes to swim. For this the scholar and the philosopher, who think it consists in knowledge, pore over their books and their apparatus, light the midnight lamp, and keep frequent vigils, when the world around them is asleep. For this the warrior, who thinks that happiness is inseparably united with fame, pursues that bubble through the gory fields of conflict, and is as lavish of his life as if it were not worth a soldier's pay. The worldling, with whom happiness and *wealth* are kindred terms, worships daily at the shrine of Mammon, and offers earnest prayers for the golden shower. The voluptuary gratifies every craving sense, rejoices in the midnight revel, renders himself vile, and yet tells you he is in the chase of happiness. The am-

13*

bitious man, conceiving that the great desideratum blossoms on the sceptre, and hangs in rich clusters from the throne, consumes one half of his life, and embitters the other half in climbing the giddy elevation of royalty. All these, however, have confessed their disappointment; and have retired from the stage exclaiming, in reference to happiness, as Brutus, just before he stabbed himself, did in reference to virtue, "I have pursued thee everywhere, and found thee nothing but a name." This, however, is a mistake; for both virtue and happiness are glorious realities, and if they are not found, it is merely because they are not sought from the right sources.

We may affirm of pleasure what Job did of wisdom, "There is a path which no fowl knoweth, and which the vulture's eye hath not seen; the lions whelps have not trodden it, nor the fierce lion passed by it. But where shall" *happiness* "be found, and where is the place of" *enjoyment?* "Man knoweth not the price thereof, neither is it found in the land of the living. The depth saith, It is not in me; and the sea saith, It is not with me. It cannot be gotten for gold, neither shall silver be weighed for the price thereof. It cannot be valued with the gold of Ophir, with the precious onyx, or the sapphire. Whence, then, cometh" *happiness,* "and where is the place of" *enjoyment?* "seeing it is hid from the eyes of all living, and kept close from the fowls of the air. Destruction and death say, We have heard the fame thereof with our ears.

God understandeth the way thereof, and he know.
eth the place thereof. When he made a decree for
the rain, and a way for the lightning of the thunder ;
then did he see it, and declare it, he prepared it,
yea, and searched it out. And unto man he said,
Behold, the fear of the Lord, that is wisdom ; and
wisdom's ways are ways of pleasantness, and all her
paths are peace."

Happiness has no other equivalent term than religion, and this is a moral synonyme. If, indeed,
the case were *otherwise,* and religion, so far as the
present world is concerned, entailed nothing but
wretchedness, yet, as it leads to eternal felicity in
the world to come, it is most manifestly our interest
to attend to its claims. The poor Hindoo devotee,
who endures all kinds of tortures, under the idea
that it is the only way to eternal felicity, acts with
perfect rationality, if you allow his data. A life
protracted to the length of Methuselah's, and filled with penances and pilgrimages, should be willingly and thankfully endured, if salvation could be
procured by no other means. In the prospect of
eternity, with heaven spreading out its ineffable
glories, and hell uncovering its dreadful horrors, the
only question which a rational creature should allow
himself to ask is, " What is necessary to avoid the
torments of the one, and secure the felicities of the
other ?" and on being told " Religion," he should apply with all the energies of his soul to this great
business, without scarcely allowing himself to ask
whether its duties are pleasant or irksome. The

man who is journeying to take possession of a kingdom, scarcely thinks it worth his while to inquire
whether the road be through a wilderness or a paradise.   It is enough for him to know, that it is the
only road to the throne.   Hence the representation of the *pleasures* of religion, is a sort of gratu-
ity in this subject.   It serves, however, to leave
those still more destitute of excuse who live in the
neglect of piety, and in this view may have still
greater power to rouse the conscience.

1. That religion is pleasure, will appear, if you
consider *what part of our nature it more particularly employs and gratifies.*

It is not a gratification of the *senses,* or of the
animal part of our nature, but a provision for *the
immaterial and immortal* MIND.   The mind of man
is an image not only of God's spirituality, but of
his infinity.   It is not like the senses, limited to
this or that kind of object, as the sight intermed-
dles not with that which affects the smell ; but with
a universal superintendence, it arbitrates upon, and
takes them in, all.   It is as I may say, an ocean,
into which all the little rivulets of sensation, both
external and internal, discharge themselves.   Now,
this is that part of man to which the exercises of
religion properly belong.   The pleasures of the understanding, in the contemplation of truth, have
been sometimes so great, so intense, so engrossing
all the powers of the soul, that there has been no
room left for any other kind of pleasure.   How
short of this are the delights of the epicure !   How

vastly disproportionate are the pleasures of the eating and of the thinking man ! " Indeed," says Dr. South, " as different as the silence of an Archimides in the study of a problem, and the stillness of a sow at her wash." Nothing is comparable to the pleasures of mind; these are enjoyed by the spirits above, by Jesus Christ, and the great and blessed God.

Think what objects religion brings before the mind, as the 'sources of its pleasure; no less than the great God himself, and that both in his nature and in his works. For the eye of religion, like that of the eagle, directs itself chiefly to the sun, to a glory that neither admits of a superior or an equal. The mind is conversant in the exercises of piety, with all the most stupendous events that have ever occurred in the history of the universe, or that ever will transpire till the close of time. The creation of the world; its government by a universal providence; its redemption by the death of Christ; its conversion by the power of the Holy Spirit; its trial before the bar of God; the immortality of the soul; the resurrection of the body; the certainty of an eternal existence; the secrets of the unseen state; subjects, all of them, of the loftiest and sublimest kind, which have engaged the inquiries of the profoundest intellects, are the matter of contemplation to real piety. What topics are these for our reason, under the guidance of religion, to study; what an ocean to swim in, what a heaven to soar in; what heights to measure, what depths to fathom.

Here are subjects which, from their infinite vast-
ness, must be ever new, and ever fresh ; which can
be never laid aside as dry or empty.   If novelty is
the parent of pleasure, here it may be found ; for
although the subject itself is the same, some new
view of it, some fresh discovery of its wonders, is
ever bursting upon the mind of the devout and attentive inquirer after truth.

How, then, can religion be otherwise than pleasant, when it is the exercise of the noble faculties of
the mind, upon the sublimest topics of mental investigation ; the voluntary, excursive, endless pursuits of the human understanding in the region of
eternal truth ?   Never was there a more interesting
or important inquiry than that proposed by Pilate
to the illustrious Prisoner at his bar ; and if the latter thought it not proper to answer it, it was not to
show that the question was insignificant, but to condemn the light and flippant manner in which a subject so important was taken up.   Religion can
answer this question, and with an ecstasy greater
than that of the ancient mathematician, exclaims,
" I have found it : I have found it."   The Bible is
not only true, but TRUTH.   It contains that which
deserves this sublime emphasis.   It settles the dis-
putes of ages, and of philosophers, and makes known
what is truth, and where it is to be found.   It brings
us from among the quicksands, and shelves, and
rocks of scepticism, ignorance, and error, and shows
us that goodly land, in quest of which myriads of
minds have sailed, and multitudes have been wrecked;

and religion is setting our foot on this shore, and dwelling in the region of eternal truth.

2. That a religious life is pleasant, is evident from *the nature of religion itself.*

Religion is a principle of *spiritual life* in the soul. Now, all the exercises and acts of vitality are agreeable. To see, to hear, to taste, to walk, are all agreeable, because they are the voluntary energies of inward life. So religion, in all its duties, is the exercise of a living principle in the soul; it is a new spiritual existence. Piety is a spiritual *taste.* Hence it is said, " If so be ye have *tasted* that the Lord is gracious." No matter what the object of a taste is, the exercises of it are always agreeable. The painter goes with delight to his picture; the musician to his instrument; the sculptor to his bust—because they have a *taste* for these pursuits. The same feeling of delight attends the Christian to the exercises of godliness; and this is his language, " It is a good thing to give thanks, and to draw near to God. O, how I love thy law ! it is sweeter to my taste than honey. How amiable are thy tabernacles !" Religion, where it is real, is the natural element of a Christian; and every creature rejoices in its own appropriate sphere. If, my children, you consider true piety with disgust, as a hard, unnatural, involuntary thing, you are totally ignorant of its nature, entirely destitute of its influence, and no wonder you cannot attach to it the idea of pleasure; but viewing it as a *new nature*, you will perceive that it admits of most exalted delight.

3. Consider *the miseries which it prevents.*

It does not, it is true, prevent sickness, poverty, or misfortune; it does not fence off from the wilderness of this world, a mystic enclosure, within which the ills of life never intrude. No; these things happen to all alike; but how small a portion of human wretchedness flows from these sources, compared with that which arises from the dispositions of the heart. " The mind is its own place, can make a heaven of hell—a hell of heaven." Men carry the springs of their happiness or misery in their own bosom. Hence it is said of the wicked, " that they are like the troubled sea which cannot rest, which is never at peace, but continually casting up mire and dirt." In contrast with which it is affirmed, that " the work of righteousness is peace; and that the good man shall be satisfied from himself." Would you behold the misery entailed by *pride,* look at Haman; by *covetousness,* look at Ahab; by *malice,* look at Cain; by *profaneness* and *sensuality,* united with the forebodings of a guilty conscience, look at Belshazzar; by *envy* and a consciousness of being rejected of God, look at Saul; by *revenge,* look at Herodias writhing beneath the accusations of John, and thirsting for his blood; by *apostasy,* look at Judas. Religion would have prevented all this, and it will prevent similar misery in you. Hearken to the confessions of the outcast in the land of his banishment; of the felon in his irons and in his dungeon; of the prostitute expiring upon her bed of straw; of the malefactor at the gallows :—" Wretched creature that I am, abhorred of men, accursed of God! To what have my crimes brought me!"* Religion, my children, prevents all this ; all that wretchedness, which is the result of crime, is cut off by the influence of genuine piety. Misery prevented is happiness gained.

4. Dwell upon the *privileges it confers.*

To the man who is a partaker of its genuine influence, all the sins he has committed, be they ever so numerous or so great, are all forgiven, and he is introduced to the bliss of pardoned guilt; he is restored to the favor of that Great Being whose smile is life, and lights up heaven with joy ; whose frown is death, and fills all hell with woe. But I cannot describe these privileges in such brilliant language as has been employed by a Transatlantic author : " Regeneration is of the highest importance to man, as a subject of the divine government. With his former disposition he was a rebel against God, and with this he becomes cheerfully an obedient subject. Of an enemy he becomes a friend ; of an apostate he becomes a child. From the debased, hateful, and miserable character of sin, he makes a final escape, and begins the glorious and eternal career of virtue. With his *character* his destination is equally changed ; in his native condition he was a child of wrath, an object of abhorrence, and an heir of woe. Evil, in an unceasing and interminable progress, was his lot ; the regions

* See more on this subject in the chapter on the Temporal Advantages of Piety.

of sorrow and despair his everlasting home ; and
fiends, and fiend-like men his eternal companions.
On this character good beings looked with detesta-
tion, and on his ruin with pity ; while evil beings
beheld both with that satanic pleasure, which a re-
probate mind can enjoy at the sight of companionship in turpitude and destruction.

" But when he becomes a subject of this great
and happy change of character, all things connected
with him are also changed. His unbelief, impenitence, hatred of God, rejection of Christ, and resistance of the Spirit of Grace, he has voluntarily
and ingenuously renounced ; no more rebellious, impious, or ungrateful, he has assumed the amiable
spirit of submission, repentance, confidence, hope,
gratitude, and love.   The image of his Maker is en-
stamped upon his mind, and begins there to shine
with moral and eternal beauty.   The seeds of immortality have there sprung up, as in a kindly soil ;
and warmed by the life-giving beams of the Sun of
Righteousness and refreshed by the dewy influence
of the Spirit of grace, rise, and bloom, and flourish,
with increasing vigor.   In him sin and the world
and the flesh daily decay, and daily announce their
approaching dissolution ; while the soul continually
assumes new life and virtue, and is animated with
superior and undying energy.   He is now a joint
heir with Christ, and the destined inhabitant of
heaven ; the gates of glory and of happiness are
already opened to receive him, and the joy of saints
and angels has been renewed over his repentance ;

all around him is peace—all before him purity and transport.　God is his Father; Christ is his Redeemer; and the Spirit of Truth his Sanctifier. Heaven is his eternal habitation; virtue is his immortal character; and cherubim and seraphim, and all the children of light, are his companions forever. Henceforth he becomes of course a rich blessing to the universe; all good beings, nay, God himself, will rejoice in him forever, as a valuable accession to the great kingdom of righteousness, as a real addition to the mass of created good, and as a humble but faithful and honorable instrument of the everlasting praise of heaven.　He is a vessel of infinite mercy; an illustrious trophy of the cross; a gem in the crown of glory, which adorns the Redeemer of mankind."*

Who, my children, can read this animated description of the privileges of true piety (and it is not an exaggerated account) without secretly longing to be a child of God?　What are all the brightest distinctions of an earthly nature, after which envy pines in secret, or ambition rages in public, compared with this?　Crowns are splendid baubles, gold is sordid dust, and all the gratifications of sense but vanity and vexation of spirit, when weighed against such splendid immunities as these.

5. Consider *the consolation religion imparts.*

Our world has been called in the language of poetry, a vale of tears, and human life a bubble, raised from those tears, inflated by sighs, which, af-

* Dwight's Sermon on Regeneration.

ter floating a little while, decked with a few gaudy colors, is touched by the hand of death, and dissolves. Poverty, disease, misfortune, unkindness, inconstancy, death, all assail the travellers as they journey onward to eternity through this gloomy valley ; and what is to comfort them but RELIGION ?

The consolations of religion are neither few nor small ; they arise in part from those things which are already mentioned in this chapter ; *i. e.* from the exercise of the understanding on the revealed truths of God's word, from the impulses of the spiritual life within us, and from a reflection upon our spiritual privileges ; but there are some others, which though partially implied in these things, deserve a special enumeration and distinct consideration.

A good conscience, which the wise man says is a perpetual feast, sustains a high place amongst the comforts of genuine piety. It is unquestionably true, that a man's happiness is in the keeping of his conscience ; all the sources of his felicity are under the command of this faculty. " A wounded spirit who can bear ?" A troubled conscience converts a paradise into a hell, for it is the flame of hell kindled on earth ; but a quiet conscience would illuminate the horrors of the deepest dungeon with the beams of heavenly day ; the former has often rendered men like tormented fiends amidst an elysium of delights, while the latter has taught the songs of cherubim to martyrs in the prison or the flames. Religion furnishes a good conscience ; by faith in the blood of Christ it takes away guilt towards God, and by a holy life it keeps the conscience clear towards man. It first makes it good by justification, and then keeps it good by sanctification. What trouble may not a man bear beneath the smiles of an approving conscience! If this be calm and serene, the storms of affliction, which rage without, can as little disturb the comfort of the mind as the fury of the wintry tempest can do, to alarm the inhabitants of a well-built, well-stored mansion.

In addition to this, religion comforts the mind, with *the assurance of an all-wise, all-pervading Providence,* so minute in its superintendence and control, that not a sparrow falls to the ground without the knowledge of our heavenly Father; a superintendence which is excluded from no point of space, no moment of time, and overlooks not the meanest creature in existence. Nor is this all; for the word of God assures the believer that " *all things work together for good to them that love God, who are the called according to his purpose.*" Nothing that imagination could conceive is more truly consolatory than this, to be assured that all things, however painful at the time, not excepting the failure of our favorite scheme, the disappointment of our fondest hopes, the loss of our dearest comforts, shall be overruled by infinite wisdom, for the promotion of our ultimate good. This is a spring of comfort whose waters never fail.

Religion consoles also *by making manifest some of the benefits of affliction, even at the time it is endured.* It crucifies the world, mortifies sin,

14*

quickens prayer, extracts the balmy sweets of the promises, endears the Saviour; and to crown all, *it directs the mind to that glorious state where the days of our mourning shall be ended:* that happy country where God shall wipe every tear from our eyes, and there shall be no more sorrow or crying. Nothing so composes the mind, and helps it to bear the load of trouble which God may lay upon it, as the near prospect of its termination. Religion shows the weather-beaten mariner the haven of eternal repose, where no storms arise, and the sea is ever calm; it exhibits to the weary traveller the city of habitation, within whose walls he will find a pleasant home, rest from his labors, and friends to welcome his arrival; it discloses to the wounded warrior his native country, where the alarms of war, and the dangers of conflict will be no more encountered, but undisturbed peace forever reign. In that one word, HEAVEN, religion provides a balm for every wound, a cordial for every care.

Here, then, is the pleasure of that wisdom, which is from above; it is not only enjoyed in prosperity, but continues to refresh us, and most powerfully to refresh us, in adversity; a remark which will not apply to any other kind of pleasure.

In the hour of misfortune, when a man, once in happy circumstances, sits down, amidst the wreck of all his comforts, and sees nothing but the fragments of his fortune for his wife and family, what, in this storm of affliction, is to cheer him but religion? and this *can* do it, and enable him to say, "although the

fig-tree shall not blossom, neither shall fruit be in
the vines; the labor of the olive shall fail, and the
fields shall yield no meat; the flocks shall be cut off
from the fold, and there shall be no herd in the
stalls; yet I will rejoice in the Lord, I will joy in
the God of my salvation." What but *religion* can
comfort the poor laborer in that gloomy season when
times are bad, and work is scarce, and he hardly
knows where to procure his next meal? What can
comfort the suffering female in that long and dreadful season, when, wasting away in a deep decline, she
lies, night after night, consumed by fever, and day
after day convulsed by coughing? Tell me, what
can send a ray of comfort to her dark scene of woe,
or a drop of consolation to her parched and thirsty
lips, but *religion?* And when the agonized parent,
with a heart half broken by the conduct of a prodigal son, exclaims—" Oh! who can tell how sharper
than a serpent's tooth it is, to have a thankless
child?" what, in that season of torture, can pour a
drop of balm into the wounded spirit but *religion?*
And when we occupy the bedside of a departing
friend, " the dreadful post of observation darker
every hour," what but *religion* can sustain the mind,
and calm the tumult of the soul? what, but this,
can enable us to bear with even common composure
the pang of separation? And we, too, must die;
and here is the excellence of piety; it follows us
where no other friend can follow us, down into the
dark valley of the shadow of death, stands by us
when the last hand has quitted his grasp, reserves

its mightiest energies for that most awful conflict, presents to the eye of faith the visions of glory rising up beyond the sepulchre, and angels advancing to receive us from the hand of earthly friends, and bear us to the presence of a smiling God.

Other sources of pleasure are open only during the season of health and prosperity. Admitting that they are all which their most impassioned admirers contend for, what can balls, routs, plays, cards, do in the season of sickness, misfortune, or death? Alas! alas! they exist then only in recollection, and the recollection of them is painful.

6. The pleasures of religion appear in the *graces it implants*.

"And now abideth these three,—Faith, Hope, Charity."

FAITH is the leading virtue of Christianity. To believe, in any case, where the report is welcome, and the evidence of its truth convincing, is a pleasing exercise of the mind: how much more so in this case, where the testimony to be believed, is the glad tidings of salvation, and the evidence of its truth most entirely satisfactory? HOPE is a most delightful exercise. The pleasures of hope have formed a theme for the poet; and it is evident that these pleasures must be in proportion to the importance of the object desired, and the grounds that exist to expect its accomplishment. What, then, must be the influence of that hope which is full of immortality, which has the glory of heaven for its object, and the truth of God for its basis! which, as it

looks towards its horizon, sees the shadowy forms
of eternal felicity rising, expanding, brightening,
and advancing, every moment.   LOVE is a third virtue, implanted and cherished in the soul by religion.
Need I describe the pleasures connected with a pure
and virtuous affection?   Religion is love—love of
the purest and sublimest kind; this is its essence, all
else but its earthly attire, which it throws off as
Elijah did his mantle, when it ascends to the skies.
The delight of love must be in proportion to the
excellence of its object, and the strength of its own
propensity towards that object.   What, then, must
be the pleasure of that love which has *God* as its
object, and which consists in complacency in *his* glories, gratitude for his mercies, submission to his will,
and the enjoyment of his favor!   This is a heavenly
feeling, which brings us into communion with angels,
and anticipates on earth the enjoyments of eternity.
Submission, patience, meekness, gentleness, justice,
compassion, zeal, are also among the graces which
true religion implants in the human soul; which,
like lovely flowers, adorn it with indescribable beauty, and refresh it with the most delicious fragrance.

7. Consider the *duties which religion enjoins* and
you will find in each of these a spring of hallowed
pleasure.

How delightful an exercise is *prayer!* "Prayer
is the peace of our spirits, the stillness of our
thoughts, the evenness of recollection, the seat of
meditation, the rest of our cares, and the calm of
our tempests; it is the daughter of charity, and

the sister of meekness." It is pleasant to tell our sorrows to any one; how much more to him who is omnipotent in power, infallible in wisdom, and infinite in compassion! With prayer is connected *praise,* that elevated action of the soul, in which she seems at the time to be learning motion and melody from an angel. How pleasant an exercise is the *perusal of the Scriptures!* In prayer we speak to God, and in the Bible God speaks to us, and both confer upon us honor indescribable. Passing by the antiquity of its history, the pathos of its narratives, the beauty of its imagery, how sublime are its doctrines, how precious its promises, how free its invitations, how salutary its warnings, how intense its devotions! "Precious Bible! when weighed against thee, all other books are but as the small dust of the balance." Nor less pleasant is *the holy remembrance of the Sabbath!* "I was glad," exclaims the Christian, "when they said unto me, let us go into the house of the Lord;" and there, when standing within the gates of Zion, surrounded with the multitude that keep holy day, he repeats, amidst the years of his manhood, the song of his childhood, and from the fulness of his joy, he exclaims—

> " Lord how delightful 'tis to see
> A whole assembly worship Thee;
> At once they sing, at once they pray,
> They hear of heaven and learn the way."

The sweetly-solemn engagements of *the sacramental feast;* the flow of brotherly love, called forth by *social prayer*, together with the *ardor of be-nevolence*, inspired by the support of public relig-ious institutions ; in these exercises is true happi-ness to be found, if indeed it is to be found any-where on earth.

8. As a last proof of the pleasures derived from religion, I may appeal to *the experience of its friends*. Here the evidences accumulate by myriads on earth, and millions in heaven. Who, that ever felt its influence, will doubt its tendency to produce delight ? Go, go, my children, to the saints of the most high God, and collect *their* testimony, and you shall be convinced that "light is sown for the righteous, and gladness for the upright in heart." Go not to the Christian of *doubtful* character, for he has only just religion enough to make him miser-able ; go to the most holy, and you shall find *them* the most happy.

And then there are also two or three other cir-cumstances which are connected with the pleasures of religion that deserve attention. *It is pleasure that never satiates or wearies.* Can the epicure, the voluptuary, the drunkard, the ball-frequenter, say this of *their* delights ? " How short is the interval, how easy the transition between a pleasure and a burden. If sport refreshes a man when he is weary, it also wearies when he is refreshed. The most de-voted pleasure-hunter in existence, were he bound to his sensual delights every day, would find it an intolerable burden, and fly to the spade and the mattock for a diversion from the misery of an unintermitted pleasure. Custom may render continued labor tolerable, but not continued pleasure. All pleasures that affect the body must needs weary, because they transport; and all transportation is violence; and no violence can be lasting, but determines upon the falling of the spirits, which are not able to keep up that height of motion, that the pleasure of the sense raises them to; and therefore how generally does an immoderate laughter end in a sigh, which is only nature's recovering herself after a force done to it; but the religious pleasure of a well-disposed mind moves gently, and therefore constantly; it does not affect by rapture and ecstasy, but is like the pleasure of health, which is still and sober, yet greater and stronger than those which call up the senses with grosser and more affecting impressions."

And as all the grosser pleasures of sense weary, and all the sports and recreations soon pall upon the appetite, so, under some circumstances, do the more elevated enjoyments of exalted rank, agreeable company and lively conversation; it is religion alone that preserves an unfading freshness, an undying charm, an inexhaustible power to please; it is this alone of all our pleasures which never cloys, never surfeits, but increases the appetite the more it gratifies it, and leaves it, after the richest feast, prepared and hungry for a still more splendid banquet.

And then another ennobling property of the pleasure that arises from religion is, *that as the sources and the seat of it are in a man's own breast, it is*

*not in the power of anything without him to de-
stroy it, or take it away.* Upon God alone is he
dependent for its enjoyment. Upon how many other
agents, and upon what numerous contingencies, over
which he can exercise no control, is the votary of
worldly pleasure dependent for *his* bliss. How
many things which he cannot command are necessary to make up the machinery of his schemes !
What trifles may disappoint him of his expected
gratification, or rob him of his promised delights !
A variable atmosphere, or a human mind no less
variable ; a want of punctuality in others, or a want
of health in himself : these, and a thousand other
things, might be enumerated as circumstances, upon
the mercy of each one of which, the enjoyment of
worldly pleasure depends. " But the good man
shall be satisfied from himself." " Whoever shall
drink of the water that I shall give him," said Jesus
Christ, "shall never thirst, but the water that I shall
give him shall be *in him* a well of water springing
up into everlasting life." The piety of his heart,
produced by the Holy Ghost, is this well-spring of
pleasure, which a good man carries every where
with him, wherever he goes. He is independent of
all the contingencies of life for his bliss. " It is an
easy and a portable pleasure, such an one as he carries about in his bosom, without alarming the eye or
the envy of the world. A man putting all his
pleasures into this one, is like a traveller putting all
his goods into one jewel ; the value is the same, and
the convenience greater."

15

"Nor is this kind of pleasure out of the reach of any outward violence only; but even those things also, which make a closer impression upon us, which are the irresistible decays of nature, have yet no influence at all upon this. For when age itself, which of all things in the world will not be baffled or defied, shall begin to arrest, seize, and remind us of our mortality, by pains, aches, and deadness of limbs, and dulness of senses, yet then the pleasure of the mind shall be in its full youth, vigor, and freshness. A palsy may as soon shake an oak, or a fever dry up a fountain, as either of them shake, dry up, or impair the delight of conscience; for it lies within, it centres in the heart, it grows up into the very substance of the soul, so that it accompanies a man to his grave; he never outlives it, and that for cause only, because he cannot outlive himself."

How comes it to pass, then, that, in opposition to all this, the opinion has gained ground that religion leads to melancholy? *The irreligious judge of it by their own feelings;* and as *they* are not conscious of any pleasurable emotions excited by sacred things, they conclude that others in like manner are destitute of them. But is *their* testimony to be received, before that of the individual who has tried and found it by experience to be bliss? Again, irreligious people form their opinion *by what they see in many professors,* some of whom, though professing godliness, are destitute of its power; and being more actuated by a spirit of the world than of piety, are strangers to the peace that passeth understanding ; others are not yet brought out of that deep dejection, with which the earlier stages of conviction are sometimes attended. The sinner, when first arrested in his thoughtless career, is filled with dismay and the most poignant grief ; reviewed in this state of mind, his appearance may produce the idea that religion is the parent of melancholy. But wait, he that sows in tears shall reap in joy. His tears, like showers in summer from a dark and lowering cloud, carry off the gloom which they first caused, portend a clearer and cooler atmosphere, and are ultimately followed by the bright shining of the sun.

An unfavorable impression against religion is sometimes produced by *the constitutional gloom* of some of its genuine disciples. It should be recollected, that, in these cases, religion does not cause the dejection, for this would have existed had there been no piety. All that can be said is, that it does not cure it, which is not to be expected, unless piety pretended to exert an influence over the physical nature of man.

The supposition that piety leads to melancholy is also founded, in part, *on the self-denying duties which the word of God enjoins.* Penitence, self-denial, renunciation of the world, willingness to take up the cross and follow after Christ, are unquestionably required, and must be truly found in the genuine Christian. Hence the worldling thinks it impossible, but that with such duties should be associated the most sullen and miserable state of

mind. Little does he imagine, that the pleasures
which religion has to offer for those she requires us
to abandon, are like the orb of day to the glow-worm
of the hedge, or the meteor of the swamp ; and that
for every moment's self-denial she requires us to
endure, she has a million ages of ineffable delight to
bestow.

" And now upon the result of all, I suppose that
to exhort them to be religious, is only in other words
to exhort them to take their pleasure—a pleasure,
high, rational, and angelical—a pleasure embased
with no appendant sting, no consequent loathing, no
remorses or bitter farewells ; but such an one, as
being honey in the mouth, never turns to gall in the
belly ; a pleasure made for the soul, and the soul for
that ; suitable to its spirituality, and equal to its
capacities ; such an one as grows fresher upon enjoyment, and though continually fed upon, is never de-
voured ; a pleasure that a man may call as properly
his own, as his soul and his conscience ; neither liable
to accident, nor exposed to injury ; it is the foretaste of heaven, and the earnest of eternity ; in a
word, it is such an one as being begun in grace,
passes into glory, blessedness, and immortality ; and
those joys that neither eye hath seen, nor ear heard,
nor have entered into the heart of man to conceive !"*

---

* This, and the other quotations, are from Dr. South's sermon on Prov. iii. 7, which is so striking that I could not
avoid giving these extracts from it.

See also an excellent volume of sermons, by the Rev. H.
F. Burder, on the Pleasures of Religion.

XI.

The Advantages of Early Piety.

A QUAINT but eminently spiritual poet of the last century, has a poem entitled, "Strife in Heaven:" a singular idea to attach to that region of untroubled repose. The design of the piece, however, is ingenious and interesting. A company of the redeemed above, are represented as discussing, in a spirit of perfect love, the question, "which of them was most indebted to divine grace for his salvation?" Amongst these grateful and holy litigants, two appeared to have claims for the greatest weight of obligation to sovereign mercy, so nearly balanced, as to render it difficult to say which owed most. One was a glorified spirit, converted in old age, after a long life of sin; the other was a saint redeemed in youth, and who spent as long a life in holiness. The one contended, that his forgiveness, after such a lengthened course of vice and destructive conduct, made him the greatest monument of saving love in heaven; "except," exclaimed the other, "myself; who, by divine grace, was prevented from that course of sin, and was enabled by religion to spend my years in

15*

holiness and usefulness." I think the happy throng must have confessed the justice of the younger seraph's claims; Omniscient wisdom from the throne must have confirmed their judgment; and in heaven it must have been decided that *they* owe most to sovereign grace, who have been called by its power to the service of God in their youth.

Youth is a season which presents peculiar advantages for the *pursuit* of piety.

It is attended in general, with more leisure and less care, than any subsequent period of life. As yet, my children, you are not entangled in the concerns of business, nor the cares of a family. The ten thousand tumultuous anxieties of a father or a mother, a master or mistress, do not yet fill your minds, and exclude all other topics. Tell us, ye fathers, struggling with the difficulties of a precarious trade; and ye mothers, absorbed in the duties of a rising family; which, think ye, is the best time to begin the pursuit of eternal life? With tears they respond, "Seize! O seize, young people, the halcyon days of youth!"

Youth is a season of *greater susceptibility of mind* than any which follows it.

In the spring-time of nature, the soil is best prepared for the reception of the seed; and the energies of vegetation are most vigorous; so it is with the mind. In youth the heart is more easily impressed, the affections more readily moved, the imagination is more lively. You have an ardor and fervency most remote from the timid, hesitating caution of age, and eminently favorable to conversion. Disdaining all resistance, ambitious of great achievements, full of high resolves, and leaping over opposing obstacles, youth surveys, with sparkling eyes, the crown of its wishes, braces itself for action, and flies to the goal; whilst age, creeping fearfully along, afraid of every difficulty, discouraged by the least resistance, can scarcely be impelled to move. I know that these things of themselves are not sufficient to make you holy; but when grace sanctifies them, and directs them to proper objects, they must render your entrance on religion more easy, your progress more rapid, and your enjoyment more strong.

Youth are *less hardened in sin*, than persons of riper years.

The depravity of our nature grows with our growth, and strengthens with our strength. Like a tree, it strikes its roots deeper, and takes a faster hold on the soil every year. You have principles of corruption already in your hearts, my children, but they have not, by long indulgence, become so stiffened into habit, as they may be at some future time. Your prejudices and prepossessions are yet few, and feeble. As yet the sentiments of modesty and propriety, and a regard to the opinions of others, would make you blush for acts of vice, and endeavor to conceal them from the world. In riper years you will assume a boldness in iniquity, disregard the censures of others, and cease to be restrained by them. Conscience has not yet been deeply corrupted; it still preterves something of its tremulous delicacy, and nice sensibility; it still elevates its warning voice, and strongly remonstrates against your least deviation from the path of virtue; but in the aged sinner, weary of useless reproof, it is almost silent, or totally disregarded. We know that without divine grace, conversion, even in any case, cannot take place; but we know, at the same time, by observation, that divine grace very often follows in the order of nature.

Youth are *pre-eminently encouraged to seek the possession and influence of piety.*

There are many invitations, promises, and injunctions, specially addressed to them. " Remember thy Creator in the days of thy youth." " I love them that love me, and they that seek me early shall find me." Under the Jewish dispensation, God called for the *first-fruits* of all things, intending, no doubt, to teach, amongst other lessons, his delight in the dedication of the first fruits of our life to his service. How pleased was the Redeemer with the hosannas of the children, and how deeply was he interested in the case of that hopeful youth, who came to inquire of him the way to life! And does not the parable of the prodigal son teach us how welcome is the return of the young to the Father of Mercies? God chose David, the youngest son of the family; and set his love upon Jacob, while Esau the elder is passed by. Amongst all the disciples, John was the most beloved, and he was, at the same time, the youngest.

But still the principal design of this chapter is to set forth the advantages attendant on the *possession* of early piety.

1. Of these some relate to *others*.   This will cause you to be a source of ineffable delight to your parents ;* and probably render you a blessing to

* In the memoirs of that truly apostolic missionary, the Rev. Henry Martyn, occurs the following anecdote, which most forcibly illustrates the subject of the influence of filial conduct upon parental and domestic comfort and respectability.

" Visited the hospital this day, and read the eleventh chapter of John to a poor man, in whose room, at the workhouse, I was struck with the misery that presented itself. He was lying with his clothes and hat on, upon the bed, dying.   His wife was cleaning the room, as if nothing was the matter ; and upon the threshold was the daughter, about thirty years old, who had been delirious thirteen years." What a scene of wretchedness !   What a miserable group ! It is a picture from which the mind turns with the deepest emotions of distressful pity.   But, oh ! the cause of this misery !   " The dying man," continued Mr. Martyn, " was once a respectable innkeeper in the town ; *but the extravagance of a son* brought him to poverty, and his daughter, who foresaw it, to insanity."   What must have been the feelings (except, indeed, vice had turned his heart to stone) of the guilty author of this complicated misery, when he saw the consuming grief of his broken-hearted father, and heard the wild ramblings of his maniac sister, whilst conscience thundered in his ear, " Thou art the cause of this dreadful calamity !"   How many broken hearts, and insane minds, has similar conduct produced !   How many are at this moment bending to the grave, or shut up in the cells of a lunatic asylum, who, but for profligate children, might have been living in health, sanity, and respectability !

your brothers and sisters.   Piety in youth will render you a benefactor to your species, and a blessing
to society.   Instead of seducing others by a bad
example, you will benefit them by the influence of a
good one; instead of poisoning others by corrupt
principles, you will scatter along your path the seed
of truth, piety, and morality; instead of drawing
down the vengeance of God upon society by your
crimes, you will bring down his blessing by your
prayers.   You will be a patriot of the most elevated
and successful nature; and by your good conduct,
and the support of all religious institutions, do more,
in connection with others of a similar disposition,
for the good of your country, than fleets and armies
can achieve.

2. Innumerable advantages will result from early
piety to *yourself*.

It will exert a friendly influence over your temporal interests.*   It will open *springs of consolation*
all along your path through the vale of tears, whose
waters adapted to every condition, shall never fail.
Religion, chosen in youth as your guide, companion,
and friend, will attend you through all the journey
of life; will go with you where you go, and dwell
with you wherever you dwell; she will accompany
you when with many tears you quit the parental
roof, and you go forth, a young adventurer, into the
world.   She will travel with you in the wilderness,
or sail with you on the ocean; she will abide with
you in a mansion, or inhabit with you the cottage :

* See the chapter on this subject.

when every other friend forsakes you, she will cling
to you the closer ; smile, when every other face is
covered with a frown ; and put forth all her energies
to comfort you in the time of your humbled for-
tunes ; in seasons of perplexity, she will guide you
to the fountain of light; when oppressed with care,
will place you on the rock of ages ; in the storms of
affliction will cast forth for you the anchor of hope ;
and in times of dreary desolation, will enable you,
by faith, to see the land which is afar off,—the land
of promise and of rest.

Early piety is *a distinguished honor.*

If there be true honor in the universe, it is to be
found in religion.   Even the heathens were sensible
of this ; hence the Romans built the temples of
virtue and honor close together, to teach that the
way to honor was by virtue.   Religion is the image
of God in the soul of man.   Can glory itself rise
higher than this ?   What a distinction ! to have *this*
lustre put upon the character in youth.   It was mentioned by Paul as a singular honor to the believing
Jews that they first trusted in Christ ; and in referring to Andronicus and Junia, he mentions it to
their praise that they were in Christ before him.
To be a child of God, an heir of glory, a disciple of
Christ, a warrior of the cross, a citizen of the New
Jerusalem, from our youth up, adorns the brow with
amaranthine wreaths of fame.   A person converted
in youth, is like the sun, rising on a summer's morning to shine through a long bright day ; but a person converted late in life, is like the evening star, a

lovely object of Christian contemplation, but not appearing till the day is closing, and then seen but for a little while.

Early piety *will be of immense importance to you in the various relations of life in which you may stand*.

If you are parents it will dispose and enable you to train up your children and servants in the fear of God. It will prevent you from neglecting the immortal interests of those who are committed to your care. How many parents are accessary to the murder of their children's souls; blood-guiltiness rests upon their conscience, and the execrations of their own offspring will be upon them through eternity. In those cases where persons are redeemed late in life, what anguish is sometimes felt on seeing their children wandering in the broad road that leadeth to destruction; and on remembering that they were the means of leading them astray. " Oh, my children ! my children !" they exclaim, " would God I had known religion earlier for your sakes. Why did I not seek the Lord in youth ? Then I should have trained you up in the fear of God, and have been spared the agony of seeing you walking in the path of destruction ; or, at least, have been spared the torturing reflection, that it was through my neglect you despised religion."

Early piety will be *a guard to you against the temptations to which we are all exposed in this life*.

Temptations to sin, like the wind, come from every quarter. In company, in solitude ; at home, abroad, in God's house, and in our own; we are always open to attack.   Business, pleasure, companions all may become a snare.   We never know when, or from what, or in what way to expect the assault.   At one time we may be tempted to infidelity, at another to immorality; now to licentiousness, then to intemperance   Piety is the only effectual guard of our character.   Luther tells us of a young believer who used to repel all temptations with this exclamation, " Begone, I am a Christian."   My children, adopt the same character, and maintain it with the same constancy and success. When Pyrrhus tempted Fabricius, the first day with an elephant, and the next day with promises of honor, the Roman nobly replied, " I fear not thy force, I am too wise for thy fraud."   Religion will enable you to say the same to every one who threatens or allures.   Neglect piety in youth, and who shall say how long in the scale of vice and infamy you may be found in after life?   Omit to take with you this shield, and your moral character may be destroyed, or receive a wound, the scar of which you may carry to the grave.

Early piety *will thus leave you fewer sins to bewail in after life.*

Amongst other things which the illustrious BEZA gave thanks for to God in his last will and testament, was this, that he became a real Christian at the age of sixteen, by which he was prevented from the commission of many sins, which would otherwise have overtaken him, and rendered his life less happy.

Every year's impenitence, must cause many years' repentance If you neglect religion in youth, God may give you up to the delusions of infidelity, or to the practices of immorality ; and during this unhappy season of what remediless mischief may you be the occasion, how many companions may you lead astray by your crimes ; who, admitting that *you* are afterwards reclaimed by grace, are not so easily led back by your virtues. Instances have occurred in which young men, during the days of their irreligion, have perpetrated the horrid crime of corrupting female virtue, and then abandoned the hapless victim of their passion. Cast off as a guilty worthless thing, the injured partner of his sins has added iniquity to iniquity, and she who, but for her betrayer, might have lived a long and virtuous life, has sunk amidst disease, and want, and infamy, to an early and dishonored grave. God, in the mysteries of his grace, has, in after years, given repentance to the greater criminal of the two. But can *he* forget his crime? Oh no. God has forgiven him, but never, never can he forgive himself. Not even the blood which has washed away the guilt from his conscience, can efface the history of it from the page of memory ; nor floods of tears deaden the impression which it has left upon the heart. He cannot restore the virtue he destroyed, nor refund the peace which with felon hand he stole from a bosom tranquil till it knew him ; he cannot build up the character he demolished, much less can he rekindle the life which he extinguished ; or call back from the regions of the damned the miserable ghost which he hurried to perdition.   Ah! that ghost now haunts his imagination, and as she exhibits the mingled agony, fury, revenge, and despair of a lost soul, seems to say, " Look at me, my destroyer !" For awhile he can see nothing but her flames, and hear nothing but her groans.

Early piety would have saved him from all this. Late piety brings him salvation for another world, but it comes not soon enough to save him from remorse in this.

Early piety will procure for you, if you live so long, *the honor of an aged disciple.*

A person converted late in life is a young disciple, though a gray-headed man.   An aged hero, who has spent his days contending for the liberties of his country ; or a philosopher, who has long employed himself in improving its science ; or a philanthropist, who has become old in relieving its wants, are venerable sights, but far inferior, if they are destitute of religion, to the aged Christian who has employed half a century in glorifying God, as well as doing good to man.   An old disciple is honored in the church, and respected even in the world.   His hoary head is lifted like a crown of glory among other and younger disciples, over whom his decaying form throws its venerated shade.   How rich is he in expereince of all the ways of godliness !   Like a decrepit warrior, he can talk of conflicts and of victories.   Younger Christians gather round him to learn wisdom from his lips, and courage from his feats, and to show him tokens of respect. By his brethren in Christ he is regarded with veneration ; his presence is always marked with every demonstration of respect, and his opinion is listened to with the profoundest deference. He is consulted in emergencies, and the fruits of his experience are gathered with eagerness. His virtues have been tried by time, the surest test of excellence, and they have passed with honor the ordeal. That suspicion and scepticism, which innumerable moral failures have produced in some minds, as to the reality of religion in general, and the sincerity of any of its professors, retire from the presence of such a man, convinced of the injustice of its surmises ; and even the infidel and the profane bear a testimony to his worth, which his long-tried consistency has extorted. " There, at least," say they, " is one good man, whose sincerity has been tried by the fluctuating circumstances and varying situations of half a century. His is no mushroom piety, which springs up in a night, and perishes in a day. The suns of many summers, and the storms of many winters have passed over it ; and both adversity and prosperity have assailed and demonstrated its stability. We begin, after all, from that very character, to believe that there is more in religion than we have been apt to imagine."

Early piety, if persisted in, *prepares for a comfortable old age.* The condition of an old man without piety, is wretched indeed. He presents to the eye of Christian contemplation a melancholy spec-

tacle.   As to all the grand purposes of existence,
he has passed through the world in vain.   Life to
him has been a lost adventure.   Seventy years he
has sojourned in the region of mercy, and is going
out of it without salvation.   Seventy years he has
dwelt within reach of redemption, and yet is going
to the lost souls in prison.   If he is insensible to
his case, he is going to ruin asleep; but if a little
awakened, how bitter are his reflections.   If he
looks back upon the past, he sees nothing but a wide
and dreary waste, where the eye is relieved by no
monuments of piety, but is scared by memorials of
a life of sin; if he looks at his present circumstances, he sees nothing but a mere wreck of himself, driving upon the rock of his destiny and
destruction; —but the future! oh! how can he look
on that, which presents to him death, for which he
is not prepared; judgment, from which he can expect nothing but condemnation; heaven which he
has bartered for pleasure, the remembrance of which
is now painful, or insipid; hell, which he has merited,
with its eternity of torments, by his iniquities.   The
ghost of spent years and departed joys flit before
him, and point to these regions of woe, whither sinful delights conduct the sensualist and voluptuary.
Miserable old man! the winter of life is upon him,
and he has nothing to cheer his cold and dreary
spirit; nor any spring to look forward to; the *night*
of existence has come on; not a star twinkles from
heaven upon his path; nor will any morning dawn
upon the gloom which enwraps him.   Such is the

16*

old age of those who remember not God in their youth, and carry on their oblivion of religion, as such persons generally do, to the end of life.

But should any one be called at the eleventh hour, such a convert will be subject, at times, to the most painful doubts and apprehensions; he questions the reality of his religion; he fears that it is the result of circumstances, not of a divine change; he is afraid that, like a half-shipwrecked vessel driven into port by the violence of the storm, rather than by the effort of the crew, he has been forced to religion more by the terrors produced by approaching death, than by the choice of his own will; he often concludes that he never forsook the world, till he could no longer retain it; and that he renounced the enjoyments of earth only because, from the decay of his body, from the feebleness of his mind, and the weakness of his fancy, he is unable to indulge in them. These, and other similar fears, generally occasion, in persons converted in old age, a painful hesitancy concerning the security of their state; prevent them from going on their way rejoicing, and hang like a cloud upon the prospect of immortality.

How much more cheering and consolatory are the reflections of the aged Christian, who remembered his Creator in the days of his youth. He too has arrived at the wintry days of existence, but, like the inhabitant of a well-stored mansion, he has a thousand comforts which enable him to hear the howling of the tempest without a fear, and to look on the dreariness of the scene unconscious of a want;

and then, in addition to this, the days of everlasting
spring approach. He too is overtaken by the evening; his shadow lengthens on the plain, but the
heavens pour upon him the glory of God, while the
word in which he trusted is a lamp unto his feet;
and an eternal day is about to dawn upon his soul.
In the past he sees the long interval between the
season of youth, and the furrowed countenance of
age, filled up, in some good degree, with works of devotion, righteousness, and benevolence, whereby he has
glorified God, benefited his species, and prepared a
balm for his memory. No sins of youth fill his
bones with pain, nor his spirit with remorse. He
has little doubt of his sincerity; for his life, though
it affords him no ground of dependence for salvation, furnishes him with numerous evidences of the
faith which justifies the soul, and purifies the heart.
He forsook the world when most capable of enjoying it; he was not driven by violence to religion,
but deliberately weighed anchor, and, with every
sail set, steered for the haven of piety. He has resisted innumerable attacks upon his principles, and
against every foe has held fast his integrity. On
the verge of life he can say, " I have kept the faith.
I have fought a good fight, I have nearly finished
my course; henceforth there is laid up for me a
crown of life, which God the righteous Judge will
bestow upon me."

Surely, surely, my children, an old age thus placid
and venerable, is an object worthy of your desires !
surely these peaceful recollections, these sublime

prospects, amidst the dreariness of age, are deserv-
ing your exertions!

Early piety *will have a considerable influence on
your eternal felicity.*

In dwelling upon the two different and contrary
states of heaven and hell, we are not to conceive of
them as conditions of being, where all persons in
the former will be equally happy, and all in the latter equally miserable. There are different degrees
of glory in one, and different degrees of torment in
the other. This is proved by scripture, and accords
with reason. Grace is glory in the bud; glory is
grace in a state of fructification; and as in the natural world, so it is in the spiritual world, where
there is little blossom, there cannot be much fruit.
Life is the seed-time for eternity; what a man sow-
eth, that shall he also reap, not only in kind, but in
degree. Late sowings, as well as scanty ones, are
generally followed with short crops. The reward
of the righteous is all of grace, but then that grace
which rewards the righteous rather than the wicked,
may, with equal consistency, reward righteousness
according to its degrees. We cannot think that the
reward of the dying thief, who was converted in the
dark valley of the shadow of death, will be equal to
that of Timothy or of Paul, who spent a long and
laborious life in the service of Christ. Nor is it to
be imagined that the crown of the aged convert will
be as bright, or as heavy as that of the Christian
who is converted in youth, and continues, till a good
old age, in a course of consistent piety.

But there is one consideration which should come
home to the bosom of young people with overwhelm-
ing force ; I mean, *that unless they become partakers of piety in early life, the probability is, that
they will never partake of it at all.* Is it of consequence that you should become pious at any time ?
then does all that consequence attach to the *present*
time ?   Let me sound this idea again and again in
your ears, let me detain your attention upon the
awful and alarming sentiment.   The probability of
your salvation becomes weaker and weaker as the
years of youth roll by.   It is less probable this year
than the last, and will be less probable next year
than this.   I do not now argue upon the uncertainty of life, *that* I have considered before, I *appeal* to
FACTS, which in reference to the sentiment I have
now advanced, are of the most alarming aspect.
Consider, only two individuals of the six hundred
thousand, who left Egypt above the age of twenty
years, entered Canaan.   Of those who are converted at all, by far the greater part are brought to seek
religion in their youth ; and of the few who are reclaimed in adult, or old age, how rare a case is it to
find one who has been religiously educated.   It is
easy to observe, generally speaking, that sinners who
have been brought under the means of grace, or under some new and impressive preaching, which they
never enjoyed before, if they do not *soon* profit by
their privileges, rarely profit by them at all.   God's
time of conversion seems to be the morning of religious privilege.   The churches mentioned in the

New Testament, were chiefly made up of persons converted by the *first* efforts of the apostles. Hence, when these servants of the cross were unsuccessful in their *early* labors in a city, or province, they looked upon it as a bad omen and a strong indication that it would be useless to continue their ministrations there ;* so that the usual order of divine grace is, for its showers to fall on what might be called morning sowings. The seasons of youthful years, or youthful means, are the usual times of conversion ; and those who misimprove either of these, are in general found to neglect religion forever after.

I am aware, that instances to the contrary are *sometimes* found ; and therefore none who are inclined to seek God at any age should despair : yet they but rarely occur, and therefore let none presume. True repentance is never too late ; but late repentance is seldom true.

It is very probable, that some who may read these pages, deliberately and sincerely make up their minds to serve God at some future time, after they have a little longer enjoyed the world. Mistaken youth ! Sinful young people ! Let them consider what their intention amounts to ; " I will go on sinning a little longer, and then I will repent. I will serve Satan, and the world, and sin as long as I can, and when I am worn out in their service, or weary of it, I will turn to God, and try the ways of religion. O Lord ! the preserver of my days, spare my life a little longer to disobey thee, to insult thee, and then

* See Acts, xiii. 46, 48 ; xxii. 18 ; xxviii. 23—28.

give me thy grace to assist me to turn from my wicked ways and live." What wickedness! What shocking impiety! What daring madness! Do they not tremble? Are they not terrified at this view of their own conduct? Can they live another day in this state of mind? Can they give their eyes to sleep with such a purpose in their bosom? Let them consider how just it is that God should reserve the dregs of his wrath for those, who reserve only the dregs of their time for HIM.

Now, now, my children, is the accepted time, this is the day of salvation. "To-day if ye will hear his voice, harden not your hearts." You know not what another day, hour, moment, may bring forth. Opportunity, mercy, salvation, heaven, eternal glory, are all upon the wing of the *present* hour; condemnation, hell, eternal torment, and despair, may all be in the train of the *next*. That door of grace which is open to-day, may be shut to-morrow; that sceptre of mercy which is stretched out to-day may be withdrawn to-morrow. Oh the noble purposes that have withered, the sublime prospects that have failed, the millions of immortal souls that have perished by putting off the *present* season, for a more convenient time. ."Soul opportunities," says an old author, "are more worth than a thousand worlds." And they are rapidly sliding by with the days of your youth.

XII.

The Influence of Religion upon the Temporal Interests of its Possessor.

GODLINESS has the promise of the life that is *to come*, it conducts to glory, honor, immortality : this is its *chief* commendation. Revelation has drawn aside the veil which hangs over the unseen state, and urged you, my children, upon the great business of religion, by a contemplation of the dark world of hell, and of the splendors of the celestial city. It might seem that, after such an appeal, every other were useless, and that to speak of other advantages than eternal life, were only adding a drop to the ocean, a taper to the sun ; but there are persons who are wrought upon more by present good, however small, than any future prospect of the greatest gain ; who are more governed by illustrations borrowed from things seen and temporal, than by those which are derived from things unseen and eternal. In *this* respect also, and on this ground, religion can plead its advantages, for it has " the promises of the life that *now is*" as well as that which is to come.

I do not assert, that religion will conduct all its followers to wealth, honor, and health.   No.   Still, however, it exerts a friendly influence on all the temporal interests of mankind, and protects them from many evils to which, without it, they are exposed.

1. It exercises and improves the *understanding*.

From beginning to end, religion is an intellectual process.   Whatever raises man above the dominion of the senses, and renders him independent of these, as sources of gratification, must have a salutary influence upon the mind.   Now the objects which religion exhibits, are such as the mental faculties alone can converse with ; and the moment a man begins to feel solicitude about spiritual things, he begins to experience a considerable elevation of character. And then the subjects of divine truth are of the most sublime and lofty kind.   They form the Alps in the world of mind.   The existence and attributes of the great God ; the system of Providence, embracing all worlds and all ages ; the scheme of redemption, planned from eternity for the salvation of millions of rational creatures ; the immortality of the soul ; the solemnities of judgment ; the everlasting states of the righteous and the wicked ; these are the every-day topics of thought to a Christian.   Can a man live in the daily contemplation of these vast ideas, and not feel an elevating influence upon his understanding ?   It will probably be said, that science will have the same effect.   This is admitted in part. But how many are there to whom philosophical pursuits are utterly inaccessible !   Besides this, it may be replied that nothing but religion will infallibly guard the soul from being debased by vicious indulgences.

Read the missionary records, and learn by these interesting details, what religion has done for the negroes of the West Indies, the Hottentots of South Africa, the Esquimaux of Labrador, the fur-clad Greenlanders of the Arctic regions, and the voluptuous cannibals of the South Sea Islands. It has raised them from savages into rational creatures; it has awakened their dormant understanding; sharpened their powers of perception ; taught them the art of reasoning; and invested them with the power of eloquence.

But why do I go to distant countries, while our own furnishes illustrations so numerous, and so striking?   How many persons are there, who were educated in our Sunday-schools, and who are now filling stations of importance, credit, and usefulness, who, but for religion, would never have risen in the scale of society, or ascended above the lowest level of poverty.   Education, it is true, gave the first impulse to their minds; but it was an impulse which would have soon spent its force, had it not been continued and increased by religion. It was this that gave the sober, serious, and reflective turn of mind which has led to such mental improvement; and they who but for the power of godliness, would have been still earning their bread at the plough or the anvil, are filling the place of tradesmen or clerks ; or are raised to the distinction of preaching with ability and success, the truths of salvation.*

2. Religion guards the *health.*

I do not mean to say that the rose will always bloom upon the countenance of piety, but I will affirm, that where it already displays its beauty, and sheds its fragrance, religion will prevent those vices, which, like worms at the root of a flower, consume its strength, and shorten its existence.   How many diseases are generated by sin!   It is calculated that even in time of war, there are more who perish by

---

* As a proof of the influence which religion has in strengthening and elevating the powers, of even the most cultivated understanding, I may give the following quotation from the life of the Rev. Henry Martyn, a book which I most emphatically recommend to the perusal of all young people, as one of the most interesting publications that modern times have produced.

" Since I have known God in a saving manner," he remarks, " painting, poetry, and music have had charms unknown to me before.   I have received what I suppose is a taste for them : for religion has refined my mind, and made it susceptible of impressions from the sublime and beautiful. O how religion secures the heightened enjoyment of those pleasures which keep so many from God, by their becoming a source of pride !"

And it may be fairly argued, that the sublimity of Milton's genius, was owing, in no small degree, to the influence of religion upon his mind.   This is at once far more direct and obvious in its tendency, than any natural scenery, however bold and striking may be its features, since piety not only brings the mind into the region of sublime mental scenery, but fixes the eye most intently upon it.

drunkenness and licentiousness than by the sword. "Ye victims of voluptuousness, ye martyrs of concupiscence, who formerly tasted the pleasures of sin for a season, but now are beginning to feel the horrors of it for ever; you serve us for demonstration and example. Look at those trembling hands, that shaking head, those disjointed knees, that faltering resolution, that feeble memory, that worn-out body all putrefaction; these are the dreadful rewards which vice bestows now, as pledges of what Satan will bestow presently, on those on whom he is preparing to exhaust his fury." Religion will prevent all this; that passion which wastes the strength as with a fever; that ambition which wears out the frame faster than hard labor; that malice which robs of sleep; that gambling which hurries a man backward and forward between the delirium of hope and the torture of fear; that gluttony which brings on apoplexy; that drunkenness which preys as a slow fire on the organs of life; that debauchery which corrupts the whole mass of the blood, and brings the infirmities of age on the days of youth; are all kept off by religion. "The fear of the Lord prolongeth days; it is a fountain of life to guard us from the snares of death." But of the drunkard and the fornicator it may be said, "his bones are full of the sins of his youth, which lie down with him in the dust. Though wickedness be sweet in his mouth; though he hide it under his tongue; though he spare it, and forsake it not, but keep it still within his mouth ; yet his meat within his bowels is turned, it is the gall of asps within him."*

3. Religion builds up and protects the *reputation*.

It prevents those sins which render a man dishonorable and infamous ; it promotes all those virtues which raise and cherish esteem.   How much is the liar, the extortionate and imposing tradesman, the unfaithful servant, the unkind husband, the cruel oppressive master despised ! Who respects the individual that is notoriously addicted to vice, and flagrantly neglectful of the lowest obligations of virtue ?   Whereas, a man of consistent piety, who is known to be a real Christian, and whose Christianity renders him scrupulously true, honest, and upright, such a man is always universally esteemed. The wicked may laugh at a saint, but is he not the very man with whom they love to trade ; in whose character they find sufficient vouchers for the propriety of his conduct; and in whose fidelity they can repose unbounded confidence ? This was remarkably exemplified in the instance of the missionary Schwartz, who labored to spread the gospel in the southern part of the Indian peninsula.   Such was the repute in which this holy man was held by the native princes of Hindostan, that when Tippoo Saib was about to enter into a treaty with the Company, not being disposed to place much confidence in their agents, he exclaimed, " Send to me the missionary Schwartz, I will treat with him, for I *can* confide in *his* veracity."

* Job xx. 11—14.

17*

How many persons has the want of religion brought to an untimely end! No man would ever have been exiled as a felon, or executed as a male-factor, if he had lived under the influence of piety. No jail would have been needed, no gallows erected, if all men were pious. Godliness may not, indeed, guard us from poverty, but it will certainly save us from infamy. It may not advance us to wealth, but it will assuredly raise us to respectability.

4. Religion protects *our secular interests.*

I do not pretend that piety bears into the church the cornucopia of wordly wealth, to pour down showers of gold on all who court her smiles and bend to her sway; but still there is a striking ten-dency in her influence, to improve our worldly cir-cumstances.

It certainly prevents *those vices which tend to poverty.* Penury is often the effect of vice. How many have hurled themselves and their families from the pinnacles of prosperity to the depths of adversity, by a course of wicked and profligate ex-travagance. Multitudes have spent all their sub-stance, like the prodigal son, upon harlots and riot-ous living. Pride has ruined thousands, and indo-lence its tens of thousands. It is an observation of Franklin, " that one vice costs more to keep than two children." Religion is the most economical, and sin the most expensive thing in the world. How much do the drunkard, debauchee, sabbath-breaker, and frequenter of theatres, pay for their sinful gra-tifications! What is spent in this kingdom every

year in the grosser sensual indulgences, would pay
the interest of the national debt.   Piety would save
all this to the nation.

And then it not only prevents the vices which
tend to poverty, *but enjoins and cherishes the virtues
which lead to prosperity.*   It makes a man industrious; and is not this the way to wealth?   It renders him sober; and does not sobriety tend to advance our fortune?   It enforces a right improvement
of time, and surely this is advantageous to every
one.   It prescribes frugality, which tends to increase.   If a young man is in the service of another,
piety, by causing him to speak the truth, and adhere
to the principles of honesty, renders him trustworthy
and confidential.   We have a most striking and instructive instance of this in the history of Joseph,
of whom the historian thus writes: "And the Lord
was with Joseph, and he was a prosperous man; and
he was in the house of his master the Egyptian.
And his master saw that the Lord was with him,
and that the Lord made all that he did to prosper
in his hand.   And Joseph found grace in his sight,
and he served him; and he made him overseer over
his house, and all that he had, he put into his hand.
And he left all that he had in Joseph's hand, and
he knew not aught he had, save the bread which he
did eat."   This is one of the most lively and convincing cases on record of the influence of religion
on our temporal interests.   It was his piety that secured to Joseph this elevation and prosperity: it
was religion that exalted him from a menial slave to

a steward. Innumerable are the cases in which persons, who set out on the journey of life without property, and without patronage. have by dint of those virtues which religion enjoins, risen to respectability and affluence. They were first probably in a state of servitude, where by their steadiness and good conduct they so attached themselves to their employers, as to become in their estimation almost essential to the future success of the business; and, the result has been a share, and, in some cases, the whole of the trade, which they had contributed so materially to establish.

A friend of mine was once walking in the neighborhood of a large manufacturing town on a very cold winter's morning, when he overtook a plain man, decently clad, and wrapped in a comfortable great coat. After the usual salutations, my friend said to the stranger, " I am glad to see you with such a good warm covering this cold morning."—" It was not always thus," the man replied. " I was once a poor miserable creature, and had neither good clothes nor good victuals; now I have both, and a hundred pounds in the bank."—" What produced this favorable change ?" continued my friend. " Religion, sir; I am a good workman, and, as is too commonly the case with such men, spent half my time, and all my wages nearly at the public-house. I was of course always poor, and always wretched. By God's direction I was led to hear the Methodists, when by divine grace the word reached my heart. I repented of my sins, and became a new creature in Christ Jesus : old things passed away, and all things became new.   Religion made me industrious and sober, nothing now went for sin ; and the result is, that I am comfortable, and comparatively rich."

Here then, is a proof and an illustration, that godliness is profitable for all things, having the promise of the life that now is, as well as that which is to come.   Nor are these proofs uncommon.   Many persons, now living in circumstances of high respectability, are willing to ascribe all they possess here, as well as all they hope for hereafter, to the influence of religion.

All this is seen in the case of individuals ; but if the subject be carried out to society at large, it will appear still more striking.

What but religion can raise men from a savage to a civilized state ?   What else could have achieved the wonders which have been wrought in Africa, in Otaheite ; and taught the rudest barbarians to till the ground, to learn trades, to clothe themselves in decent apparel, to read, to cast accounts, to print books, to frame laws ?

Godliness alone can expel from society the practice of cruelty, and introduce the reign and prevalence of mercy.   The dark places of the earth are full of the habitations of cruelty.   Rome and Greece in the zenith of their glory, had neither a hospital for the sick, nor an asylum for the poor ; they treated their enemies with the most insolent cruelty ; practised the most vigorous slavery ; instituted

games, in which myriads of human beings were torn
to pieces in fighting with wild beasts. What a
blessing has Christianity been to the whole world,
even in relation to its present comforts ! It has
suppressed polygamy, put a stop to the sale of children by their parents, and the abandonment and
murder of aged parents, by their children ; it has
rescued women from their abominable degradation
by the other sex, and raised them to their just rank
in society ; it has sanctified the bond of marriage,
checked the licentiousness of divorce ; it has in a
great measure destroyed slavery, mitigated the terrors of war, given a new sanction to treaties, introduced milder laws, and more equitable governments ;
it has taught lenity to enemies and hospitality to
strangers : it has made a legal provision for the
poor ; formed institutions for instructing the ignorant; purified the stream of justice ; erected the
throne of mercy. "These, O Jesus, are the triumphs and the trophies of thy gospel ; and which of
thine enemies, Paganism, Islamism, or Infidelity, *has*
done, or *could* do the like ?"

Even the avowed and inveterate opponents of the
gospel, have been reluctantly compelled to acknowledge, in this view, its excellence. Voltaire says
expressly, " that religion is necessary in every community ; the laws are a curb upon open crimes, and
religion on those that are private." " No religion,"
says Bolingbroke, " ever appeared in the world,
whose natural tendency was so much directed to
promote the peace and happiness of mankind, as the

Christian. The gospel of Christ is one continued lesson of the strictest morality, of justice, benevolence, and universal charity. Supposing Christianity to be a human invention, it is the most amiable and useful invention that ever was imposed upon mankind for their good." Hume acknowledges, " that disbelief in futurity, looses in a great measure the ties of morality, and may be supposed, for that reason, pernicious to the peace of civil society." Rousseau confesses, " that if all were perfect Christians, individuals would do their duty, the people would be obedient to the laws, the chiefs just, the magistrates incorrupt, the soldiers would despise death, and there would be neither vanity nor luxury in such a state." Gibbon admits, " that the gospel discouraged suicide, advanced erudition, checked oppression, promoted the manumission of slaves, and softened the ferocity of barbarous nations ; that fierce nations received at the same time lessons of faith and humanity, and that even in the most corrupt state of Christianity, the barbarians learnt justice from the law, and mercy from the gospel."*

And yet with such concessions, and after having paid such a tribute of praise to the excellence of Christianity, these miserable men have been so vile and perverse as to conspire for her destruction.

* See an interesting work by Dr. Ryan, entitled, " The History of the Effects of Religion on Mankind in Countries Ancient and Modern, Barbarous and Civilized." I very particularly recommend the perusal of this volume to all young persons who can procure it, and also a similar Treatise by the late Bishop Porteus.

Thus has it been most demonstrably proved, that godliness exerts a powerful and favorable influence over the temporal interests of mankind. Neglect it, my children, and you know not what awaits you, either in this world or that which is to come. You may imagine that, provided you are moral and steady, although you are not pious, you are far enough removed from the probability of that wretchedness which vice brings with it. But, ah! in some unguarded moment, temptation may be successful to lead you astray : one vice makes way for another; and the dreadful progress described in the chapter on the deceitfulness of the heart, may be realized by you. Neglect religion, and you will *certainly* be ruined for the world to come, and *may be* for the life that now is. Vice certainly brings hell in its train, and sometimes a dreadful earnest of its future torments, in present poverty, disease, and misery.

I reflect with unutterable grief, as I now write, upon many young men, who were entering life with the greatest advantages, and the brightest prospects, whom, to use a common expression, fortune favored with her brightest smiles : but, alas! they would not be happy and respectable, for taking to the ways of sin, they dashed all the hopes of their friends, and wantonly threw away the opportunities which a kind providence had put within their reach. They went first to the theatre, then to the brothel, then to the tavern. They became dissipated, extravagant, idle. Unhappy youths! I know not what they might have been ; respectable tradesmen, prosperous merchants, honorable members of society; I know what they are; bloated rakes, discarded partners, uncertificated bankrupts, miserable vagrants, a burden to their friends, a nuisance to the community, and a torment to themselves.

Seek religion, then; for, as Solomon says in a passage quoted in a former chapter, " She is more precious than rubies; and all things thou canst desire are not to be compared unto her. Length of days is in her right hand; and in her left hand riches and honor. Exalt her, and she shall promote thee : she shall bring thee to honor, when thou dost embrace her."

XIII.

The Choice of Companions.

Man was made for society, and society is thought to be essential to his happiness. Adam did but half enjoy the lovely and untainted scenes of Eden, while there was no rational companion, to whom he could impart the raptures of his soul, and Paradise was incomplete till God gave him a friend. How much more might it be expected, that now, when the human bosom is bereft of its innocence, man should look out of himself for happiness, and endeavor to find it in society. Young people, especially, are anxious to form associations of this kind, and are in imminent danger of choosing companions that will do them no good. The design of the present chapter is to put you, my children, on your guard against this evil, and to assist you in the selection of those friends with whom you take daily counsel. This subject has been already adverted to, but it is of sufficient importance to occupy a separate chapter.

1. It becomes you very seriously to reflect on the influence which your companions, of whatever kind

they are, will certainly have in the formation of your character.

"We are all," says Mr. Locke, "a kind of chameleons, that take a tincture from the objects which surround us." A still wiser man has told us, that "He that walketh with wise men shall be wise, but a companion of fools shall be destroyed." Hence he says to us; "make no friendship with an angry man, and with a furious man thou shalt not go; lest thou learn his ways, and get a snare to thy soul." These admonitions are founded on the general principle, that the example of our companions will exert a plastic influence in the formation of our own character, slow and silent, perhaps, but irresistible and successful: and this influence will be in proportion to the love and esteem we cherish for them. All nations and all ages have confessed the truth of this sentiment. The example of a beloved companion is omnipotent, more especially if he be a sinful one, because a bad model finds in the depravity of our nature, something that prepares it to receive the impression. One evil companion will undo in a month, all that parents and teachers have been laboring for years to accomplish. Here then pause, and consider that the character of your associates will, in all probability, be your own. If you do not *carry* to them a similarity of taste, you will be sure to *acquire* it; "for how can two walk together except they be agreed?"

Let me now set before you the dangers to be apprehended from *bad* company.

By bad company I mean all those who are destitute of the fear of God ; not only the infidel, the
profligate, the profane, but those who are living in
the visible neglect of religion.   Now these are no fit
companions for you.   They may be respectable and
genteel as to their rank in life ; they may be graceful and insinuating in their manners ; they may be
persons of fine taste, and cultivated understandings ;
of facetious humor, and polished wit ; but these
things, if connected with irreligious habits, only
make them the more alarmingly and successfully
dangerous ; they are like the fair speech, and lovely
form, and glowing colors, which the serpent assumed
when he attacked and destroyed the innocence of
Eve.   Look through these meretricious ornaments,
pierce this dazzling exterior, and recognise the fang
and the venom of the wily foe.   The more external
accomplishments any one has, if he be without the
fear of God, the greater is his power to do mischief ;
and remember, that when you have listened to his
wiles, and feel the sharpness of his tooth, and the
deadly agony of his venom, it will be no compen-
sation, nor consolation, that you have looked on his
many-tinted skin, and have been ruined by the fascination of his charms.   The companions you are to
avoid, then, are those who are obviously living without the fear of God.

Consider the many dangers arising from such
associates.   You will soon outlive all sense of serious
piety, and lose all the impressions you may have received from a religious education.   These you can-

not hope to preserve ; you may as soon expect to
guard an impression traced with your finger in the
sand from being effaced by the tide of the Atlantic
ocean.   Even they whose religious character has
been formed for years, find it hard to preserve the
spirituality of their mind in irreligious company.
" Throw a blazing fire-brand into snow or rain," says
Bolton, " and its brightness and heat will be quickly
extinguished, so let the liveliest christian plunge himself into sinful company, and he will soon find the
warmth of his zeal abated, and the tenderness of his
conscience injured."   How, then, can *you* expect to
maintain a sense of religion, whose habits are scarcely formed, and whose character has yet so much of
the tenderness and suppleness of youth ?   Do consider your proneness to imitate ; your dread of singularity; your love of praise ; your morbid sense of
shame.   Can you bear the sneer, the jest, the broad,
loud laugh ?   With none to defend you, none to
join in your reverence for piety, what are you to do
single and alone ?

In such company you lay yourselves open to
temptation, and will probably be drawn into a great
deal of guilt.   In private and alone, the force of
temptation and the power of depravity are very
great, but how much greater when aided by the example of intimate friends.   As united fires burn the
fiercer, and the concentrated *virus* of many persons
thrown into the same room infected with the plague,
renders the disease more malignant, so a sinful community improves and grows in impiety, and every
18*

member joins his brother's pollution to his own. Nothing is so contagious as bad morals. Evil communications corrupt good manners. Multitudes have committed those sins without scruple in society, which they could not have contemplated alone without horror. It is difficult indeed to wade against the torrent of evil example, and, generally speaking, whatever is done by the party, must either be done or approved by every individual of which it is composed.

In such company you will throw yourselves out of the way of repentance and reformation. The little relish you once had for devotional exercises will soon be lost. Your Bible will fall into desuetude, the house of God will be neglected, and pious friends carefully shunned. Should an occasional revival of your serious feelings take place under a sermon, or the remonstrances of a friend, they will be immediately lulled again to repose, or banished from your bosom by the presence and conversation of an irreligious companion.

In many cases, evil society has destroyed for ever even the *temporal* interests of those who have frequented it. Habits of dissipation, folly, and extravagance, have been acquired, character has been ruined, business neglected, poverty and misery entailed. But if this should not ensue, the influence of evil association will go far to ruin your *souls* and sink you to perdition. A companion of fools shall be destroyed; their path is the way to hell, going down to the chambers of death. Yes; if you connect

yourselves with them, they will drag you into the
vortex of their own ruin, as they sink into the gulf
of perdition. Is there the companion on earth
whose society you will seek to retain at this dreadful hazard ? Is there one, for the sake of whose
friendship you would be willing to walk with him to
the bottomless pit ? What though you could have the
society of the first poets, philosophers, wits, and
fashionables of the age, and yet were to lose your
own souls, what would this profit you ? Will it
soothe the agonies of your spirit in those regions of
horrible despair, to remember what you enjoyed in
the company of your gay companions on earth ?
Alas ! alas ! all that rendered your intercourse on
earth delightful, will then come to a final end.
There will be no opportunities granted you to gratify your sensual desires together ; no delicious food,
no intoxicating liquors ; there are no amusing tales,
no merry songs there ; no feast of reason, nor flow
of soul there ; no coruscations of wit will enliven
the gloom of hell ; no gay fancy will brighten the
darkness of eternal despair ; no sallies of humor
shall illumine the darkness of everlasting night ;
" but there shall be weeping, and wailing and gnashing of teeth : the worm that never dies, and the fire
that is never quenched."

What mind but His, who comprehends the universe in his survey, can count the multitudes that
have been ruined for both worlds by the influence
of bad company. Their names have been recorded
on every roll of infamy, and found in every memo-

rial of guilt and wretchedness. The records of the workhouse and the hospital ; of the jail and the hulks ; of the gallows and the dissecting room, would declare the mischief: and could we look into the prison of lost souls, a crowd of miserable ghosts would meet our eye, who seem to utter in groans of despair, this sad confession, " We are the wretched victims of evil association."

In the large and populous town where Providence has fixed my lot, I have had an extensive sphere of observation ; and I give it as my decided conviction, and deliberate opinion, *that improper associates are the most successful means which are employed by Satan for the ruin of men's souls.*

The advice then which I offer is this :

1. Be not over anxious about society. Do not take up the opinion that *all* happiness centres in a friend. Many of you are blessed with a happy home and an agreeable circle round your own fireside. Here seek your companions, in your parents, your brothers and sisters.

2. Determine to have *no* companion rather than have an improper one. The one case is but a privation of what is pleasant, the other is a possession of a positive evil.

3. Maintain a dignified, but not proud reserve. Do not be too frank and ingenuous. Be cautious of too hastily attaching yourselves as friends to others, or them to you. Be polite and kind to all, but communicative and familiar with few. Keep your hearts in abeyance, till your judgment has most care-

fully examined the characters of those who wish to
be admitted to the circle of your acquaintance.
Neither run nor jump into friendships, but walk
towards them slowly and cautiously.

4. Always consult your parents about your companions, and be guided by their opinions. They
have your interest at heart, and see further than you
can.

5. Cultivate a taste for reading and mental improvement ; this will render you independent of living society. Books will always furnish you with intelligent, useful, and elegant friends. No one can
be dull who has access to the works of illustrious
authors, and has a taste for reading And after all
there are but comparatively few, whose society will
so richly reward us as this silent converse with the
mighty dead.

6. Choose none for your intimate companions but
those who are decidedly pious, or persons of very
high moral worth. A scrupulous regard to all the
duties of morality ; a high reverence for the scriptures ; a belief in their essential doctrines ; a constant attendance on the means of grace, are the *lowest* qualifications which you should require in the
character of an intimate friend.

Perhaps I shall be asked one or two questions on
this subject, to which an answer ought to be returned. " If," say you, " I have formed an acquaintance with a young friend, before I had any serious
impressions upon my mind, ought I now to quit his
society, if he still remains destitute of any visible re-

gard to religion ?" First try, by every effort which affection can dictate, and prudence direct, to impress his mind with a sense of religion : if, after awhile your exertions should be unavailing, candidly tell him, that as you have taken different views of things, and acquired different tastes to what you formerly possessed ; and that as you have failed to bring him to your way of living, and can no longer accommodate your pursuits to his, conscience demands of you a separation from his society. Sir Matthew Hale, one of the most upright and able judges that ever sat upon the bench, was nearly ruined by his disolute companions. When young, he had been very studious and sober ; but the players happening to come to the town where he was studying, he became a witness of their performance, by which he was so captivated that his mind lost its relish for study, and he addicted himself to dissipated company. When in the midst of his associates one day, it pleased God to visit one of them with sudden death. Sir Matthew was struck with horror and remorse. He retired and prayed, first for his friend, that if the vital spark had not fled, he might be restored ; and then for himself, that he might never more be found in such places and company as would render him unfit to meet death From that day he quitted all his wicked companions, walked no more in the way of sinners, but devoted himself to piety and literature.

I shall be asked again probably, " What am I to do if I can find in my situation no individual of my

own rank and circumstances in life, who is a partaker of true piety ; ought I, in this case, to associate with those who are much below me, and who
cannot be my companions in any thing but piety ?'
In reply to this, I observe, that it is *character* which
constitutes respectability, and not the adventitious
circumstances of fortune or rank : and to conduct
ourselves in any degree as if we were ashamed of
the followers of.Christ, because they are poor, is an
offence against our divine Lord.   To forsake prayer-
meetings, benevolent institutions, Sunday-schools, or
places where the gospel is preached, merely because
we find none there of sufficient fortune to associate
with us ; to treat our poorer brethren with cold neglect and haughty distance; to refuse to be seen
speaking *with* them, and *to* them, as if they were beneath us ; this is most manifestly wrong; for it is
carrying the distinctions of the world into the church.
Still, however, as religion was never intended to
level these distinctions, it might not be advisable to
choose *bosom companions* from those who are far below us in worldly circumstances.   Some inconvenience would arise from the practice, and it would
occasion, in many cases, the ways of godliness to be
spoken ill of.

Young persons of good habits should take great
heed that they do not, by insensible degrees, become
dangerous characters to each other.   That social
turn of mind. which is natural to men, and especially
to young persons, may perhaps lead them to form
themselves into little societies, particularly at the

festive season of the year, to spend their evenings together. But let me entreat you to be cautious *how* you spend them. If your games and your cups take up your time till you entrench on the night, and perhaps on the morning too, you will quickly corrupt each other. Farewell, then, to prayer, and every other religious exercise in secret. Farewell, then, to all my pleasing hopes of you, and to those hopes which your pious parents have entertained. You will then become examples and instances of all the evils I have so largely described. Plead not that these things are lawful in themselves ; so are most of those in a certain degree which, by their abuse, prove destruction to men's souls and bodies. If you meet, let it be for rational and christian conversation ; and let prayer and other devotions have their frequent place among you : and if you say or think that a mixture of these will spoil the company, it is high time for you to stop your career, and call yourselves to an account ; for it seems by such a thought, that you are lovers of pleasure, much more than lovers of God. Some of these things may appear to have a tincture of severity, but consider whether I could have proved myself faithful to you, and to him in whose name I speak, if I had omitted the caution I have now been giving you. I shall now only add, that had I loved you less tenderly, I should have warned you more coldly of this dangerous and deadly snare.*

* See Dr. Doddridge's sermon, entitled " A Dissuasive from keeping bad Company."

XIV.

On Books.

THE invention of the art of printing forms an era in the history of mankind, next in importance to the promulgation of the law, and the publication of the gospel. Until this splendid gift was bestowed upon man, books, which were all in manuscript, were circulated within a comparatively narrow sphere, and knowledge was in the possession of only a privileged few. This invaluable art, however, rendered the fountains of information accessible to all, and gave opportunity to the poorest of our race, to slake their mental thirst at the deepest and purest streams of truth. There was a time when ignorance was rather a misfortune than a reproach; and when, indeed, a craving after information would, with many, have been rather a calamity than a benefit, since the means of satisfying the appetite were beyond their reach. The state of things is altered now, and almost a whole circle of science may be purchased for a few shillings. Education is also much improved and extended. Under these circumstances, ignorance is a deep reproach; and a young person who can suffer days and weeks to pass without taking up a book, is a pitiable spectacle of doltish inanity. Cultivate, then, my children, a taste for reading ; and, in order to this, there must be a thirst after information. " Knowledge," says Lord Bacon, " is power ;" and if it were not power it is pleasure. It gives us weight of character, and procures for us respect. It enables us to form an opinion with correctness, to state it with clearness, to offer it with confidence, and to enforce it with argument. It enlarges the sphere of our usefulness, by raising the degree of our influence. Other things being equal, that man will be the most useful, who has the greatest measure of information. Here I shall offer some directions for your guidance in the selection of books. Books may be divided into two classes.

First, such as relate to religion.

Of these, the BIBLE of course occupies the supreme place, an elevation exclusively its own. It is, as its title signifies, THE BOOK ;—the standard of all right sentiments ; the judge of all other works. Sir William Jones, that prodigy of learning, wrote on the fly-leaf of his Bible these remarks : " I have carefully and regularly perused these holy Scriptures, and am of opinion that the volume, independently of its divine origin, contains more sublimity, purer morality, more important history, and finer strains of eloquence, than can be collected from all other books, in whatever language they may have been written." Salmasius, the learned antagonist of

Milton, said on his death-bed, " That were he to begin life again, he would spend much of his time in reading David's Psalms and Paul's Epistles." Whatever books you neglect, then, my children, neglect not the Bible. Whatever books you read, read this. Let not a day pass without perusing some portion of holy writ. Read it devoutly; not from curiosity, nor with a view to controversy; but to be made wise unto salvation. Read it with much prayer. Read it with a determination to follow its guidance wheresoever it leads.*

In addition to the Bible, there are many uninspired religious books which I recommend. In the class of *Biography*, HUNTER's Scripture Characters is a most fascinating production; BROOK's Lives of the Puritans, GILPIN's Lives of the Reformers, Cox's Life of Melancthon, are all useful and interesting. Mr. WILLIAMS' Life and Diary will show you how the tradesman may be busy for both worlds. The life of PEARCE, by Fuller, is an excellent work. MARTYN's Memoirs is the most interesting piece of Biography published in modern times. DURANT's Life and Remains of his Son are singularly instructive.

Should you wish to read on *Doctrinal Theology*, I strongly recommend DWIGHT's System. *On the Evidences of Christianity*, Bishop WATSON's Apology, in reply to Paine; likewise BOGUE's Essay,

* I recommend to the young a diligent and serious perusal of Bickersteth's Help to the Reading of the Scriptures ; a very valuable treatise.

CHALMERS' Historical Evidences; the masterly work of PALEY; and CAMPBELL on miracles, a work which meets the subtilities of Hume. As a work of general biblical knowledge, too much praise cannot be bestowed on HORNE's Introduction to the critical study of the Bible. No young person should suffer himself to live another month without seeking to gain access to this invaluable book. TOWNSEND's Chronological Arrangements of the Old and New Testaments is a very useful work.

On *Church History*, I recommend BURNET's History of the Reformation; CAMPBELL, for his admirable description of the rise, progress, and spirit of popery; MOSHEIM, for his account of the errors and corruptions of the church; and MILNER, for his anxiety to trace true piety, wherever it is to be found, amidst the prevailing ignorance and vice of the times. He is, however, too credulous, and not so impartial in his treatment of the questions which bear on dissent, as the dignity and candor of an historian require. JONES' History of the Waldenses is a very interesting work.

Secondly the other division of books includes all the varied classes which relate to the affairs of this life.

Enjoying, as Britons, the advantages of a political constitution, which is the work of ages, and the admiration of the world, you should acquaint yourselves with its theory, and for this purpose may read CUSTANCE's short work, DE LOLME's more elaborate and philosophical productions, and the first volume of BLACKSTONE's Commentaries, together with a more modern work of Lord JOHN RUSSELL's.

Young men should acquaint themselves with the principles of *trade* and *commerce,* and of course should be acquainted with " ADAM SMITH's Wealth of Nations."

History is a class of reading in which you ought to be at home ; and as Britons, it would be to your deep disgrace to be ignorant of the details of your *own country.* In this department you ought not to be satisfied with mere facts, and names, and dates, but should read with an eye which discriminates and marks the changes which events introduce into the manners, laws, liberties, and governments of nations. History is something more than a mere chronicle of facts ; and our knowledge of its details should be such as enables us to trace the progress of society, and the march of improvement. The history of GOLDSMITH should prepare you for the larger and popular work of HUME. The beautiful simplicity of HUME's composition, together with his philosophical mode of analyzing character, and tracing events, render his work peculiarly fascinating ; but unhappily, HUME was a confirmed infidel, and must be read with a mind ever upon its guard against the poison which he has infused into his narrative ; and his views on the great question of religious liberty were not the most liberal. In his history of the Stuarts, he has suffered his high tory principles so far to prejudice his mind and bias his judgment, that this portion of his work will be a lasting reproach to him for his want of accuracy : it is in fact little better in some places than a mere historical romance. It is highly probable that his antipathy to religion led him into this error. Perceiving, as he himself confessed, that the Puritans and Non-conformists were the most zealous friends of liberty, he felt a sort of revulsion for liberal principles, because of the religious sentiments with which they were so often united. Philosophy, then, does not always emancipate the human understanding from the fetters of prejudice. Mr. Brodie, an author of considerable reputation, has exposed such a shameful want of accuracy in Hume's account of the Stuarts' reigns, that the authority of this northern sceptic as a matter-of-fact man, seems to be much on the decline. When you read HUME, remember, that although you are drinking a pleasant draught from a goblet of burnished gold, there is poison in the cup ; happily, the deleterious infusion floats upon the surface, and may be therefore easily detected. An English history, in which there shall be the most sacred regard to the principles of pure morality, evangelical religion, and rational liberty, is still a desideratum in the literature of our country.*

* Some interesting and valuable books, entitled, " Studies in History," have been published by the Rev. T. Morell, theological tutor in the dissenting academy at Wymondley. His moral reflections are rather too long, and too much detached from the history. Hume has so incorporated his infidelity with his history, that it is impossible to read one without the other. In this way, a moral and religious history should be written. To use a simile, borrowed from

The ancient history of ROLLIN, eloquent, pure and moral, should be read by every young person. It is almost impossible to recommend. this work too strongly. It has all the interest of a novel, with none of its poison. What need have we of fiction, at least, till we have read such facts as are here embodied. Rollin, however, it must be confessed, is rather too warlike in the tendency of his remarks. GOLD-SMITH'S *Greece* should prepare for the masterly work of MITFORD; and his *Rome*, for the gorgeous produciton of GIBBON. Unhappily, the same remark will apply to the latter writer, as to his contemporary HUME; he was an infidel, though in a more covert way than the Scotch historian. If you have leisure and inclination to pursue Roman history, CREVIER, who was a pupil of ROLLIN, has supplied the means, in his " Lives of Emperors;" and HOOKE also, in his Roman History, which is carried down to the death of Octavius. ROBERTSON'S historical works are eminently entitled to attention, especially his " Charles the-Fifth," the introductory volume of which contains a view of the progress of society in Europe, from the subversion of the Roman empire to the beginning of the sixteenth century, and also presents a masterly survey of the graduations by which the social institutions of antiquity have passed

weaving, the religion and the narrative should, like the warp and the woof, be wrought into each other. When they are entirely detached, young people find the thread of the history too much broken, and leave the comment in order to follow the text.

through the barbarism of the dark ages into all that characterises the state of modern Europe. Bishop BURNET's History of his own Times ought to be perused as the work of an author who wrote the narrative of events which he witnessed, whose veracity can be trusted, if not his discrimination.

In the department of *English composition*, ADDISON and JOHNSON, though moral writers, in the *usual* acceptation of the term are not always correct in their principles, if, indeed, the New Testament is the standard of moral sentiments. It is desirable to cultivate a good taste, and an elegant style of composition ; and for this purpose, the productions of these two celebrated writers may be read, together with BURKE on the Sublime, ALISON on Taste, BLAIR's Lectures, CAMPBELL on Rhetoric, and Lord KAIMES's Elements of Criticism.

Should you feel inclined, and be favored with leisure, to pursue the study of Mental Philosophy, I recommend you to begin with ISAAC TAYLOR's Elements of Thought. Then read Mr. BURDER's Hints on Mental Culture ; then Dr. WATTS on the Improvement of the Mind ; then Dr. REID's work on the Intellectual and Active powers of the Human Mind ; and then study DUGALD STEWART's beautiful work on Intellectual Philosophy.

Poetry is a bewitching, and if not of a strictly moral character, a dangerous species of writing. I by no means condemn it, for this would betray a gothic destitution of taste, as well as an ignorance of some of the first principles of our nature. The ear is tuned to enjoy the melody of numbers, and the imagination formed to delight in the creations of fancy. But still it must be recollected that the imagination is amongst the inferior faculties of mind, and that the gratification of the senses is amongst the lowest ends of a rational existence : only a *limited* perusal of poetry is therefore to be allowed ; such an indulgence in this mental luxury and recreation, as will not unfit the mind, or deprive it of opportunity for severer and more useful pursuits. We should use poetry as we do those pleasing objects of nature, from which it derives its most lovely images ; not as the regions of our constant abode, but as the scenes of our occasional resort. Although the present age can boast the noble productions of such men as SCOTT, SOUTHEY, CAMPBELL, and WORDSWORTH, whose poems every person of real taste will read, yet I recommend the more *habitual* perusal of our great MILTON among the ancients, and COWPER and MONTGOMERY among the moderns, the first for his genius, and the others for their piety.*

* As for BYRON, possessing, as he does, the very soul of poetry beyond all his contemporaries, his exquisite pathos and peerless beauty can make no atonement for his vices, and should have no power to reconcile us to his works. He is, indeed, as he has been styled, the master of a Satanic school: infidelity and immorality are the lessons which all his pages teach; and nearly all his characters embody and enforce. Never before did these dispositions receive such patronage from the poetic muse. Never was genius seen more closely allied to vice than in the productions of this popular but dangerous writer. His works are enough to

The whole wide range of *Natural History* and *Experimental Philosophy* presents a scene of interesting research, through which authors of the first respectability stand always ready to conduct you, unfolding at every step some new proof of the existence, and some fresh display of the wisdom, power, and goodness of the great First Cause. The sublime wonders of astronomy elevate the mind, and throw up an almost infinite field of contemplation and astonishment. Chemistry, by its combinations,

corrupt the morals of a nation, and seem, indeed, to have been written for this dreadful purpose. He stands like a volcano in the world of letters, grand and majestic, dark lowering, and fiery; while every new work is but another eruption of lava upon the interests beneath. He seems to have been stirred up by the evil Spirit to attempt, by his fascinating poems, that mischief which the wit of Voltaire, the subtilties of Hume, and the popular ribaldries of Paine, had in vain endeavored to achieve.

The indignation of heaven seems to have been roused even before his death, and to have scorched with its lightning the wings of this lofty but impious genius; inasmuch as his later productions evince a singular destitution of that talent by which the earlier effusions of his muse were characterized. One can scarcely suppose it possible that even *he* could read the last cantos of his most licentious work without secretly exclaiming, under a consciousness of their inferiority, "How am I fallen!"

If young people would not be cursed by the infidelity and immorality which lurks in its pages, let them beware how they touch his volumes, as much as they would to embrace a beautiful form infected with the plague. I most earnestly recommend the perusal of an admirable sermon by Dr. Styles, on the moral character of Lord Byron's Works.

affinities, and repulsions ; by its principles as a theory, and the unlimited practical uses of these principles, is an endless career of pleasing and useful study.   Optics, pneumatics, electricity, with all their attendant sciences, have been treated of by writers, whose productions assist us to explore the wonderful works of God : while botany shows that the weed we trample under our feet, no less than the mighty orb which rolls through illimitable space, obeys the laws, assumes the place, and accommodates itself to the order appointed by its Creator.

As to that class of books denominated *novels*, I join with every other moral and religious writer in condemning, as the vilest trash, the greater part of the productions, which, under this name, have carried a turbid stream of vice over the morals of mankind.   They corrupt the taste, pollute the heart, debase the mind, demoralize the conduct.   They throw prostrate the understanding, sensualize the affections, enervate the will, and bring all the high faculties of the soul into subjection to an imagination which they have first made wild, insane, and uncontrollable.   They furnish no ideas, and generate a morbid, sickly sentimentalism, instead of a just and lovely sensibility.   A wise man should despise them, and a good man should abhor them.   Of late years they have, it is true, undergone a considerable reformation.   The present EXTRAORDINARY FAVORITE of the literary world, has indeed displaced, and sent into oblivion, a thousand miserable scribblers of love stories, who still however fling back at him, as they

retire, the ancient taunt, "Art thou too become one
of us?" His works discovered prodigious talent,
astonishing information, and a power of delineating
character truly wonderful. But what is their merit
beyond the power to amuse? Whoever wrote so
much for so little usefulness? They are still, in
part, works of fiction, and in measure, exert the same
unfriendly influence on the public mind and taste as
other works of fiction do when they are made the
almost exclusive matter of our reading.

As to *religious novels*, they are rarely worth your
attention. I should be sorry to see this species of
writing become the *general* reading of the religious
public. Symptoms of a craving appetite for this
species of mental food have been very apparent of
late. These are far more likely to lead young persons of pious education to read other kinds of novels,
than they are to attract the readers of the latter to
pious tales. They have already, in many cases,
formed a taste for works of fiction, which is gratify-
ing itself with far more exceptionable productions.
They have become the harbingers, in some families,
of works, which, till *they* entered, would have been
forbidden to pass the threshold.

It is very evident that the taste of the present
age is strongly inclined for works of fiction. I am
not unacquainted with the arguments by which such
productions are justified, nor am I by any means
prepared to pronounce a sweeping sentence of condemnation upon them. Genius is elicited and cherished by writing them; and taste is formed, cor-

rected, and gratified, by reading them. Provided they are totally free from all unscriptural sentiments and antichristian tendency, they form a recreation for the mind, and keep it from amusements of a worse character. I am also aware that they may be, and have been, made the vehicle of much instruction. Johnson tells us that this, amongst many other arts of instruction, has been invented, that the reluctance against truth might be overcome; and as physic is given to children in confections, precepts have been hidden under a thousand appearances, that mankind may be bribed by a pleasure to escape destruction. In his beautiful allegory of TRUTH, FALSEHOOD, and FICTION, he represents Truth as so repeatedly foiled in her contests with Falsehood, that in the anger of disappointment, she petitions JUPITER to be called back to her native skies, and leave mankind to the disorder and misery which they deserved, by submitting willingly to the usurpation of her antagonist. Instead of granting her request, he recommended her to consult the Muses by what method she might obtain an easier reception, and reign without the toil of incessant war. It was then discovered, that she obstructed her own progress, by the severity of her aspect, and the solemnity of her dictates; and that men would never willingly admit her, till they ceased to fear her; since, by giving themselves up to FALSEHOOD, they seldom make any sacrifice of their ease or pleasure, because she took the state that was most engaging, and always suffered herself to be dressed and painted by DESIRE.

The Muses wove in the loom of *Pallas* a loose and changeable robe, like that in which FALSEHOOD captivated her admirers; with this they invested TRUTH, and named her FICTION. She now went out again to conquer with more success; for when she demanded entrance of the PASSIONS, they often mistook her for FALSEHOOD, and delivered up their charge; but when she had once taken possession, she was soon disrobed by REASON, and shone out, in her original form, with native effulgence, and resistless beauty.

This is plausible; but will not history and biography answer all the ends of fiction, unattended with its injurious effects? Here all is life, variety, and interest. Here is every thing to amuse, to recreate. Here the finest moral lessons are inculcated in the details of facts. Here are passions, motives, actions, all forming the most exquisite delineations of character, set home upon the heart with the aid of the powerful conviction that these are *facts*. I am sure that none can have attended to the more secret and subtle operations of their own minds, without perceiving that a display of virtue or vice, embodied in *fact*, has inconceivably more power over the mind, than the same character exhibited by the most extraordinary genius in a fiction. While reading the latter, we may have been deeply affected, we may have glowed with anger at the sight of vice, melted with pity at the display of misery, or soared in rapture at the exhibition of excellence; but when the book is laid down, and the mind recovers from the illusion, does not the recollection, that all this was the creation of imagination, exert a cold and chilling influence upon the heart, and go far to efface almost every favorable impression, till, by a kind of revenge for the control which a *fiction* has had over us, we determine to forget all we have felt. We cannot do this in rising from a fact.

Fiction is generally overwrought. It is vice in caricature, or virtue in enamel; the former is frequently too bad to be dreaded as likely to happen to us ; the latter too high to be an object of expectation. All the attendant circumstances are too artificially contrived. There is little that is like it in real life. Our passions are too much excited, our hopes are too much raised ; and when we come from this ideal world into the every-day scenes of ordinary life, we feel a sense of dulness, because everything looks tame and common-place. The effect of such works is great for the time, but it is not a useful effect : it is like the influence of ardent spirits, which fit men for desperate adventures, but not for the more steady and sober efforts of ordinary enterprise.

Observe then, although I do not totally condemn *all* works of fiction, for then I should censure the practice of Him who spake as never man spake, whose parables were fictitious representations ; yet I advise a sparing and cautious perusal of them, whether written in poetry or prose. History, biography, travels, accounts of the manners and customs of nations, will answer all the ends of fiction ; they will amuse, and they will in the most easy and pleasing way instruct. They will exhibit to us every possible view of human nature, and every conceivable variety of character. They will introduce us to a real world, and exhibit to us the feelings and the excellences of men of like passions with ourselves ; and who, according to the complexion of their character, may be regarded as beacons to warn us, or the polar star to guide us.

1. Again, and again, I say, cultivate, my children, a taste for the acquisition of knowledge ; thirst after information as the miser does after wealth ; treasure up ideas with the same eagerness as he does pieces of gold. Let it not be said, that for you the greatest of human beings have lived, and the most splendid of human minds have written in vain. You live in a world of books, and *they* contain worlds of thought. Devote all the time that can lawfully be spared from business to reading. Lose not an hour. Ever have some favorite author at hand, to the perusal of whose production, the hours, and half-hours, which would otherwise be wasted, might be devoted. Time is precious. Its fragments, like those of diamonds, are too valuable to be lost. Let no day pass without your attempting to gain some new idea. Your first object of existence, as I have already stated, should be the salvation of your soul ; the next, the benefit of your fellow-creatures ; and then comes the improvement of your mind.

*_** I subjoin a list of some other books of which I should advise the perusal.

Mrs. HANNAH MORE's "Practical Piety;" "Christian Morals;" "Character of St. Paul."—BOWDLER's "Select Pieces."—GREGORY's "Letters."—LOWTH "On the Sacred Poetry of the Hebrews."—NEWTON "On the Prophecies." FULLER "On Calvinism."—SHUCKFORD's "Connexions."—PRIDEAUX's "Connexions."—"Life of Sir William Jones."—JORTIN's "Life of Erasmus."—HALLAM's "Literary History of the Middle Ages."—MILTON's "Prose Works."—Lord Bacon's "Essays."—TYTLER's "Elements of History."—ENFIELD's "History of Philosophy."—FENELON's "Dialogues on Eloquence."—BOSWELL's "Life of Johnson."

20*

XV.

Amusements and Recreations.

It is a trite remark, that the mind, like a bow, will lose its power by being always strained ; and that occasional relaxation from the cares of business is necessary to preserve the vigor and elasticity of the human faculties. Allowing this to be true, it becomes a question, in what way recreation may be lawfully sought ; or, in other words, what kind of amusement may be innocently resorted to. Here two rules may be laid down.

1. All recreations are improper *which have an injurious influence upon the moral and religious character.* This is an axiom. No reasoning is necessary to support it : no eloquence is requisite to illustrate it : none but an atheist can oppose it.

2. All recreations are improper which, by their nature, *have a tendency to dissipate the mind, and unfit it for the pursuit of business;* or which encroach too much on the time demanded for our necessary occupations. This rule is as intelligible and as just as the former.

These two directions, the propriety of which all

must admit, will be quite sufficient to guide us ‾in the choice of amusements.

First, there are some diversions, which, by leading us to *inflict pain*, produce *cruelty of disposition.**

A reluctance to occasion misery even to an insect is not a mere *decoration* of the character, which we are left at liberty to wear or to neglect ; but it is a disposition which we are commanded, as matter of duty to cherish. It is not mere sensibility, but a necessary part of virtue. It is impossible to inflict pain, and connect the idea of gratification with such an act, without experiencing some degree of mental obduration. We are not surprised that he who, while a boy, amused himself in killing flies, should, when he became a sovereign, exhibit the character of a cruel and remorseless tyrant. To find pleasure in setting brutes to worry and devour each other, is a disposition truly diabolical ; and the man who can find delight in dog-fighting, cock-fighting, bull-baiting, is quite prepared to imitate those cannibals who, in the popular insurrections and massacres of the French revolution, sported with the mangled carcases and palpitating limbs of their murdered victims, and dragged them about with their teeth in the gardens of the Tuileries.

Horse-racing, in addition to the cruelty with

* The author is indebted for some thoughts in this chapter to a lecture on the same subject, which occurs in an excellent volume of Lectures to the Young, published by his friend the Rev. T. Morgan, a Baptist Minister.

which it is attended, is generally a means of assembling on the course, all the gamesters, swindlers, and black-legs in the neighborhood, and is the cause of much drunkenness, debauchery, and ruin.

All *field sports*, of *every* kind, are, in my view, condemned by the laws of humanity. Shooting, coursing, hunting, angling, are all cruel. What agony is inflicted in hooking a worm or a fish; in maiming a bird; in chasing and worrying a hare; and to find *sport* in doing this, is inhuman and unchristian. To say that these animals are given for food, and must be killed, is not a reply to my argument. I am not contending against killing them, or eating them, but against the act of killing of them for *sport*. The infliction of death, under any circumstances, and upon any creature, however insignificant in the scale of creation, is too serious a matter to be a source of amusement. No two terms can be more incongruous than death and sport. It seems perfectly monstrous, that after having subjected the irrational creation to the terrors of dissolution by his guilt, man should experience *pleasure* in executing the sentence. Death is the enemy even of brutes; and the irrational creation manifest symptoms of instinctive horror at his approach; and to find delight in throwing the shuddering victim to the devourer, is shocking. I would extend these remarks to all animals, and say, that it is unlawful to find *sport* in killing such as are *noxious*. Wolves, bears, serpents, are to be destroyed when their continuance endangers human life; but to find pleasure in the act of killing even these, has a hardening tendency on the human heart.

Secondly. Some amusements tend to cherish *selfish* and *avaricious* feelings, and at the same time to produce that *gambling taste* which leads to the utter ruin of both the temporal and eternal interests of mankind. Billiards, cards, dice, have this tendency; and indeed, all other games that are played for money. The object of the player in these games is to get money, by a hasty process. What arts of fraud and deception are often resorted to, in order to avoid the loss and shame of defeat, and secure the gain and honor of success! What anger and ill-will are often produced in the mind of the unsuccessful party! Even the rules of decorum observed in polished society, are not sufficient, in many cases, to restrain the passionate invective, and the profane oath. I may here most confidently appeal to the frequenters of the card-table, for the truth of what I say, when I affirm, that the want of success during an evening at whist is a trial of temper, which few are able to bear with honor to themselves, or the comfort of those around them. Passion, petulence, and sullenness are always waiting under the table, ready to appear in the person and conduct of the loser. I have had scenes described to me by spectators of them, which I should have thought a disgrace to the vulgar company assembled at an alehouse, much more *the genteel party in the drawing-room.* Have not the most serious misunderstandings arisen from this source between man and wife!

What wrath and fury has the latter, by her tide of
ill success, brought down upon her head from her
irritated husband.   The winner sees all this. retains
his ill-gotten gain, and knows not all the while that
a chilling frost of selfishness is upon his heart, freez-
ing up the generous feelings of his nature.   Nothing
is more bewitching than the love of gambling.   The
winner having tasted the sweets of gain, is led forward by the hope of still greater gain ; while the
loser plunges deeper and deeper into ruin, with the
delusive expectation of retrieving his lost fortune.
How many have ruined themselves and their families forever by this mad passion !   How many have
thrown down the cards or dice, only to take up the
pistol or the poison ; and have rushed, with all their
crimes about them, from the gambling-table to the—
fiery lake of hell !

To affirm that these remarks are applicable only
to those who play high, is nothing ; because it is the
nature of vice to be progressive.   Besides, it is a
fact, that many tradesmen, and even laboring people,
have ruined themselves by the love of play.   It is,
as I have said, a most ensnaring practice, leading
us from one degree to another, till multitudes who
begin with only an occasional game, end in the most
confirmed and inveterate habits of gambling.

Thirdly. Some amusements tend *to foster vanity
and pride*, while, at the same time, *they generate a
distaste for all the serious pursuits of religion, and
the sober occupations of domestic life.*

If I mistake not, these remarks will apply to balls,

routs, and concerts. I am not quite sure that the *morals* of society have not suffered considerable deterioration by assemblies. Circumstances are connected with this species of amusement, the tendency of which is more than questionable. The mode of dress adopted at these fashionable resorts ; the nature of the employment ; the dissipating tendency of the music, the conversation, and the elegant uproar ; the lateness of the hour to which the dazzling scene is protracted ; the love of display which is produced ; the false varnish which is thrown over many a worthless character, by the fascinating exterior which he exhibits in a ball room, have a tendency to break down the mounds of virtue, and expose the character to the encroachments of vice. And if it were conceded, which it certainly cannot be, that no immoral consequence results to those who occupy the upper walks of life, who are protected by the decorum of elegant society, yet what mischief is produced to their humble imitators, who attend the assemblies which are held in the barn or the ale-house ! I look upon dancing, among these, to be a practice fraught with immorality ; and my soul is horrified at this moment by remembering the details of a most tragic event which occurred in this neighborhood a few years since to an interesting female, who, after having lost her virtue on the night that followed the dance, was found, a few hours after, murdered, either by her seducer or herself. Have nothing to do then with this fascinating, though injurious species of amusement. Besides, what an en-

croachment does it make upon time, which is demanded for other pursuits! How does it dissipate
the mind, and poison it with a vain and frivolous
taste for dress and personal decoration! How com-
pletely does it unfit the soul for piety, and even the
necessary occupations of domestic life! Let there
be a love once acquired for these elegant recreations
by any female, and, from my heart, I pity the man
who is destined to be her husband.

My opinion of the STAGE I shall reserve for a separate chapter; in the meantime I shall reply to a
question which, no doubt, ere this, you are ready to
ask, "What amusements I would recommend?"

I do not hesitate at once to observe, that young
people stand in much less need than is supposed, of
any amusement properly so called. Their spirits
are buoyant, their cares are light, their sorrows are
few, and their occupations rarely very fatiguing to
the mind. What more is necessary beyond mere
change of employment, I should say, may be found
in engagements both strengthening to the body and
improving to the mind. A country ramble amidst
the beauties of nature, where, surrounded by sights
and sounds which have awakened and cherished the
spirit of poetry, we may admire the works of God
and man together, will, to every mind of taste or
piety, be quite enough to refresh and stimulate the
wearied faculties.

The perusal of an entertaining and instructive
book, where our best authors have said their best
things, and in their best manner too, will have the

same effect.   My children, acquire a taste for reading.   Aspire to an independence of the butterfly
pursuits of the pleasure hunter.   Seek for that thirst
after knowledge, which, when the soul is jaded with
the dull and daily round of secular affairs, shall conduct her to the fountains of thought contained in the
well-stocked library : where, as she drinks the pure
perennial streams of knowledge, she forgets in their
murmurs the toils of the day.   Or the study of
natural philosophy, attended, where an apparatus can
be commanded, with a course of illustrative experi-
ments, would be at once refreshing and instructive.
And where young people are happily situated beneath the wing of their parents, the pleasures of
home, the agreeable intercourse of the domestic circle are no mean or insufficient recreation from the
fatigues of business.

But perhaps many a youthful bosom will at this
thought heave a sigh, and sorrowfully exclaim, " I
am not at home.   In that beloved retreat, and with
its dear inhabitants, I should want no amusements.
My father's greeting smile ; my mother's fond embrace ; the welcome of my brothers and my sisters ;
the kind looks, the fond inquiries, the interesting
though unimportant conversation of all, would recruit
my strength, and recreate my mind.   But I am far
from these.   I am in a distant town, a stranger in a
strange place ; a mere lodger, where the attentions
which I receive are all bought and paid for.   Wearied and dispirited, I ofttimes return from the scene
of labor, and find in the cold and heartless salutation

of my host, and in the dreary solitude of my own chamber, that I am, indeed, not at home. Often and often, as I sit musing away the hour that intervenes between business and sleep, and carrying out into painful contrast my lodging and my home, I involuntarily exclaim,

' My friends, do they now and then send
A wish or a thought after me ?'

"Who can wonder that in such a situation I should occasionally pay a visit to the theatre, or the concert, and seek to forget that I am not at home, by amusements which have a tendency to drown reflection and divert my mind. Oh ! give me again the pleasures of home, and I will make a cheerful surrender of all that I have adopted as their substitutes."

I feel for such young persons. I too have been in their situation ; I have felt all that they feel. I have wept at the contrast between being a stranger or a guest, and a happy child at home. I too have returned at night to meet the silent look, or cheerless greeting of the hostess, instead of the smiling countenance and fond expression of the mother that bore me, the father that loved me. I too have retired to my room to weep at thoughts of home. I can therefore sympathize with you. And shall I tell you how, in these circumstances, I alleviated my sorrows and rendered my situation not only tolerable, but even sometimes pleasant? By the exercises and influence of true religion; by the intercourse

of a holy fellowship with pious companions; and by
the assistance of books.   Try, do be persuaded to
try the same means.

> "Religion, what treasures untold
>   Reside in that heavenly word!
> More precious than silver and gold,
>   Or all that this earth can afford."

This will find you a home, and a father and friends
in every place.   It will softens your banishment, and
open to you springs of consolation, which shall send
their precious streams into your forlorn abode.   It
will render you independent of the theatre and the
ball-room.   It will guard you from vices, which,
where they are committed, only serve to render the
recollection of home still more intolerable.   It will
give you an interest and a share in all the religious
institutions which are formed in the congregation
with which you associate, and will thus offer you a
recreation in the exercise of a holy and enlightened
philanthropy.

Amusements, in the usual acceptation of the word,
are but the miserable expedients resorted to by the
ignorant and unsanctified mind of man for happiness:
the ineffectual efforts to restore that peace which
man lost by the fall, and which nothing but true
piety can bring back to the human bosom.   In departing from God, the soul of man strayed from the
pasture to the wilderness, and now is ever sorrowfully exclaiming, as she wanders on, who will show us
any good?   To relieve her sense of want, and satisfy

her cravings, she is directed to amusements, but they prove only the flowers of the desert, which, with all their beauty, do not satisfy. No, no. It is the return of the soul to God through faith in Jesus Christ which can alone give·true and satisfying delight. Believing in him, we have peace that passeth understanding, the judgment is at rest in the contemplation of the first truth, and the heart in the enjoyment of the chief good. Peace with God, attended by peace with conscience, producing peace with the world, and affording a foretaste of peace beyond the grave, gives a feast to the soul, compared with which wordly pleasures are but as rank and gaudy flowers round the food of an hungry man, adding nothing to its relish by their colors, and only spoiling all by their odors. Religion conducts us to the fountain of living waters, and shows that these things are but broken cisterns that can hold no water. Amusements are but expedients to make men happy without piety. The mere husks, which THEY only crave after, and feed upon, who are destitute of the bread which cometh down from heaven ; and which are rejected by those who have their appetite satisfied with this celestial manna.

In addition to this, cultivate a taste for reading. Employ your leisure hours in gaining knowledge. Thus even *your* situation will be rendered comparatively comfortable, and the thoughts of home will neither destroy your happiness, nor send you for consolation to the polluting sources of wordly amusement.

But there are some who will reply, " I have neither taste for religion nor reading, and what amusements do you recommend to *me?*" *None at all.* What, that man talk of *amusement*, who, by his own confession, is under the curse of heaven's eternal law, and the wrath of heaven's incensed King? Amusement! what, for the poor wretch who is on the brink of perdition, the verge of hell, and may the next hour be lifting up his eyes in torments, and calling for a drop of water to cool his parched tongue! *Diversion!* what, for him who is every moment exposed to that sentence, "Depart from me. accursed, into everlasting fire, prepared for the devil and his angels!" What, going on to that place where the worm dieth not, and the fire is never quenched; where there is weeping and wailing, and gnashing of teeth, and calling for amusements! Oh monstrous inconsistency! We have heard of prisoners dancing in their chains, but who ever heard of a poor creature asking for amusements on his way to the place of execution? This is your case. While you have no taste for religion, you are certainly under sentence of eternal death. You are every day travelling to execution. Yet you are asking for amusements! And what will be your reflections in the world of despair, to recollect that the season of hope was employed by you, not in seeking the salvation of the soul, and everlasting happiness, but in mere idle diversions, which were destroying you at the very time they amused you. Then will you learn, when the instruction will do you no good, that you voluntarily relinquished the fulness of joy which God's presence affords, and the eternal pleasures which are to be found at his right hand, for the joy of fools, which as Solomon truly says, is but as " the crackling of thorns beneath the pot." *Before you think of amusement seek for* RELIGION.

XVI.

On Theatrical Amusements.

I DO not hesitate for a moment to pronounce the THEATRE to be one of the broadest avenues which lead to destruction; fascinating, no doubt it is, but on that account the more delusive and the more dangerous. Let a young man once acquire a taste for this species of entertainment, and yield himself up to its gratification, and he is in imminent danger of becoming a lost character rushing upon his ruin. All the evils that can waste his property, corrupt his morals, blast his reputation, impair his health, embitter his life, and destroy his soul, lurk in the purlieus of a theatre. Vice, in every form, lives, and moves, and has its being there. Myriads have cursed the hour when they first exposed themselves to the contamination of the stage. From that fatal evening they date their destruction. Then they threw off the restraint of education, and learned how to disregard the dictates of conscience. Then their decision, hitherto oscillating between a life of virtue and of vice, was made for the latter. But I will attempt

to support by arguments and facts these strong assertions.

The stage cannot be defended as an *amusement ;*
for the proper end of an amusement is to recreate
without fatiguing or impairing the strength or spirit.
It should invigorate, not exhaust the bodily and
mental powers ; should spread an agreeable serenity
over the mind and be enjoyed at proper seasons. Is
midnight the time, or the heated atmosphere of a
theatre the place, or the passionate, tempestuous excitement of a deep tragedy the state of mind, that
comes up to this view of the design of amusement?
Certainly not. But what I wish particularly to insist upon is, the *immoral and antichristian tendency
of the stage.* In order to judge of this immoral and
antichristian tendency, let us look at the precepts of
God's word. Here I will select a few out of many
passages of the Holy Scriptures.

*Texts which relate to our conversation, or the right
use of speech.*

Thou shalt not take the name of the Lord thy
God in vain, for the Lord will not hold him guiltless
that taketh his name in vain. Exod. xx. 7

I say unto you that every idle word that men shall
speak, they shall give an account thereof in the day
of judgment, for by thy words thou shalt be justified,
and by thy words thou shalt be condemned. Matt.
xii. 36, 37.

Be not deceived, evil communications corrupt
good manners. 1 Cor. xv. 33.

Let no corrupt communications proceed out of

your mouth, but that which is good to the use of edifying that it may minister grace to the hearers. Ephes. iv. 29.

Let your speech be always with grace, seasoned with salt. Col. iv. 6.

But above all things, my brethren, swear not. James, v. 12.

It is evident then, from these passages, that the Bible forbids all conversation which is idle, impure, or obscene, and commands us to employ the gift of speech in no other way than that which is good and to the nse of edifying. Now I confidently ask if there is scarcely one popular play ever performed which is not polluted, in very many places, with the grossest and most shocking violations of these sacred rules. What irreverend appeals to heaven, what horrible abuse of the thrice holy name of God, what profane swearing, what filthy conversation, what lewd discourse, are poured forth from the lips of almost every actor that comes upon the stage. Can it be a lawful entertainment to be diverted by hearing men and women insult God by cursing, swearing, and taking his holy name in vain? It is nothing to say that this is only done by the actors and' not by the spectators, because we are commanded not to be partakers, even by countenance, of other men's sins.

Passages which condemn all impurity of mind and conduct..

Blessed are the pure in heart for they shall see God. Matt. v. 8.

I say unto you that whosoever looketh on a woman

to lust after her, hath committed adultery with her already in his heart.   Matt. v. 28.

Now the works of the flesh are these, adultery, fornication, uncleanness, lasciviousness, of the which I tell you before, as I have told you in time past, that they which do such things shall not inherit the kingdom of God.   Gal. v. 20.

It must be evident to every one who reads with impartiality the word of God, that the most remote approach to lewdness is forbidden by the scriptures, even the excursions of the imagination, and the wanton exercise of the senses.   It is obviously the design of the Bible to form a character of the most elevated and refined purity, in which the concupiscible passions shall be in a state of entire subjection to undefiled religion.   Now, I ask, is it possible to comply with this design, if we attend the theatre, where, in every possible way, appeals are made to these animal propensities of our nature ? Will any man in his senses contend that a playhouse is the place where men are taught to be pure in heart, and assisted to oppose and mortify " those fleshly lusts which war against the soul ?"   " It is as unnecessary," says Law, " to tell the reader, that the playhouse is in fact the sink of corruption and debauchery ; that it is the general rendezvous of the most profligate persons of both sexes ; that it corrupts the neighborhood ; and turns the adjacent places into public nuisances ; this is as unnecessary as it is to tell him that the exchange is a place of merchandize."

Let me set before you also, *a few passages which are given in scripture to regulate our general conduct.*

" Lead us not into temptation, but deliver us from evil."

" Whether you eat or drink, or whatsoever ye do, do all to the glory of God."

" If ye live after the flesh ye shall die.'

" Flee youthful lusts."

" Blessed are they which do hunger and thirst after righteousness."

" Pray without ceasing."

" Watch the heart with all diligence, for out of it are the issues of life."

" Add to your faith virtue, to virtue knowledge, to knowledge temperance, to temperance patience, to patience godliness, to godliness brotherly kindness, to brotherly kindness charity."

"Let your affections be set on things above, and not on things on earth."

" To be spiritually minded is life and peace, but to be carnally minded is death."

From these passages it is evident that the spirit enjoined and the character to be formed by revelation, consist of meekness, purity,' spirituality of mind, heavenliness of affection, devotion, watchfulness against sin, caution not to go in the way of temptation. Now it would be to insult the common sense of every one who is conversant with the stage, to ask if such dispositions as these are enjoined and cherished by dramatic representations. I suppose no one ever pretended, that these saintly virtues are taught by the tragic or the comic muse. If our Lord's sermon on the mount, or the twelfth chapter to the Romans, or any other portion of inspired truth, be selected as a specimen and a standard of Christian morals, then certainly the stage must be condemned. Light and darkness are not more opposed to each other, than the Bible and the play book. If the one be good the other must be evil; if the scriptures are to be obeyed, the theatre must be avoided. The man who at church on the Sabbath day, responds to the third or the seventh commandment, " Lord have mercy upon us, and incline our hearts to keep this law;" who presents so often on that day the petition, " Lead us not into temptation, but deliver us from evil," is, to say the least of his conduct, the most glaring instance of absurdity in the world, if he on other days attends the theatre.

The only way to justify the stage, as it is, as it ever has been, as it is ever likely to be, is to condemn the Bible: the same individual cannot defend both. The one is too strict, or the other is too lax. Now the Bible, the Bible, my dear children, is the standard of morals. No matter by what plausible arguments a practice may be defended; no matter by what authority it may be sanctioned, if it be in opposition to the letter or the spirit of the Bible, it is wicked and must be abandoned. Even were the stage as friendly as its warmest admirers contend, to the cultivation of taste; if in some things it tended to repress some of the minor faults or vices of society, yet if, as a whole, its tendency is to encourage immorality, it must be condemned, and abandoned, and deserted. All I ask you is to weigh its pretensions in the balance of the sanctuary, and to try its merits by the only authorized standard of morals, the Bible, and sure I am you will never hesitate for a moment, to pronounce it unlawful.

It is an indubitable fact that the stage has flourished most in the most corrupt and depraved state of society ; and that in proportion as sound morality, industry and religion, advance their influence, the theatre is deserted. It is equally true, that amongst the most passionate admirers, and most constant frequenters of the stage, are to be found the most dissolute and abandoned of mankind. Is it not too manifest to be denied, that piety as instinctively shrinks from the theatre, as human life does from the point of a sword, or the draught of poison ? Have not all those who have professed the most elevated piety and morality, borne an unvarying and uniform testimony against the stage ? Even the more virtuous pagans have condemned this amusement, as injurious to morals, and the interests of nations : Solon, Xenophon, Plato, Aristotle, Cicero, Livy, Valerius Maximus, Cato, Seneca, Tacitus, the most venerable men of antiquity ; the brightest constellation of virtue and talents which ever appeared upon the hemisphere of philosophy, have all denounced the theatre as a most abundant source of moral pollution, and assure us that both Greece and Rome had their ruin accelerated by a fatal pas-

22

sion for these corrupting entertainments. William Pyrnne, a satirical and pungent writer, who suffered many cruelties for his admirable productions in the time of Charles I., has made a catalogue of authorities against the stage, which contains every name of eminence in the heathen and Christian world: it comprehends the united testimony of the Jewish and Christian churches; the deliberate acts of fifty-four ancient and modern, general, national, provisional councils and synods, both of the Western and Eastern churches; the condemnatory sentence of seventy-one ancient fathers, and one hundred and fifty modern popish and protestant authors; the hostile endeavors of philosophers and even poets; with the legislative enactments of a great number of pagan and Christian states, nations, magistrates, emperors, and princes.

The American Congress, soon after the declaration of Independence, passed the following motion:

" Whereas, true religion and good morals are the only solid foundation of public liberty and happiness,

" Resolved, that it be, and hereby is, earnestly recommended by the several States, to take the most effectual measures for the encouragement thereof, and for the suppression of *theatrical entertainments*, horse-racing, gaming, and such other diversions as are productive of idleness, dissipation, and a general depravity of principles and manners."

Now must not this be regarded in the light of very strong presumptive evidence of the immoral tendency of the stage? Does it not approach as near as can be to the general opinion of the whole moral world?

But let us examine *the average character of those productions which are represented on the stage.* If we go to *tragedy,* we shall find that pride, ambition, revenge, suicide, the passionate love of fame and glory, all of which Christianity is intended to extirpate from the human bosom, are inculcated by the most popular plays in this department of the drama. It is true, gross cruelty, murder, and that lawless pride, ambition, and revenge, which trample on all the rights and interests of mankind, are reprobated; but I would ask, who needs to see vice acted, in order to hate it? or will its being acted for our *amusement* be likely to increase our hatred of it upon right principles? As to *comedy,* this is a thousand times more polluting than tragedy. Love and intrigue; prodigality dressed in the garb of generosity; profaneness dignified by the name of fashionable spirit; and even seduction and adultery; these are the usual materials which the comic muse combines and adorns, to please and instruct her votaries. This department of the drama is almost unmixed pollution. How often is some profligate rake introduced to the spectators, furnished with a few traits of frankness and generosity, to interest them by his vicious career; and who so far reconciles them all to his crimes, as to tolerate his atrocities, for the sake of his open hearted, good-humored virtues. Who can wonder that young women should be prepared by such stuff, for any intrigue with a bold and wily adventurer ; or that young men should be encouraged to play the good-natured heroic rake, which they have seen such a favorite with the public on the stage ? Besides, how saturated, as I have already observed, are both tragedies and comedies with irreverant appeals to heaven, profane swearing, and all the arts of equivocation, and false-hood, and deception ! What lascivious allusions are made, what impure passages are repeated ! What a fatal influence must this have upon the deli-cacy of female modesty. Think too of a young man coming at the hour of midnight from such a scene, with his passions inflamed by everything he has seen, and everything he has heard; and then hav-ing to pass through ranks of wretched creatures waiting to ensnare him, and rob him of his virtue; does it not require extraordinary strength of princi-ple to resist the attack ?

I admit that modern plays are, in some measure, purified from that excessive grossness which polluted the performances of our more ancient dramatists. But who knows not that vice is more mischievous in some circles of society, in proportion as it is more refined. The *arch equivoque*, and *double entendre*, of modern plays, " are well understood, and applied by a licentious audience ; and the buzz of approba-tion, which is heard through the whole assembly, furnishes abundant proof that the effect is not lost." Little will go down with the public in the shape of comedy, farce or opera, but what is pretty highly seasoned with indelicate allusions. Hence it is that even the newspaper critics, whose morality is, in general, not of the most saintly character, so often mention the too-barefaced indecencies of new plays. Dramatic writers know very well how to cater for the public taste.

How many sentiments are continually uttered on the stage, how many indelicate allusions are made which no man who had any regard to the virtue of his sons, or the feelings of his daughters, would allow to be uttered at his table. Are not whole passages repeatedly recited, which no modest man would allow to be read before the family? Nothing but the countenance of numbers could induce many females to sit and listen to that which they hear at the theatre. Were any man to quote in company some of the expressions which are in constant iteration at the play-house, would he not be regarded as a person most dangerous to the virtue of others? And yet these nauseating exhibitions are heard with pleasure, when they are heard with the multitude. Can this be friendly to modesty, to virtue, to piety? must there not be an insensible corrosion going on under such an influence upon the fine polish of female excellence, and upon the moral principle of the other sex? Is this avoiding the appearance of evil? Is it in accordance with that morality which makes an unchaste feeling to be sin, and that injunction which commands us to watch the heart with all diligence?

Then remember *all the accompaniments of the*

22*

stage, the fascinations of music, painting, action, oratory; and say if when these are enlisted in the cause of fiction, *they do not raise the passions above their proper tone, and thus induce a dislike to grave and serious subjects, and a distaste for all the milder and more necessary virtues of domestic life.*

Add to this *the company which is generally attracted to the theatre.* I do not say that all who frequent the theatre are immoral; but I do affirm, that the most polluting and polluted characters of the town are sure to be there. Is it not a fact that a person who could not wish to have his eyes and ears shocked with sights and sounds of indecency, must keep at a distance from the avenues of the stage? for these are ever crowded with the loosest characters of both sexes. Sir John Hawkins, in his Life of Johnson, has a remark which strikingly illustrates and confirms what I have now advanced. "Although it is said of plays, that they teach morality, and of the stage, that it is the mirror of human life, these assertions have no foundation in truth, but are mere declamation; on the contrary, a play house, and the region about it, are the hot-beds of vice. How else comes it to pass, that no sooner is a theatre opened in any part of the kingdom, than it becomes surrounded by houses of ill-fame? Of this truth, the neighborhood of the place I am now speaking of (Goodman's Fields Theatre) has had experience; one parish alone, adjacent thereunto, having, to my knowledge, expended the sum of £1300 in prosecutions, for the purpose of removing these inhabitants, whom, for instruction in the science of human life, the play-house had drawn thither."

The arguments against the stage are strengthened *by a reference to the general habits of the performers and the influence which their employment has in the formation of their character.* And here I may assert, that the sentiments of mankind have gener ally consigned this wretched class of beings to infamy. The story of the unfortunate Laberius exhibits, in a strong point of view, the odium which was attached to the profession of an actor among the Romans. Compelled by Cæsar, at an advanced period of life, to appear on the stage to recite some of his own works, he felt his character as a Roman citizen insulted and disgraced; and in some affecting verses, spoken on the occasion, he incensed the audience against the tyrant, by whose mandate he was obliged to appear before them. "After having lived," said he, "sixty years with honor, I left my house this morning a Roman knight but shall return to it this evening an INFAMOUS STAGE PLAYER. Alas! I have lived a day too long."

As to the feelings of *modern times*, is there a family in Britain, of the least moral worth, even amongst the middling classes of tradesmen, which would not feel itself disgraced, if any one of its members were to embrace this profession? I ask, if the characters of players is not in general so loose, as to make it matter of surprise to find one that is truly moral? A performer, whether male or female, that maintains an unspotted reputation, is

considered as an exception to the general rule. Their
employment, together with the indolent line of life to
which it leads, is most contaminating to their morals.
The habit of assuming a feigned character, and exhibiting unreal passions, must have a very injurious effect on their principles of integrity and truth. They
are so accustomed to represent the arts of intrigue
and gallantry, that it is little to be wondered at, if
they should practise them in the most unrestrained
manner.*

SHUTER, whose facetious powers convulsed whole

---

* Of the truth of this description of the moral character
of actors and actresses, most convincing evidence is afforded
by the disgusting disclosures which have been made in
a court of law, in reference to two of the most celebrated
performers of the day. In speaking of one of them, the
Times paper observes, " The conduct of persons who appear
on the stage has never been the most irreproachable ; and
it may be doubted whether such a mass of living vice as the
actors and actresses but too generally present in their private lives, is not more injurious to public morals, than the
splendid examples of virtue which they exhibit in their theatrical characters, are useful. It appears, however, that
Kean, the defendant in the cause which was tried yesterday,
is advanced many steps in profligacy beyond the most profligate of his sisters and brethren of the stage. Some of
Kean's letters are of so filthy a description that we cannot
insert them. Yet have the managers of Drury Lane Theatre the effrontery to present, or to attempt presenting, such
a creature to the gaze of a British audience, on Monday next.
It is of little consequence to the nation whether the character of *King Richard* or *Othello* be well or ill acted ; but it is
of importance that public feeling be not shocked, and public

audiences with laughter, and whose companionable qualities often " set the table in a roar," was a miserable being.   The following anecdote, told from the best authority, will confirm this assertion ; and I am afraid, were we acquainted with many of his profession, we should find that his case is by no means singular.   " Shuter had heard Mr. Whitfield, and trembled with apprehension of a judgment to come ; he had also frequently heard Mr. Kinsman, and

decency be outraged."—*Times Newspaper, Tuesday, Jan. 18th*, 1825.

Doubtless our morals and taste as a nation will be wonderfully improved by such lectures and examples as these. These are the characters which young men and young women are sent to the play-houses to admire ; which husbands and wives, and sons and daughters are to witness, as teaching not only by theory but by practice, the vices that corrupt the mind and pollute society.   An admirable school for morals truly !   When will the virtuous part of the community, with unanimous and indignant voice, condemn the play-house as a moral nuisance, which no wise and good man ought to tolerate ?   When ! do I ask ?   The time is at hand, as is evident from the pecuniary situation of almost every theatre in the kingdom.

I was visited some years ago by an individual who had been for a loug time engaged as an actor, but who was then most anxious to be liberated from, what he had at length been brought to confess and to loathe, as a most immoral profession.   In considerable distress, he implored me to assist him in endeavoring to flee from a situation, of which he felt it difficult to say whether the vice or the misery was the greater.   Never did a captive more detest his fetters, or more covet to be free, than this poor creature did to be liberated from the thraldom in which he groaned.

sometimes called upon him in London. One day,
accidentally meeting him in Plymouth, after some
years of separation, he embraced him with rapture,
and inquired if that was the place of his residence;
Mr. Kinsman replied, 'Yes, but I am just returned
from London, where I have preached so often, and
to such large auditories, and have been so indisposed,
that Dr. Fothergill advised my immediate return to
the country for change of air.' 'And I,' said Shuter, 'have been acting Sir John Falstaff so often,
that I thought I should have died, and the physicians
advised me to come into the country for the benefit
of the air. Had *you* died, it would have been in
serving the best of masters; but had *I*, it would
have been in the service of the devil. Oh, sir, do
you think I shall ever be called again? I certainly
was once; and if Mr. Whitfield had let me come to
the Lord's table with him, I never should have gone
back again. But the caresses of the great are exceedingly ensnaring. My Lord E— sent for me
to-day, and I was glad I could not go. Poor things!
they are unhappy, and they want Shuter to make
them laugh. But oh, sir! such a life as yours;—
As soon as I leave you, I shall be King Richard.
This is what they call a good play, as good as some
sermons. I acknowledge there are some striking
and moral things in it; but after it, I shall come in
again with my farce of "A Dish of all Sorts," and
knock all that in the head. Fine reformers we!'
Poor Shuter! once more thou wilt be an object of
sport to the frivolous and the gay, who will now

laugh at thee, not for thy drollery, but for thy seriousness; and this story, probably, will be urged against
thee as the weakness of a noble mind; weakness let
it be called, but in spite of himself, man must be serious at last.   And when a player awakes to sober reflection, what agony must seize upon his soul.   Let
those auditories, which the comic performer has convulsed with laughter, witness a scene in which the
actor retires and the man appears; let them behold
him in the agonies of death, looking back with horror on a life of guilt, while despair is mingled with
forebodings of the future.   Players have no leisure
to learn to die; and if a serious thought wander
into the mind, the painful sigh which it excites is
suppressed, and, with an awful desperation, the
wretched creature rushes into company to be delivered from himself.   A more careless, a more un-
reflecting being than a player cannot exist; for if an
intense impression of the dignity of reason, the importance of character, and future responsibility be
once felt, he can be a player no longer."

To send young people therefore to the play-house
to form their manners, is to expect they will learn
truth from liars, virtue from profligates, and modesty
from harlots.

Can it then be right, even on the supposition that
we could escape the moral contagion of the stage,
to support a set of our fellow-creatures in idleness,
and in a profession which leads to immorality, licentiousness, and profligacy?

But, my dear children, I have not only arguments

to bring in proof of the immoral tendency of the
stage, but I have *facts*. It is useless to contend
against these. I am distressed while I write, to
think of the once promising young men, who, to my
certain knowledge, have been utterly ruined by re-
sorting to this scene of polluting amusement. I am
not allowed to disclose the details, or I could a tale
unfold that would shock every right feeling in your
hearts.

It was but a few days since, that a venerable and
holy man, now the deacon of a Christian church, said
to me :—" Sir, the theatre had nearly brought me to
the gallows. There I found associates who introduced me to every crime. When likely to be prevented by want of money from going to meet them
at the theatre, I robbed my father, to gain a shilling
for admission into the gallery."

Take warning then, and have nothing to do with
the theatre. Avoid it as one of the avenues to the
broad road that leadeth to destruction. Run not
with the multitude to do evil. Be not thrown off
your guard, and enticed to sin, by being directed to
some who have never been injured by such amusements. Would it be any inducement to you to venture near a lazaretto, to be pointed to some person
who had breathed an atmosphere tainted with the
plague, without receiving the infection? I admit
that the danger is not the same in all cases. Individuals, whose connexions, habits, characters,
are formed, may not receive so much injury as
younger persons : though the most virtuous and

moral cannot, I am sure, escape all harm ; even they must have their mental purity injured, and their imagination corrupted ; *they* must acquire a greater and greater distaste for religion, and irreverence towards God ; but to young people, and to young *men* especially, the danger is greater than I describe ; to them the doors of the theatre are as the jaws of the devouring lion.*

* I most earnestly recommend to all young persons, who have any doubts upon this subject, or any taste for theatrical representations, the perusal of an admirable treatise on this subject by Dr. Styles, from whose work it is necessary to say a large portion of this chapter is taken.

See also a very striking representation of the unlawfulness of the stage, in Law's Treatise upon Christian Perfection.

23

XVII.

On the period which elapses between the time of leaving school and the age of Manhood.

YOUNG people, while at school, generally look forward with much desire, and longing anticipation, to the happy time when they shall terminate their scholastic pursuits, throw off the restraints of the seminary, and enter upon the engagements which are to prepare them for their future station in life. They are seldom aware of the immense importance of this period of their existence; and but rarely consider, *that it is at this time the character usually assumes its permanent form.*

I will suppose, my dear children, that you have now quitted the school-room, for the warehouse, the office, or the shop; exchanged grammars and dictionaries for journals and ledgers; and the researches of learning for the pursuits of business. All is new and all is interesting. Youthful feelings are subsiding into something like a consciousness of approaching manhood; and the comparative insignificance of the schoolboy is giving way to the incipient import-

ance of the man of business. At this very point
and period of your history, it becomes you to halt and
reflect. Instead of being led on in joyous thoughtlessness, by the new scenes that are opening before
and around you, and leaving your habits and your
character to be formed by accident or by chance, I
beseech you to ponder on the very critical circumstances in which you are now placed.

*The period which elapses from fourteen to eighteen
years of age, is indeed the crisis of your history and
character.* It is inconceivably the most eventful and
influential term of your whole mortal existence.
Comparing the mind to substances which, under the
influence of heat, are capable of being moulded to
any form, it is at this period of its history that it is
in the most suitable temperature and consistency to
yield to the plastic influence of external causes, and
to receive its permanent form and character : before
this, it is too fluid and yielding, and afterwards too
stiff and unbending. This, this is the very time,
when the ever variable emotions, passions, and pursuits of boyhood begin to exhibit something like the
durable and settled forms of manhood.

In reference to the affairs of this life ; if a young
person ever become a good mechanic, or a good
tradesman, he gains the elements of his future excellence about this period. So it is in poetry, painting,
learning. *Before* this, the first decisive and unequivocal traits of genius *sometimes* appear, and even
after this they are sometimes developed ; but generally speaking, it is from the age of fourteen to

eighteen, that the marks of future eminence are put
forth.   It is the vernal season of mind, and habits,
and genius.   The same remarks will apply *to the
formation of character.*   Then the passions acquire
new vigor, and exert a mighty influence; then the
understanding begins to assert its independence, and
to think for itself; then there is a declaration of its
liberty on the part of the mind, and a casting away
of the trammels of education; then there is a self-
confidence and a self-reliance, which have received as
yet few checks from experience ; then the social impulse is felt, and the youth looks round for companions and friends ; then the eye of parental vigilance
and the voice of parental caution are generally at a
distance.   Then, in fact, the future character is
formed.   At this time, generally speaking, *religion
is chosen or abandoned ;* and the heart is given to
God or the world.   Can anything be more awfully
important, than such reflections to those who are yet
about this age?   You are now deciding for both
worlds at once.   You are now choosing to become a
Christian on earth, and a seraph in heaven, or a
worldling here, and a fiend hereafter   You are now
setting out on a journey, which is to conduct you to
glory, honor, immortality, and eternal life, or to the
blackness of darkness forever.   Yes, the starting
point for the realms of eternal day, or the regions of
eternal night, has generally been found to be within
the period which I have named.

   These remarks apply more strictly to young men
than to persons of the opposite sex ; inasmuch, as

females generally remain at home, under the eye, and voice, and example of parental piety, and are far less exposed than boys to the temptations and sins of youth. All young men, therefore, of this age, should pause and reflect thus :—" I am now arrived at that period which must be considered as the most eventful era of my whole existence ; when my character, both for time and eternity, will, in all probability, be formed ; when I may be said to be commencing the career which is to terminate in heaven or hell ; as well as that path which is to lead me to respectability and comfort, or to depression and poverty in the present world. How critical my age ! How important that I should consider wisely my situation, and decide aright !"

Permit me to give you a little advice, in some measure suited to your circumstances.

1. *Most sacredly observe the Sabbath, and constantly attend the means of grace.*

Let nothing induce you to prostitute the hallowed day to worldly pleasure. Never listen to the enticements of a companion, who would tempt you, even once, to forsake the house of God. Abandon such an acquaintance. He is unfit for you, and will ruin you. Sabbath-breaking is a sin of most hardening tendency.—When tempted to commit it, imagine you hear the awful voice of divine prohibition, followed with the loud deep groan of a holy father, and the exclamation of a pious mother, " Oh, my son ! my son ! do not pierce my heart with anguish." Attach yourselves to a sound, evangelical ministry, and

23*

listen not to those who subvert the very foundations of the gospel. Avoid those preachers who oppose all that is peculiar to Christianity.

2. *Keep up attention to the private duties of religion.*

Never let a day pass without reading the scriptures and private prayer. Whilst these practices are continued, I have hope of you: they show that piety has still some hold upon your heart. Secure some portion of every day, if it be but a quarter of an hour in the morning, and in the evening, for this most important duty. Should you not have a chamber to yourselves, let not the company of others prevent you from keeping up this practice. It would be better, however, in this case, to retire to your room when you can have it to yourself.

3. *Be very careful in the selection of companions.*

All that I have before said on the subject of company, applies with great force to this period of your life. It is now that the mischief of evil associations will be felt in all its devastating influence. One bad companion at this time, when the character is assuming its permanent form, will give a most fatal direction. Your company will probably be courted; but resist every overture which is not made by individuals of well-known, unbending virtue.

4. *Strive to excel in the business or profession to which your life is to be devoted.*

It is quite a laudable ambition for a man to aspire to eminence in his secular vocation. Be not satisfied with *mediocrity* in anything that is lawful.

Even as a tradesman, you should endeavor to be distinguished. It will give you weight in society, and thus, by increasing your influence, augment the means of your usefulness. A dolt, however pious he may be, possesses but little weight of character. Give your mind, therefore, to business. Penetrate into all its secrets, comprehend all its principles, study all its bearings. Care nothing about pleasure ; but find *your* recreation in your employment. It is astonishing how few rise to eminence in their calling, either in trade or in the professions. The summits are gained by a very small number ; the multitude grovel below. Why ? Because they did not seek nor begin to ascend, during their apprenticeship. They did not give themselves wholly to these things during this important season. Excellence in any department of human affairs can be looked for only from diligent and early culture. Industry and close application will keep you out of the way of temptation. Let your mind be occupied with business, and there will be neither leisure nor inclination for polluting amusements.

5. If your attention to business leave any time unoccupied, I advise you *to carry on a course of reading.*

Make companions of useful books, and you will need no other. And as it is every man's chief praise to excel in his own profession, let your reading bear a relation to that in which you are engaged.*

---

* The author hopes he shall be pardoned for the frequency with which he urges a taste for reading. He knows the importance of the subject.

6. *If you can find a pious and intelligent associate, embrace the opportunity of innocent and pleasurable companionship :* " for as iron shapeneth iron, so a man sharpeneth the countenance of his friend." With such a friend carry on some course of intellectual improvement, and both give and receive the stimulus which fellowship affords.

Again and again, remember the tremendous importance which attaches to the period to which this chapter more particularly refers ; and believing, as you must, that it is from fourteen to eighteen, the character, in relation to both worlds, is generally formed, judge what manner of persons ye ought to be at that time, if you wish to be a good tradesman, and real Christian upon earth, or a glorified and happy spirit in heaven.*

* See an excellent little work, entitled " Character essential to Success in Life, addressed to those who are approaching to Manhood," by the Rev. Isaac Taylor, of Ongar.

XVIII.

Public Spirit.

You are born, my dear children, in no common age of the world. You have entered upon the stage of existence, when some of the most interesting scenes of the great drama are being presented. There are eras, when the moral world seems to stand still, or to retrograde; and there are others, when it is propelled with accelerated movements towards the goal. Ours is of the latter kind. After the dark and stormy epoch, which was terminated by the glorious revolution of 1688, the churches of Christ, blessed with religious liberty, sunk to inglorious repose. Little was done, either to improve the moral condition of our own population at home, or the state of heathen countries abroad. WHITFIELD and WESLEY broke in upon this slumber, when it seemed to be most profound. From that time, the spirit of religious zeal awoke, and increasing its energies, and multiplying its resources till our days, it now exhibits a glorious array of means and instruments, from which in the long run, may be expected the conversion of the world.

Christendom presents at this moment a sublime and interesting spectacle in its Bible Societies, Missionary Societies, Tract Societies, with all the other institutions adapted to the moral wants of every class and condition of mankind. War is not only declared, but prosecuted with vigor, against the powers of darkness; the hosts of the Lord are marching forth to the field of conflict; the sound of the trumpet is heard, and the call of warriors floats on the gale. Spiritual patriotism is breathed into the souls of all denominations of Christians. Instruments of the holy warfare are invented and distributed, which suit the hands of persons of every rank, condition, stature, and strength; while females are invited to emulate the Spartan women of antiquity, and to assist in this conflict by the side of their fathers, husbands, and brothers.

All young people ought to enlist themselves in this cause. They should rise up into life, DETERMINED TO DO ALL THE GOOD THEY CAN, AND TO LEAVE THE WORLD BETTER THAN THEY FOUND IT. To see them reluctant to come forward, is an indelible disgrace to them. It is a poor, miserable kind of life to live only for ourselves; it is, in fact, but half-living. It is an opposition both to reason and revelation. He that does nothing to bless others, starves his own soul. You must therefore set out in life, my children, with a resolution, by God's help, to act the part of a religious philanthropist. "He that converteth a sinner from the error of his ways, shall save a soul from death, and hide a multitude of sins." Aspire to this honor. Think how many things you can already do. You can instruct a class of ignorant children in a Sunday School.* You can teach adults to read. You can distribute religious tracts. You can join in the labors of Bible associations, or in the exertions of juvenile missionary societies.

Here, however, I must suggest a caution or two. Females who are employed in the labor of collecting gratuitous contributions to public societies of any kind, should be very watchful against the least infringement on that delicacy and modesty of character which is the chief ornament of their sex. Their exertions, I know, are the life's blood of some causes ; be it so : but let their benevolence flow like the vital fluid through the veins—unseen, unheard. I believe that *in general* the strictest rules of modesty have been observed by the female collectors of our Missionary Societies ; but I have heard of instances very much to the contrary. Happily, such cases are rare. I think it quite questionable whether *very* young females, whose characters are scarcely formed, should be thus employed. It would be a source of mischief and regret, if the present mode

---

* It is to the great dishonor of many young people in affluent circumstances, that they are retiring from our Sunday schools, and leaving the work to those who are in humbler life. Well, we must do without them ; but let them remember that for their indolence, or pride, or whatever else be the cause of their secession, they must give an account at the bar of Christ.

of employing females in collecting for public institutions should abate one jot of that retiredness of
disposition, and love of home, which are so essential
to the beauty and excellence of their character.   A
gossiping, unsettled, roving temper, that can be better pleased with wandering round the town from
door to door, than performing the duties which fall
to the lot of a grown-up daughter at home, is no
present ornament, and affords but a folorn hope of
future worth.   I confess I look with some degree
of jealousy upon the efforts of female zeal, for if
public spirit is to be maintained at the expense of
private usefulness, the world will be no great gainer
in the end.   Exertions for the public should be regarded not as a substitute for, but a recreation from,
the more stated duties of home.

It is more necessary still, perhaps, to caution
young *men* against acquiring, by their activity, *a
bold, forward, obtrusive, and dictatorial temper.* If
zeal should render them conceited, vain, and med-
dling, it would be a heavy deduction from its clear
amount of usefulness.   There is some little danger
lest Satan, perceiving it to be impossible to *repress*
the ardor of youth, should attempt to *corrupt* it

Observing these cautions, you cannot be too ardent in the cause of religion, and the interests of
the human race.   Those who are likely to occupy
the middling classes of society, who are the sons
and daughters of persons in comparatively affluent
circumstances, and are likely, by the blessing of
God, to occupy the same rank themselves, should

feel most specially bound to consecrate their energies to the public welfare, inasmuch as they possess
far more means of usefulness than others, and are
likely to have greater influence in society. But
even the poorest can do something. There is no
one who is destitute of all the means of doing good.
In France, during the reign of the late emperor, the
conscription law extended to persons of all ranks
in society; and in the same regiment, the sons of
the rich and of the poor contended, side by side, for
the glory of their country: nor did the former think
themselves degraded by such an association; they
felt that to fight under the imperial and victorious
eagle, was an honor sufficient to annihilate every
other consideration. How much more justly will
this apply to persons who are marshalled under the
banner of the cross!

It is of the utmost importance that young people
should begin life with a considerable portion of public spirit in their character; since it is rarely found
that this virtue, if planted late, attains to any considerable magnitude, beauty, or fruitfulness. The
seeds of benevolence should be sown, together with
those of piety, in the first spring of our youth; then
may we expect a rich autumnal crop. The first
lesson which a child should learn from his parents
is, *how to be blessed;* and the second, *how to be a
blessing.*

You have been taught this, my children, from the
very dawn of reason: now then practice it. Live
for some purpose in the world. Act your part well.

24

Fill up the measure of your duty to others. Conduct yourselves so that you shall be missed with sorrow when you are gone. Multitudes of our species are living in such a selfish manner, that they are not likely to be remembered a moment after their disappearance. They leave behind them scarcely any traces of their existence, but are forgotten almost as though they had never been. They are, while they live, like one pebble lying unobserved amongst millions on the shore; and when they die, they are like that same pebble thrown into the sea, which just ruffles the surface, sinks, and is forgotten, without being missed from the beach. They are neither regretted by the rich, wanted by the poor, nor celebrated by the learned. Who have been the better for their life? Who are the worse for their death? Whose tears have they dried up, whose wants supplied, whose miseries have they healed? Who would unbar the gate of life, to re-admit them to existence; or what face would greet them back again to our world with a smile? Wretched, unproductive mode of existence? Selfishness is its own curse—it is a starving vice. The man that *does* no good, *gets* none. He is like the heath in the desert, neither yielding fruit, nor seeing when good cometh; a stunted, dwarfish, miserable shrub.

We are sent into the world to do good; and to be destitute of public spirit, is to forget one half of our errand upon earth. Think what opportunity there is for the increase and operations of this noble disposition. We are in a world which abounds with evil. There are six hundred millions of immortal souls, yet enslaved in their minds by the chains of Pagan superstition or Mahometan delusion, aliens to the commonwealth of Israel, strangers to the covenant of promise, without God, and without hope in the world; there are one hundred and twenty millions following the *Papal Beast*, and bearing his image; there are nine millions of the seed of Abraham, wandering as vagabonds over the face of the whole earth, with the thick veil of unbelief upon their hearts. In our own country, many towns and villages are yet unblessed with the faithful preaching of the gospel; multitudes of adults are still without Bibles to read, and myriads of children without a knowledge of letters; ignorance of the grossest kind, vice of the most abominable forms, are to be found in every street. And then, as to positive misery, what aboundings are to be seen in every collection of human abodes; where can we go and not hear the groans of creation ascending round us, and not see the tears of sorrow flowing in our path? Poverty meets us with its heart-breaking tale of want and woe; disease in a thousand shapes appeals to our compassion; widows, orphans, destitute old men, and fatherless babes, with numbers ready to perish, are almost everywhere to be seen. Shall we live in the centre of so much sin, ignorance, and wretchedness, and not feel it our duty to do good? What a wretch must he be, who, in such a world, is destitute of PUBLIC SPIRIT! For all that selfishness ever hoarded, may you, my children, never be cursed

with an unfeeling heart. Here is something for all
to do, and all should do what they can.

Consider *the felicity of doing good.* Public spirit
is a perennial source of happiness in a man's own
bosom. The miser is rightly named; the word signifies miserable, and miserable he is. Benevolence
is happiness. Its very tears are more to be desired
than the most exulting smiles which avarice ever
bestowed upon its accumulating treasures. Who
does not covet that exquisite delight which Job must
have experienced in the days of his prosperity, and
of which he thus speaks: " When the ear heard me,
then it blessed me; and when the eye saw me, then
it gave witness unto me; because I delivered the
poor that cried. and the fatherless, and him that had
none to help him. The blessing of him that was
ready to perish came upon me; and I caused the
widow's heart to sing for joy. I was eyes to the
blind, and feet was I to the lame. I was a father to
the poor, and the cause that I knew not I searched
out." O tell me, what are all the pleasures of sense
or appetite, all the gay festivities of worldly amusements, when compared with this? To do good, is to
be like God in operation and bliss; for he is the
blessed God, because he is the *merciful* God.

Public spirit *is most honorable.* Even the heathen
accounted a benefactor a most honorable character.
Never does humanity appear adorned with so bright
a crown of glory, as when distinguished benevolence,
united with humble piety, enters into the character.
When a young lady, instead of frittering away her

time in frivolous pursuits, parties of pleasure, personal decorations, or scenes of vanity, employs her hours in visiting the cottages of the poor, alleviating the sorrows of the wretched, reading to the sick, how like an angel does she appear ; and one can almost fancy that she is watched with exalted delight, on her visits of mercy, by the heavenly messengers who minister to the heirs of salvation, and who hail her as a coadjutor in their embassies of love. What is the most celebrated beauty that ever became the centre of attraction, the object of voluptuous gaze, the subject of general envy to one sex, and of admiration to the other, when, amidst the blaze of diamonds, and the perfumery of the East, she displayed her charms in the ball-room ; compared with that modest and retiring young woman, who, in her woollen cloak and miry shoes, is seen on a cold wintry day at the sick bed of the poor expiring mother, first reviving the sinking frame of the sufferer with the cordials she has prepared with her own hands, then dispensing bread to the clamorous hungry babes, then comforting the agitated mind of the departing wife with the consolations of religion, and, last of all, soothing the troubled breast of the distressed husband with the prospect of a country, where there shall be no more death !

Or what is the man of polished manners, insinuating address, sparkling wit, and endless anecdote, whose society is courted, and who is the life of every company into which he enters ; who everywhere receives the incense of praise, and the worship of

admiration ; I say, what is this man, in real grandeur, utility, and moral beauty of character, to the
unassuming youth, who though well educated and
extensively read, and with a mind that could luxu-
riate in all the pleasures of literary pursuits, devotes
a large portion of his time to the exercises of benevolence : who on a sabbath journeys to some neigh-
boring village on foot, sustaining the storms of winter, and the sultry heats of summer, to teach a school
of ignorant children, bound to him by no tie but that
of our common nature, to read the word of God:
who is often seen in the retired streets and alleys of
his own town, checking the torrents of wickedness by
the distribution of tracts, or the circulation of the
Bible : who, when fatigued with business, would
gladly seek the repose of home, or else, thirsting for
knowledge, would fain converse with books, yet instead of this, devotes his evening hours to assist in
managing the business of public institutions !

Need I ask which of these two is the most honorable character ? They admit of no comparison. The
wreath of literary fame, the laurel of the warrior, the
tribute of praise offered to superior wit, are empty
and worthless compared with the pure bright crown
of the philanthropist. There is a time coming when
the former shall be of no value in the eyes of their
professors, or the world; but the distinctions of superior beneficence belong to an order which shall be
acknowledged in heaven, and shall be worn with unfading brilliancy through eternity.

I exhort, therefore, my children, that you do all

the good you can, both to the souls and bodies of
your fellow-creatures : for this end, as I have already
said, you were born into the world, and society has
claims upon your attention, which you cannot neglect
without disregarding the authority of God. Give
your *property* for this purpose. Begin life with a
conviction that every one ought to devote a fair
portion of his worldly substance for the benefit of
others. No man ought to set apart a less proportion
of his income for the good of the public than a tenth.
Whatever estate yours may be, whether great or
small, consider that it comes to you with a reserved
claim of one-tenth for the public. Consider yourself
as having a right to only nine-tenths. Pay tithes of
all you possess to the cause of God and man Be
frugal in your general expenditure, that you may
have the more to do good with. Waste not that
upon unnecessary luxuries of dress or living, which
thousands and millions want for necessary comfort
and religious instruction. The noblest transformation
of property is not into personal jewels, or splendid
household furniture, or costly equipages ; but into
clothing for the naked, food for the hungry, medicine
for the sick, knowledge for the ignorant, holiness for
the vicious, salvation for the lost.

Give your *influence*, whatever it be, to the cause
of the public. We have all a circle of influence, and
it is more extensive than we imagine. We are all,
and always, doing good or harm. Two persons never
meet, however short the duration, or whatever be the
cause of the interview, without exerting some in-

fluence upon each other. An important transaction,
a casual hint, a studied address, each and all may
become the means of controlling the mind of those
with whom we have to do. Let *your* influence be
all thrown into the scale of the public good. Do
your own duty, and endeavor to rouse others to do
theirs.

Let your exertions in the public cause be the result of *deliberate purpose*, not of mere accident. *Set
yourselves* to do good. Pursue a system, and act
not from caprice. Let not your zeal be a blaze at
one time, and a mere spark at another. *Study your
situation, circumstances, talents, and let your benevolence flow through that channel which Providence has more especially opened before you.* All
are not fitted for, nor are they called to, the same
work. In the division of the labor of mercy, occupy that station, and be content with that work, to
which you are obviously destined. Avoid the disposition *which will be first in the front rank, or no-
where.* This is selfishness, not benevolence : selfishness operating in the way of activity, instead of
indolence : of giving, instead of hoarding. Be
anxious to do good, though, like the ministering
angels, your agency should never be seen, but only
felt. Do not be discouraged by difficulty, nor dis-
heartened by ingratitude ; seek your reward in the
approbation of conscience, and the smile of God, not
in the acknowledgments of men. Persevere to the
end of life ; and be not weary in well doing. Be
diligent, for the world is dying around you, and

you are dying with it. You are young; but you are mortal. Your time of working may be short, and therefore strive to do much in a little time ; for a man's life is to be measured not so much by the years that he lives, as by the work he does. You may die, but if you do good, your work lives; lives and multiplies its kind on earth, and then follows you to heaven, to live in your own remembrance, and the happiness of others through everlasting ages.

" As therefore we have opportunity, let us do good unto all men, especially unto them that are of the household of faith ; and let us not be weary in well doing, for in due season we shall reap if we faint not."*

* Every young person ought to read that incomparable work of Cotton Mather's, entitled " Essays to Good," edited by the Rev. G. Burder

XIX.

Female Accomplishments, Virtues, and Pursuits.*

As the perusal of this volume is intended for those who may be supposed to have finished, or are near the completion of scholastic pursuits, all that can be designed in this chapter, is to follow up the object of a good education, which, most probably, it has been the felicity of many of my female readers to receive; or, in the opposite case, to correct the faults, and point out in what way to supply the defects of a bad one.

" A young lady may excel in speaking French and Italian, may repeat a few passages from a volume of extracts; play like a professor, and sing like a syren; have her dressing-room decorated with her own drawings, tables, stands, screens, and cabinets: nay, she may dance like Sempronia herself, and yet may have been very badly educated. I am far from

* The author has departed in this chapter from the style of direct and particular address to his children, to a more general form of instruction.

meaning to set no value whatever on any or all of these qualifications ; they are all of them elegant, and many of them properly tend to the perfecting of a polite education.   These things in their measure and degree may be done, but there are others which should not be left undone.   Many things are becoming, but ' one thing is needful.'   Besides, as the world seems to be fully apprized of the value of whatever tends to embellish life, there is less occasion here to insist on its importance.

   " But, though a well-bred young lady may lawfully learn most of the fashionable arts, yet it does not seem to be the end of education to make women of fashion *dancers, singers, players, painters, actresses, sculptors, gilders, varnishers, engravers,* and *embroiderers.*   Most *men* are commonly destined to some profession, and their minds are consequently turned each to its respective object.   Would it not be strange if they were called out to exercise their profession, or to set up their trade, with only a little general knowledge of the trades of other men, and without any previous definite application to their own peculiar calling ?   The profession of ladies, to which the bent of *their* instruction should be turned, is that of daughters, wives, mothers, and mistresses of families.   They should be therefore trained with a view to these several conditions, and be furnished with a stock of ideas and principles, and qualifications and habits, ready to be applied and appropriated, as occasion may demand, to each of these respective situations ; for though the arts which merely embellish life, must claim admiration, yet when a man of sense comes to marry, it is a companion whom he wants, and not an artist. It is not merely a creature who can paint, and play, and dress, and dance; it is a being who can comfort and console him ; one who can reason and reflect, and feel, and judge, and act and discourse, and discriminate; one who can assist him in his affairs, lighten his cares, soothe his sorrows, purify his joys, strengthen his principles, and educate his children."*

This is sound reasoning and unquestionable dis-cretion ; it proceeds on the obvious and indisputa-ble principle, that the excellence of means is to be judged of by their adaptation to the end to be pro-duced ; and the value of an instrument to be appre-ciated by its fitness for the work contemplated. *That* is a perfect female education, which best pre-pares women for the station in society which Provi-dence has destined them to occupy. And what is that station ? To be wives, mothers, and mistresses. Think not that this is degrading woman below her just rank, or that such a station requires nothing more than an initiation into the mysteries of the kitchen, or a memory well stored with the responses of the " Cook's Oracle." If to be the suitable com-panion of a sensible man ; the judicious mother of a rising family ; the neat and orderly and frugal mis-tress of an extensive household ; if to be qualified to counsel her husband in the intricacies of life, to soothe him in his troubles, to lighten his heart of

* Mrs. Hannah More.

half its load of care, to enliven his solitude with the
charm of her conversation, and render his home " the
soft green," on which his weary spirit shall love to
repose; if to be qualified to train up her children in
the paths of religion, to form them to habits of virtue, to preside over their education, and the formation of their character, so as to multiply in them her
own image of female excellence, and raise in each of
them her second lovely self; if to be qualified to
render her house attractive, both to its stated inhabitants, and the friends who may occasionally resort to it; I say, if this be a low station, and fitness
for it be nothing more than mean qualifications,
where, in all this world, shall we find any one that
is high, or noble, or useful?

For these sacred occupations has Providence destined the female sex, and say, what kind of education fits for such a scene of endearing and important
duties? For such a circle of obligations, she should
indeed be *accomplished :* " no term however has
been more abused than this. *Accomplishment* is a
word that signifies completeness, perfection. But I
may safely appeal to the observation of mankind,
whether they do not meet with swarms of youthful
females, issuing from our boarding schools, as well
as emerging from the more private scenes of domestic education, who are introduced into the world,
under the broad and universal title of *accomplished ladies,* of whom it cannot very truly be pronounced that they illustrate the definition, by a complete-

25

ness which leaves nothing to be added, and a perfection which leaves nothing to be desired.

" This frenzy of accomplishments, unhappily, is no longer restricted within the usual limits of rank and of fortune ; the middle orders have caught the contagion, and it rages downward with increasing violence, from the elegantly dressed but slenderly portioned curate's daughter, to the equally fashionable daughter of the little tradesman, and of the more opulent, but not more judicious farmer. And is it not obvious, that as far as this epidemical mania has spread, this very valuable part of society is declining in usefulness, as it rises in its unlucky pretensions to elegance ? And this revolution of the manners of the middle class has so far altered the character of the age, as to be in danger of rendering obsolete the heretofore common saying, ' that most worth and virtue are to be found in the middle station.' For I do not scruple to assert, that in general, as far as my observation has extended, this class of females, in what relates both to religious knowledge, and to practical industry, falls short both of the very high and the very low. Their new course of education, and the habits of life, and elegance of dress, connected with it, peculiarly unfits them for the active duties of their own very important condition ; while with frivolous eagerness and second-hand opportunities, they run to snatch a few of those showy acquirements which decorate the great. This is done apparently with one or other of these views ; either to make their fortune by marriage, or if that fail to qualify them to become teachers of others : hence the abundant multiplication of superficial wives, and of incompetent and illiterate governesses."*

By accomplishments, I believe, are usually intended, dancing, music, drawing, the languages, &c. &c.

As for *Dancing*, if it be allowable at all in a system of Christian education, it cannot be permitted ·to rise to a higher rank than that of a mere *physical training*, which should be strictly confined to the school, and laid aside forever when the school is quitted for home. Balls of every kind, public and private, *baby* assemblies and adult ones, are in my judgment, reprehensible and injurious; and if our Lord's exposition of the seventh commandment be correct, I am perfectly sure that an assembly-room is no place for *Christian* morals : the half-naked costume there exhibited has the same effect as Montesquieu ascribed to the dances of the Spartan virgins, which taught them " to strip chastity itself of modesty." Piety looks round in vain in a ball-room, for one single object congenial with its nature.

Music has not the same objection. The acquisition of this pleasing science requires a vigorous exercise of that faculty of the mind which is the foundation of all knowledge,—I mean *attention;* and therefore, like the mathematics, is valuable, not merely for its own sake, but as a part of mental education.† Besides this the ear is tuned by its Maker to

* Mrs. More.

† This, however, supposes that the pupil is really made to comprehend the theory of music as she goes on, and is made

harmony, and the concord of sweet sounds is a pleasant and innocent recreation. Music becomes sinful, only when too much time is occupied in acquiring the science, or when it is applied to demoralizing compositions. I am decidedly of opinion, that in general, far more time is occupied in this accomplishment than ought to be thus employed. Many pupils practise three, four, five hours a day. Now suppose *four* hours a day be thus spent, commencing from six years of age, and continuing till eighteen, then leaving out the Sundays, and allowing thirteen days annually for travelling, there will be 14,400 hours spent at the piano-forte, which, allowing ten hours a day for the time usually devoted to study, will make nearly four years out of twelve given to music. Can this be justified, my female friends, on any principle of reason or revelation? What ideas might have been acquired, what a stock of knowledge amassed, what habits of mental application formed in this time! And what renders this the more culpable is, that all this time is spent in acquiring a science which, as soon as its possessor is placed at the head of a family, is generally neglected and forgotten. If it be really true, therefore, that music cannot be acquired without practising four hours a day, I do not hesitate to say that the sacrifice is far too costly;

to play by the *notes*, and not merely from memory. The ignorance of some teachers, and the indolence of others, deprive music of all its salutary power to strengthen the mind, and reduce it to the mere business of teaching a child to play a few tunes, which, bull-finch like, she has learned by note.

and females should forego the accomplishment, rather than purchase it at such a rate. If the great design and chief excellence of the female character, were to make a figure for a few years in the drawing-room, to enliven the gay scene of fashionable resort, and, by the freshness of her charms, and the fascination of her accomplishments, to charm *all* hearts, and conquer *one*, then let females give all their precious hours till they can play like Orpheus, or sing like a syren; but if it be what I have already stated, then indeed it will sound like a meagre qualification for a wife, or a mother, to say, " She is an exquisite performer on the harp or piano "

Drawing, with all the fancy operations of the brush, the pencil, the needle, and the scissors, are innocent and agreeable, provided they are kept in the place of recreations, and are not suffered to rise into occupations. Of late years they have acquired a kind of hallowed connection, and FANCY has been seen carrying her painted and embroidered productions to lay on the altar of MERCY and of ZEAL. These things are sinful only when they consume too much time, and draw the mind from the love and pursuit of more important, or more necessary duties. They are little elegant trifles, which will do well enough to fill up the *interstices* of time, but must not displace the more momentous objects which require and occupy its larger portions.

The *Languages* are accomplishments, for which there is a great demand in. the system of modern education. I confess plainly at once, that I rate

25*

the importance of French at a much lower value than many do. I believe not one in a hundred who pretend to learn it, ever derive the least advantage from it. The object of acquiring a foreign language is to converse with those who speak it, or to be as a key to all the literature which it contains. To be able to hammer out a few sentences, ill pronounced, and worse constructed; to tell what a table, or a house, or door is, or pass the usual compliments in French, is a miserable reward for years of dreaming or yawning over Levizac or Du Fief. If, then, you have begun French, or Italian, and still retain anything of what you have learned, give a moderate portion of your time to recover what else will soon be utterly lost; for nothing is so soon lost from the mind as a *little* of a foreign language. Pursue the study till you can, at least, read it with nearly as much ease as your mother tongue. Perhaps the chief advantage from this accomplishment is, that it raises our reputation a little in elegant society, and so far increases our weight of character, and thus enlarges the sphere of our usefulness.

On the subject of accomplishments, then, my views are sufficiently explicit. The greater part of them I by no means condemn. Custom has rendered them necessary, religion allows them to be innocent, and ingenuity can render them useful. Piety is not in a state of hostility with taste, and would not look more lovely in Gothic barbarity than in Grecian elegance. Provided she maintain all her sanctity, dignity, spirituality, and benevolence, she does not appear less inviting when attired by the MUSES, and attended by the GRACES. Females may play, and draw, and paint, and write Latin, and speak Italian and French, provided the time, the money, and the admiration lavished on these external acquirements, be all within reasonable limits; provided they are regarded as sources of private entertainment, not as arts of public display; are considered as recreations from more severe and necessary pursuits, not as the chief end of education; and are viewed as mere appendages of excellence, not its substitute.

It unfortunately happens, however, that the female who has in reality received the worst education, often makes the best figure in society. There are many schools which (to adopt a simile borrowed from the trades of my own town) instead of resembling the jeweller's workshop, where sterling gold and real diamonds are polished, are nothing more than gilders, varnishers, and platers, whose object is to give the brightest surface in the shortest time, and at the least expense. The paste and the gilt look very well, perhaps better than the gem and the gold, because more of it can be obtained for the same sum; but which will wear best, and last the longest? It requires much self-denial, sturdy attachment to solid excellence and nobleness of mind, for a female of few accomplishments, but many virtues, to go home from a company, where some gilded, varnished mind has received, for her music or singing, the tribute of admiration, and still to prefer the uncom-

manding excellence of character to all the fascinations of exterior decoration. But look onward in
life. See the future career of both. The syren
wins the heart, for which, as a prize, she has sung
and played. She marries, and is placed at the head
of a rising family. But, alas! the time she should
have spent in preparing to be a companion to her
husband, a mother to her children, a mistress to her
servants, was employed at the piano, in qualifying
her to charm the drawing-room circle. She suc-
ceeded, and had her reward, but it ended when she
became a wife and a mother. She had neither good
sense, nor information ; neither frugality, order, nor
system ; neither ability to govern her servants, nor
to guide her children ; her husband sees everything
going wrong, and is dissatisfied ; he caught the
nightingale to which he listened with such transport in her native bower ; but she is now a misera-
ble-looking, moping, silent bird in her cage. All is
discontent and wretchedness, for both at length find
out that she was better qualified to be a public
singer than a wife, or a mother.

Far different is the case with the unostentatious
individual of real moral worth. She too wins a
heart more worth winning than the prize last spoken
of. Some congenial mind, looking round for an individual who shall be a help-meet indeed, sees in her
good sense and prudence, in her well-stored understanding, in her sobriety of manners, in her sterling
piety, the virtues likely to last through life, with
foliage ever verdant, fruit ever abundant. They

are united ; the hopes of lovers, rational, unromantic, founded on kindred minds, and kindred hearts, are realized in all the fond endearments of wedded life. Although the first bloom and freshness of youthful affection fade away, its mellowness still remains, and mutual esteem still continues and grows. Their family increases, over which she presides in the meekness of wisdom, the order of system, and the economy, not of meanness, but of prudence. To her children, whom her husband trusts with confi- dence to her care, she is the instructor of their minds, the guide of their youth. Their father sees them rising up to prove the wisdom of his choice, when he selected a wife rather for virtues than ac- complishments ; their mother delights in a husband who is one with her in all her views, and approves of all her doings. They pass through life together, blessing and being blessed ; mutual comforters, and mutual counsellors, often saying, if not *singing*,

> " Domestic happiness, thou only bliss
> Of Paradise that has survived the Fall !
> Thou art not known where PLEASURE is adored,
> That reeling Goddess with the zoneless waist."

How true and how beautiful are the words of Solo- mon ; " Who can find a virtuous woman ? for her price is far above rubies. The heart of her husband doth safely trust in her, so that he shall have no need of spoil. She will do him good and not evil all the days of her life. She layeth her hands to the spindle, and her hands hold the distaff She stretcheth out her hands to the poor; yea, she reacheth forth her hands to the needy. Her husband is known in the gates, when he sitteth among the elders of the land. Strength and honor are her clothing; and she shall rejoice in time to come. She openeth her mouth with wisdom, and in her tongue is the law of kindness. She looketh well to the ways of her household, and eateth not the bread idleness. Her children rise up and call her blessed, her husband also, and he praiseth her. Many daughters have done virtuously, but thou excellest them all. Favor is deceitful, and beauty is vain; but a woman that feareth the Lord, she shall be praised. Give her of the fruit of her hands and let her own works praise her in the gates."

A beautiful comment on this lovely passage is to be found in the "Friend," by COLERIDGE, amongst some "*Specimens of Rabbinical wisdom, selected from the* MISNA." It is entitled, "Whoso hath found a virtuous wife, hath a greater treasure than costly pearls."

"Such a treasure had the celebrated teacher RABBI MEIR found. He sat during the whole of one sabbath day in the public school, and instructed the people. During the absence from his house, his two sons died, both of them of uncommon beauty, and enlightened in the law. His wife bore them to her bedchamber, laid them upon the marriage-bed, and spread a white covering over their bodies. In the evening, RABBI MEIR came home. 'Where are my sons,' he asked, 'that I may give them my blessing ?'—' They are gone to the school,' was the answer,—' I repeatedly looked round the school,' he replied, ' and I did not see them there.'—She reached to him a goblet, he praised the Lord at the going out of the Sabbath, drank, and again asked, ' Where are my sons, that they too may drink of the cup of blessing ?'—' They will not be far off,' she said, and placed food before him that he might eat. He was in a gladsome and genial mood, and when he had said grace after the meal, she thus addressed him :— ' Rabbi, permit me one question.'—' Ask it then, my love,' he replied.—' A few days ago, a person intrusted some jewels to my custody, and now he demands them again; should I give them back to him ?'—' This is a question,' said Rabbi Meir, ' which my wife should not have thought it necessary to ask. What! wouldst thou hesitate or be reluctant to restore to every one his own ?'—' O no,' replied she, ' but I thought it best not to restore them without acquainting thee therewith.'—She then led him to their chamber, and stepping to the bed, took the white covering from the dead bodies. ' Ah, my sons! my sons!' thus loudly lamented the father, ' my sons, the light of mine eyes, and the light of my understanding! I was your father, but ye were my teachers in the law!' The mother turned away and wept bitterly. At length she took her husband by the hand, and said, ' Rabbi, didst thou not teach me that one must not be reluctant to restore that which was intrusted to our keeping? See, the Lord gave, the Lord hath taken away, and blessed be the name

of the Lord !'—' Blessed be the name of the Lord !'
echoed RABBI MEIR, 'and blessed be his name for
thy sake too ; for well is it written, Whoso hath
found a virtuous wife hath a greater treasure than
costly pearls : she openeth her mouth with wisdom,
and her tongue is the law of kindness.' "

My young female friends, have you no ambition
to answer, in future life, these beautiful patterns of
female excellence? Have you no desire, that if
Providence should place you at the head of a family,
you may shine forth in all the mild radiance of domestic, feminine excellence? Is there not, as you
read, some spirit-stirring desires in your soul? Does
not all the glitter of mere external accomplishments
fade away into darkness before such effulgent virtue? Does not all the painted insignificance of
mere drawing-room charms dwindle into nothing before that solid excellence which is a

"Perpetual fountain of domestic sweets."

If so, and ye would thus bless and be blessed, make
up your mind deliberately to this opinion, and abide
by it, *That what is useful is infinitely to be preferred to what is dazzling ; and virtuous excellence to be more ardently coveted than fashionable
accomplishments.* A right aim is of unspeakable
consequence. Whatever we propose as the grand
paramount object, will form the character. We
shall subordinate everything else to it ! and be this
your aim, TO EXCEL RATHER IN THE SOLID AND USE-

FUL ATTAINMENTS, THAN IN EXTERNAL SHOWY DECO-
RATIONS.

Seek a large portion of what is usually denominated GOOD SENSE.

It is very difficult to define what I mean, and
perhaps it is not necessary, for every one knows
what I intend, by this quality. It is that sobriety
of character, that quick perception of all the propri-
eties of life, that nice discernment of what is best to
be done in all the ordinary circumstances of human
society, which shall enable us to act with credit to
ourselves, and comfort to others. It is a thought-
ful, cautious way of judging and acting, and is
equally opposed to that rashness which acts with
precipitancy, and that ignorance which cannot act at
all. It is, in fact, *prudence*, accommodating itself
to all the relations of life, and the ever-varying circumstances of society.

To store your mind with USEFUL INFORMATION.

Read much, and let your reading be of a right
kind. Reject with disdain, as you ought, the libel
which has been circulated by some against your understanding, that poetry and novels are the books
most adapted to the understanding and feelings of
young ladies. On this topic I refer you to the
chapter on Books. I cannot, however, but insert
here a few additional hints on the subject.

To assist in the right formation of your character,
I very urgently recommend the perusal of Mrs.
HANNAH MORE'S " *Strictures on the Modern System
of Female Education ;*" for although this work is
26

more particularly intended for mothers, it may be read with immense advantage also by daughters. The views of this incomparable woman are so correct, and also enlarged, so accordant with reason, and what is still more important, so harmonious with revelation, that you cannot look up to a better guide. GISBORNE'S " *Duties of Women*" may also be read with great advantage.　Cox's " *Female Biography*," and GIBBON'S " *Lives of Pious Women*," with WILLIAMS' " *Life of Mrs. Savage*," in this department of reading, will be found interesting books.

History should of course occupy much of your time.　Here you should be at home.　But do not read merely to acquire a mental chronicle of names and dates.　To know when such a king reigned, by whom such a country was conquered, or where such a battle was fought, is one of the lowest ends of reading the annals of nations.　In Mrs. MORE's work you will find an admirable chapter, " On the religious and moral use of History and Geography," to which with great pleasure I refer you.

Poetry should be resorted to as a recreation, and a recreation only.　On this subject I need not repeat what I have already stated, except to add, that as ,you have not learned the dead languages, I should advise you to add to the productions of your own national muse, the immortal poems of HOMER and VIRGIL, which may be read, the former in the translations of POPE and COWPER, and the latter in that of DRYDEN.

Botany seems, if not to belong to your sex, to be

peculiarly appropriate to it. The elementary treatises of *Chemistry*, such as " Conversations on Chemistry, by a Lady," and PARKES' Catechism, might
be read with great benefit ; and indeed the elementary treatises of the whole range of natural philosophy, if you have leisure, should be studied.

As you may be one day called to train the minds
of your own children, you should not have the philosophy of education to learn, when you want it to use,
and therefore should now become acquainted with all
that is connected with this invaluable science. Miss
EDGEWORTH's Treatise on Practical Education,*
with Mrs. MORE's work, will be found most interesting as well as instructive. And if you are willing
to go still further, I would advise you to study WATTS'
" *Improvement of the Mind*," and his "*Logic ;*" Mr.
BURDER's " *Hints on Mental Culture ;*" DUGALD
STEWART's work on " *The Philosophy of the Human
Mind ;*" and some parts of LOCKE's treatise " *On
the Human Understanding.*" Some of these works

---

* Never was there a writer that better understood the
philosophy of education than this extraordinary woman ; an
she has written, from the work above-mentioned down to
" Early Lessons," may be read with advantage, not only by
those who are to learn, but by those who are to teach. I regret, in common with many others, the exclusion of religion
from her productions ; but on the general principles of education, and the formation of the character, in every other
view of it than in reference to religion, Miss Edgeworth remains unequalled. How deeply to be deplored, that from
the works of *such* a writer, the spirit and genius of Christianity should be systematically excluded.

will certainly require close application, and hard thinking; but they will amply reward the labor of research ; and the powers of the mind, like those of the body, strengthen by exercise. " Serious study serves to harden the mind for more trying conflicts ; it lifts the reader from sensation to intellect; it abstracts her from the world and its vanities; it fixes a wandering spirit, and fortifies a weak one ; it divorces her from matter ; it corrects that spirit of trifling, which she naturally contracts from the frivolous turn of female conversation, and the petty nature of female employments ; it concentrates her attention, assists her in a habit of excluding trivial thoughts, and thus even helps to qualify her for religious pursuits."

Thus would I have a female qualified for her station as a wife, mother, and mistress of a family ; but this is not all; for mental improvement should be associated with A CORRECT KNOWLEDGE OF HOUSEHOLD AFFAIRS. She who is to preside over a family, should be most intimately acquainted with everything that can preserve its order, or promote its comfort. That must be a most injudicious *mother*, who is not anxious to teach a daughter how to manage a family to the greatest advantage; and that must be a weak and silly girl, who is not willing to be taught. *All* the time, therefore, must not be given to books; for *learned ladies*, without neatness, without order, without economy, without frugality,

"May do very well for maidens or aunts,
    But believe me they'll never make wives."

A husband's home should be rendered comfortable for himself and his children, or else they are both very likely to wander *from* home for comfort. Cleanliness, neatness, frugality, order, are all of great importance in the habits of a wife, mother, and mistress, for the want of which, no knowledge, however profound or extensive, can be a substitute. It is not at all requisite that a wife should be either an accomplished housemaid, or a perfect cook, but she ought to be able to judge of these qualifications in others ; and the want of this ability has led many a man, who was blessed with a *learned* wife, to exclaim, with something betweeen disgust and despair, " I now find, to my cost, that knowledge alone is as poor a qualification for a wife, as personal beauty or external accomplishments."

Before I close this chapter, I must mention one or two dispositions, which young females should assiduously cherish and unostentatiously exhibit.

The first is FILIAL OBEDIENCE; not that this is binding upon daughters only, for what son is he that honoreth not, loveth not, comforteth not, his father and his mother ? Wherever Providence should cast his lot, or in whatever circumstances he should be placed, let him continue in every possible way to promote the happiness of his parents. Young people are but too apt to think, that the obligations to filial piety diminish in number and strength as years increase. I am afraid, that really one of the signs of the times, and it is no bright one, is the decrease of this amiable and lovely virtue. I think I see rising

26*

—I wish I may be in error—a spirit of independence, which is aiming to antedate the period of manhood, and to bring as near to fourteen as possible, the time when the yoke of parental control may be thrown off. This is neither for the comfort of the parents, nor the advantage of the children. It is not obedience only that should not be refused; for where *this* is denied, there can be neither religion nor virtue; but all that public way of showing them honor, and all that private way of promoting their comfort, for which, opportunities are constantly presented. There is no period in the life of a father or mother, when the obligation to be in some measure subject to them, and in all measure to promote their happiness, ceases. It has been brought as an allegation against the BARD, whom an Englishman might be proud to name, that he was so severe a father, as to have compelled his daughters, after he was blind, to read aloud to him, for his sole pleasure, GREEK and LATIN authors, of which they did not understand a word. Compelled his daughters! What daughters must they be who need *compulsion* in such a case.

The following is the description of a daughter which I have somewhere met with :—" M. E. S. received her unhappy existence at the price of her mother's life, and at the age of seventeen she followed, as the sole mourner, the bier of her remaining parent. From her thirteenth year, she had passed her life at her father's sick bed, the gout having deprived him of the use of his limbs, and beheld the arch

of heaven only when she went forth to fetch food or
medicines.   The discharge of her filial duties occupied the whole of her time and all her thoughts.
She was his only nurse and for the last two years
they lived without a servant.   She prepared his
scanty meal, she bathed his aching limbs, and, though
weak and delicate from constant confinement, and the
poison of melancholy thoughts, she had acquired an
unusual power in her arms, from the habit of lifting
her old and suffering father out of and into his bed
of pain.   Thus passed away her early youth in sorrow ; she grew up in tears, a stranger to the amusements of youth, and its more delightful schemes and
imaginations.   She was not, however, unhappy ; she
attributed no merit to herself for her virtues ; but
for that reason were they more her reward.   'The
peace which passeth all understanding,' disclosed itself in all her looks and movements.   It lay on her
countenance like a steady unshadowed moonlight;
and her voice, which was at once naturally sweet and
subtile, came from her like the fine flute tones of a
masterly performer, which, still floating at some uncertain distance, seemed to be created by the player
rather than to proceed from the instrument.   If you
had listened to it in one of those brief sabbaths of
the soul, when the activity and discursiveness of the
thoughts are suspended, and the mind quietly eddies
round instead of flowing onward (as at late evening
in the spring, I have seen a bat wheel in silent circles round and round a fruit tree in full blossom, in
the midst of which, as within a close tent of the

purest white, an unseen nightingale was piping its purest notes,) in such a mood, you might have half fancied, half felt, that her voice had a separate being of its own—that it was a living something whose mode of existence was for the ear only: so deep was her resignation, so entirely had it become the habit of her nature, and in all she did or said so perfectly were her movements, and her utterance without effort, and without the appearance of effort. Her dying father's last words, addressed to the clergyman who attended him, were his grateful testimony, that during his long and sore trial, his good MARIA had behaved to him like an angel; that the most disagreeable offices, and the least suited to her age and sex, had never drawn an unwilling look from her; and that whenever his eye had met hers, he had been sure to see in it either the tear of pity, or the sudden smile expressive of her affection and wish to cheer him. 'God,' said he, ' will reward the good girl for all her long dutifulness to me !' He departed during the inward prayer, which followed these his last words. His wish will be fulfilled in eternity !"

What daughter can read this and not admire, and if need be, imitate the conduct of MARIA ? Few are called to these self-denying acts of filial piety; but who would not do all they could to sweeten, as far as may be, the dregs of life to an aged mother, or a blind father? It has been observed, that a good daughter generally makes an exemplary wife and mother.

SENSIBILITY, *when blended with a sound judgment,*

*and guided in its exercises by good sense and pru-
dence*, is a lovely ornament of the female character·
By sensibility, I mean a susceptibility of having emotion excited by external objects ; a habit of mind, in
which the affections are easily moved, by objects
calculated and worthy to produce feeling.   Of course,
this is an *evil* or an *excellence*, according as it is
united with other mental habits.   An excess of sensibility, is one of the most injurious ingredients which
can enter into the formation of character.   Where it
is united with a weak judgment, and a wild imagination, it exposes its possessor to the greatest possible
dangers, and opens in her own bosom a perpetual
source of vexation, misery, and self-torment.   If we
were to trace to their source many of those quarrels
which have alienated friends, and made irreconcilable enemies; those mortifications of pride and
vanity, which have ended in lunacy : those hasty
and imprudent marriages which have terminated in
universal wretchedness ; those acts of profligacy,
suicide, and even murder, which have stained the
annals of mankind ; we should find the germ of all
these mischiefs, in an excess of morbid sensibility.
Feeling, like fire, is a good servant, but a bad master :
a source of comfort, and a means of usefulness, if
well governed ; but if left to rage without control,
an engine of destruction, and a cause of misery.
Every heart should have an altar, on which this fire
should be perpetually kept burning, but then prudence should ever be on the watch, lest it should
consume the temple.

Young females are in imminent danger of being led away by the representation, that an unfeeling woman, though she be pure as a statue of Parian marble, yet withal, if she be as cold, is a most unlovely character. This I admit, and therefore I class a well-governed sensibility amongst the decorations of the female character. But then, the tendency of this remark is certainly mischievous, since, according to the spirit in which it is usually both made and received, it means, that an *excess* of feeling rather adorns than injures the character. It will be found, generally speaking, that young people rather force the growth, than check the luxuriance of their feelings; which is just in the inverted order of nature, since the affections generally grow without culture, the judgment scarcely ever. The voice of flattery, also, is all on the side of feeling. A warm-hearted girl, carried away by her feelings, and misled by a wild and ardent imagination, will find many more admirers than the sensible, prudent, and reserved one; and for this plain reason, because there are more fools in the world than wise men. Follow out the history of the two characters. It is the end that proves all.*

Imprudent attachments, rash friendships, misdirected anxieties, eccentric charities, fickle schemes, groundless anticipations, mortifying disappointments, harassing litigations, with innumerable other evils, come in the train of excessive and ungoverned sensibility. Let young women therefore remember,

* See Mrs. More.

that the understanding is the queen amongst the
faculties of the soul, beneath whose despotic sway,
the imagination and affections may be as active and
as ardent as they please, so that they never offend
against the laws of their sovereign.

With these limitations, I will admit that sensibility is an ornament of female character. A cold,
unfeeling, heartless woman, who has no tear for sorrow, no smile for excellence; who has no power but
that of niggardly calculation, and no emotions but
those which, by a sort of centripetal force, are all
drawn to self as the centre of gravity, is a libel upon
her sex. She may have prudence, but it is likely to
degenerate into cunning; frugality, but it will in all
probability soon become avarice; caution, but it will
be changed to suspicion; intellect, but it will be
proud, censorious, and cynical. Pure sensibility is
the soil in which the generous affections grow : it
cherishes that mercy which is full of good fruits ;
gives birth to all the enterprises of benevolence, and
when touched and purified with a " live coal from
the altar," will give a keener taste for the spirit of
religion, a richer enjoyment of its privileges, and a
quicker zeal in discharging its duties ; but then it
must be feeling associated with principle, and guided
in all its exercises by a sound judgment.

A RETIREDNESS OF DISPOSITION is also an exquisite
ornament of the female character. Even the most
distant approach to whatever is forward in manner,
and vain in conversation, should be most studiously
avoided. Delicate reserve, without awkward bash-

fulness, is no small part of the loveliness of every young female ; especially in all her conduct *towards the opposite sex.* A lady who takes pains to be noticed, generally gains her object without its reward : for she is noticed, but at the same time she is despised. Nothing can be more disgusting than a bold obtrusiveness of manners in a female, except it be that affectation of retiredness which retreats only to be followed. Flippancy and pertness are sometimes mistakenly substituted, by their possessor, for smartness and cleverness. These latter qualities never look well when they are studied : they are never tolerable but when they are natural ; and are amongst the last things which we should seek to *acquire :* for when obtained in this way, they appear no better than ornaments stuck on, instead of being wrought in. I am not contending against that *ease of manners* which the most retiring female may and should adopt, even in the company of gentlemen : that artless and elegant freedom which is compatible with the most delicate reserve ; but merely that *obtrusive mode of address,* which determines to attract attention.

A love of display has been thought to be amongst the blemishes which usually attach to female character in general. I do not now refer to the petty concerns of dress, for this is truly pitiable, and an individual silly enough to indulge such a butterfly, peacock taste as this, is too weak to afford any rational hopes of having her follies corrected. Arguments are lost upon that little mind whose ambition cannot comprehend, or value, or covet, a distinction of greater worth, than a richer silk, a more graceful plume, or a more modern fashion. This Lilliputian heroine, armed at every point with feathers, flowers, and ribbons ; supported by all her auxiliary forces of plumassiers, frisseurs, milliners, mantua makers, perfumers, &c., &c., contending for the palm of victory, on the arena of fashion, must be left to her fate, to conquer or to fall : I have no concern with HER. But there is vanity of another kind, against which I would caution young females, and that is *a fondness for exhibiting their fashionable accomplishments or mental acquirements.* Pedantry in a man is bad enough, but in a woman is still worse. Few things are more offensive than to see a female laboring to the uttermost to convince a company, that she has received a good intellectual education, has improved her advantages, and is really a sensible, clever woman ; at one time almost vociferating about nitrogen, oxygen, and caloric ; then boasting her acquaintance with some of the greatest geniuses of the age ; and last of all entering into a stormy debate on politics and finance.

Now observe, I am not contending against a woman's acquainting herself with these subjects, for I reject with indignation the calumny that the female mind is unequal to the profoundest subjects of human investigation, or should be restricted in its studies to more feminine pursuits ; much less am I anxious to exclude the stores of female intellect, and the music of female tongues, from the feast of

27

reason and the flow of soul. No. Too long have the softer sex been insulted by the supposition, that they are incapable of joining or enriching the mental communion and conversation of the drawing-room. I most unequivocally, unhesitatingly say, that they have a much smaller share of conversational intercourse than their natural talents, and their acquired information, entitle them to.

All I am contending against is, that *love of display* which leads some to force themselves upon the attention of a company, which is not contented with sharing, but is ambitious of monopolizing the time and opportunities of rational discourse. Some silversmith and jewellers, who wish to attract public attention, make a splendid display of gems and jewels in their window ; but their window contains their whole stock, they have no store besides : there are others, who, making all proper exhibition, can conduct their customers from room to room within, each filled with stores of inestimable value. Not unlike the former, some persons make a grand display in conversation, but their tongue, like the shop-window, exhibits all they possess, they have very little besides in the mind ; but there are others who, like the latter tradesman, are not deficient in respectable display, but then, besides the ideas which they exhibit in conversation, they have a valuable stock of knowledge in the mind.

To conclude this long chapter, I must again remind you that TRUE RELIGION is the deep basis of excellence ; SOUND MORALITY its lofty superstructure ; GOOD SENSE, GENERAL KNOWLEDGE, CORRECT FEELING, the necessary furniture of the fabric ; and UNAFFECTED MODESTY and FASHIONABLE ACCOMPLISHMENTS its elegant decorations.

XX.

On Prudence, Modesty, and Courtesy.

RELIGION, my dear children, is the first and the principal thing which I am anxious that you should possess, but it is not the *only one.* It is the basis of excellence which should be well laid, to bear whatsoever things are lovely, or of good report, or, changing the metaphor, it is that firmness and solidity of character which, like the substance of the diamond, best prepares it to receive a polish, and is rendered more beautiful and more valuable by *being* polished. The religion of some persons is like the gem in the rough, the excellence of which is concealed and disfigured by many foreign adhesions: there is real principle at the bottom, but it is so surrounded by imprudence, rudeness, ignorance, slovenliness, and other bad qualities, that it requires a skilful eye to discern its worth. I most earnestly admonish you, therefore, to add to your piety

1. PRUDENCE.

By prudence, I mean a calculating and deliberative turn of mind, as to the tendency of our words and actions ; coupled with a desire so to speak and

act, as to bring no inconvenience either upon ourselves or others.   It is that right application of
knowledge to practice, which constitutes wisdom.
A person may have an immensity of knowledge, with
scarcely a grain of prudence ; and, notwithstanding
the stores of his understanding, may always have
his peace destroyed.   I am aware that prudence is
too often regarded by the ardent and sanguine
minds of the young, as a cold and heartless virtue ;
a sort of November flower, which, though regular in
its growth, and mild in color, has neither glow nor
fragrance, but stands alone in the garden as the memorial of departed summer, the harbinger of approaching winter.   Youth are captivated by what is
frank and generous, even when it leads to " Head-
long Hall."   If by prudence I meant mere cold reserve, or that selfishness which chills the ardor of
kindness, and freezes the spring of benevolence in
the heart, you might well beware of a disposition so
unlovely ; but when I simply mean a habit of thinking before you speak or act, lest your thoughtlessness should prove injurious to the comfort of your
own mind, or the comfort of others ; when I only
require you to exercise that judgment upon the tendencies of your conduct, which is one of the chief
distinctions of a rational creature ; when I merely
call upon you to put forth the power of foresight
which God has planted in your nature, surely, surely,
there is nothing unsuited either to your age, or to
the most generous mind, in this.   That rashness of
speech, or of conduct, which is always involving a

person, and his friends too, in difficulties, inconveniences, and embarrassments, has little to commend
itself to your admiration, with whatever good temper or gay fancy it may happen to be associated;
society must be a chaos, if all its members were
formed upon this model.

You must have seen, my dear children, the mischiefs which imprudence has brought in its train.
What strifes have been engendered by a rash, unguarded use of the tongue; by persons giving a
hasty opinion of the character, conduct, and motives
of others: I believe that a moiety of the quarrels
which exist, may be traced up to this source.   If
then you would journey along through life in honor
and in peace, I cannot give you a more important
piece of advice than this: "Be very cautious how
you give an opinion of the character, conduct, or
motives of others. *Be slow to speak.*   For one that
has repented of having held his tongue, myriads have
bitterly grieved over the imprudent use of it."   Remember what Solomon says, " A prating fool shall
fall;" and almost all fools do prate: silence is generally a characteristic of wise men, especially in
reference to the concerns of others.   I know not a
surer mark of a little, empty mind, than to be always talking about our neighbors' affairs.   A collector of rags is a much more honorable, and certainly a far more useful member of society, than a
collector and vender of tales.

But let your prudence manifest itself in reference
to your *conduct*, as well as t*o* your *words*.   Never

act till you have deliberated.   Some persons invert
the order of nature and reason ; they act first, and
think afterwards ; and the consequence very generally proves, as might have been expected, that *first
impressions are fallacious guides to wise actions.*   I
scarcely know anything against which young people
should be more seriously warned than this habit of
acting from first impressions ; nor anything which
they should be more earnestly advised to cultivate,
than an almost instinctive propensity to look forward, and to consider the probable results of any
proposed line of conduct.   This calculating temper
is to be preferred, far more than the knowledge of
the rash ; for it will preserve both the peace of its
possessor, and that of others who have to do with
him.   Multitudes, by a want of prudence in the
management of their pecuniary affairs, have ruined
themselves, plunged their families into want, and involved their friends in calamity.   They have engaged in one rash speculation after another, and
formed one unpromising connection after another ;
scarcely recovered from the complicated mischief of
one, before they were involved in the embarrassment
of the next, till the final catastrophe came in all its
terrors, which might have been forseen, and *was* pre-
dicted by every one except the rash projector himself.   When we consider that in such cases a man
cannot suffer alone, but must extend the effects of his
conduct to others, prudence will appear to be not only
an *ornament* of character, but a *virtue ;* and imprudence not only *near* to immorality, but a *part* of it.

Begin life, then, with a systematic effort to cultivate a habit of sound discretion, and prudent foresight ; and for this purpose, observe attentively the
conduct of others ; profit both by the sufferings of
the rash, and the tranquillity of the cautious : render
also your own past experience subservient to future
improvement. I knew a person, who having impru-
dently engaged in a litigation which cost him a considerable sum of money before it could be compro-
mised, made the following entry in his diary :—
" March —Paid this day, one hundred and fifty pounds
for *wisdom*." Experience, it has been said, keeps a
dear school ; but some people will not learn in any
other, and *they* are fortunate who improve in this.
I most emphatically recommend to you the diligent
study of the book of Proverbs, as containing more
sound wisdom, more prudential maxims for the right
government of our affairs in this life, than all other
books in the world put together.

2. MODESTY is a very bright ornament of the
youthful character : without it the greatest attainments and the strongest genius cannot fail to create
disgust.

Conceitedness I have already stated to be one of
the obstacles to youthful piety, and even where its
mischief does not operate so fatally as this, it certainly disfigures religion. Young people should consider, that even if they have much knowledge, they
have but little experience. Everything pert, flippant, obtrusive, and self-confident, is highly unbe-
coming in those who, whatever they may know of scho-

lastic literature, have but little acquaintance either with themselves or mankind. Strong intellect and great attainments will soon commend themselves, without any pains being taken to force them upon our attention ; and they never appear so lovely, nor attract us with such force, as when seen through a veil of modesty. Like the coy violet, which discloses its retreat rather by its fragrance than by its color, youthful excellence should modestly leave others to find out its concealment, and not ostentatiously thrust itself on public attention.

I do not wish to inculcate that diffidence which makes young people bashful and timid, even to awkwardness and sheepishness ; which prevents even the laudable exertion of their powers ; and which is not only distressing to the subjects of it themselves, but painful to others.   Nothing can be further from my views than this ; for it is a positive misery to be able neither to speak nor be spoken to, without blushing to the ears, and trembling to the very toes ; but there is a wide difference between this bashfulness and genuine modesty.   " *Modesty* is a habit, or principle of the mind, which leads a man to form a humble estimate of himself, and prevents him from ostentatiously displaying his attainments before others : *bashfulness* is merely a state of timid feeling : *modesty* discovers itself in the absence of everything assuming, whether in look, word, or action ; *bashfulness* betrays itself by a downcast look, a blushing cheek, and a timid air : *modesty*, though opposed to assurance, is not incompatible with an unpretending confidence in ourselves; *bashfulness* altogether unmans us, and disqualifies us for our duty."

Modesty shields a man from the mortifications and disappointments which assail the self conceited man from every quarter. A pert, pragmatical youth, fond alike of exalting himself and depreciating others, soon becomes a mark for the arrows of ridicule, censure, and anger; while a modest person conciliates the esteem of all, not excepting his enemies and rivals; he disarms the resentment even of those who feel themselves most injured by his superiority; he makes all pleased with him by making them at ease with themselves; he is at once esteemed for his talents, and loved for the humility with which he bears them. Arrogance can neither supply the want of talents nor adorn them where they are possessed.

It is of importance to cultivate modesty in youth, for if wanting then, it is seldom obtained afterwards. Nothing grows faster than conceitedness; and as no weed in the human heart becomes more rank, so none is more offensive than this. I have known individuals, who, by their extensive information, and strong sense, might have become the delight of every circle in which they moved, have yet by their positive, dogmatical and overbearing temper, inspired such a dread, that their arrival in company has thrown a cloud-shadow on every countenance. *A disputatious temper* is exceedingly to be dreaded. Nothing can be more opposed to the peace of socicty than that disposition, which converts every room into the arena of controversy, every company into competitors, and every diversity of sentiment into an apple of discord.   There are times when a man must state and defend his own opinions ; when he cannot be silent, when he must not only defend, but attack ; but even in such cases he should avoid everything dogmatical and overbearing; all insulting contempt of others, and all that most irritating treatment, which makes an antagonist appear like a fool.   Our arguments should not fall and explode with the noise and violence of thunder-bolts, but insinuate themselves like the light or the dew of heaven.

Take it, my dear children, as the result of nearly a quarter of a century's observation and experience in no contracted circle of human life, that verbal controversy in company produces very little good, and a great deal of harm.   In such a situation men contend for victory, not for truth ; and each goes into the war of words, determined to avoid, if possible, the disgrace of a public defeat.

3. COURTESY is a most valuable disposition.

This is enjoined not only by those authors who are the legislators of the drawing-room, but by Him who has published laws for the government of the heart.

" Be courteous," saith the word of God. By courtesy, I mean that benevolence of disposition which displays itself in a constant aim to please those with whom we associate, both by the matter

and manner of our actions ; in little things as well
as great ones.   Crabbe, in his English Synonyms,
has given us this definition of courtesy and complaisance :—" *Courteous* in one respect comprehends
more than *complaisant ;* it includes the manner, as
well as the action ; it is, properly speaking, polished
complaisance : on the other hand *complaisance* includes more of the disposition in it than courteousness ; it has less of the polish, but more of the reality of kindness.   *Courteousness* displays itself in
the address and the manners ; *complaisance* in direct good offices : *courteousness* is most suitable for
strangers ; *complaisance* for friends, or the nearest
relatives : among well bred men, and men of rank,
it is an invariable rule to address each *courteously*
on all occasions whenever they meet, whether acquainted or otherwise ; there is a degree of *complaisance* due between husbands and wives, brothers and sisters, and members of the same family,
which cannot be neglected without endangering the
harmony of their intercourse."   It is my earnest
desire, my children, that you should be both courteous and complaisant.   The union of both these constitutes true politeness.   I do not wish you to study
the works of Lord Chesterfield, which have been
aptly described as teaching the manners of a danc-
ing-master, and the morals of a prostitute ; but *true*
politeness, such as consists of the union I have already mentioned, is excellence carried to its highest
polish.

Life is made up for the most part of petty transactions, and is checkered more by the light and shade of minor pains and pleasures, than by the deeper hues of miseries and ecstacies. Occasions rarely happen, when we can relieve or be relieved by the more splendid efforts of benevolence; while not a day, scarcely an hour, passes without an opportunity of giving or receiving gratifications of complaisance. " Politeness," says our great essayist, in the *Rambler*, " is one of those advantages which we never estimate rightly but by the inconvenience of its loss. Its influence upon the manners is constant and uniform, so that like an equal motion, it escapes perception The circumstances of every action are so adjusted to each other, that we do not see where any error could have been committed, and rather acquiesce in its propriety, than admire its exactness.

" Wisdom and virtue are by no means sufficient without the supplemental laws of good breeding, to secure freedom from degenerating into rudeness, or self-esteem from swelling into insolence ; a thousand incivilities may be committed, and a thousand offices neglected without any remorse of conscience, or reproach from reason."

The true effect of genuine politeness seems to be rather case than pleasure. The power of delighting must be conferred by nature, and cannot be delivered by precept, or obtained by imitation ; but though it be the privilege of few to ravish and to charm, every man may hope, by rules and cautions, not to give pain, and may therefore, by the help of good breeding, enjoy the kindness of mankind, though he should have no claim to higher distinctions.

"The universal axiom in which all complaisance is included, and from which flow all the formalities that custom has established in civilized nations, is, *That no man shall give any preference to himself;* a rule so comprehensive and certain, that perhaps it is not easy for the mind to imagine an incivility, without supposing it to be broken."

Think not, however, that politeness is only to be acquired by frequenting what is called fashionable company, and places of public entertainment; complaisance is the offspring of benevolence, the tiny daughter of kindness; and this may be found in the cottage, where I have often seen as much real courtesy as ever graced a mansion. Hear the testimony of Dr. Johnson on this subject: "I have indeed not found, among any part of mankind, less real and rational complaisance, than among those who have passed their time in paying and receiving visits, in frequenting public entertainments, in studying the exact measures of ceremony, and in watching all the variations of fashionable courtesy.

"They know, indeed, at what hour they may be at the door of an acquaintance, how many steps they must attend him towards the gate, and what interval should pass before his visit is returned; but seldom extend their care beyond the exterior and unessential parts of civility, nor refuse their own vanity any gratification, however expensive, to the quiet of another."

By a neglect of complaisance, many persons of substantial excellence have deprived their virtues of much of their lustre, and themselves of much kindness : of whom it is very common to have it said— " Yes, he is a good man, but I cannot like him." Surely such persons, by an ill economy of reputation, have sold the attachment of the world at too low a price, since they have lost one of the rewards of virtue, without even gaining the profits of wickedness.*

4. ON ADMIRATION OF THE CHARACTERS OF OTHERS, I think it important to say a few things. To observe, admire, and imitate the excellences of those around us, is no less our duty than our interest. It is a just tribute to *their* moral worth, and the means of promoting *our own*. It is of great consequence, however, that our admiration of character should be well directed ; for as we naturally imitate what we admire, we should take care that we are attracted and charmed only by *real* excellence. Do not be led astray, my children, by a mere speciousness, or showiness of character. Let nothing be regarded by you as worthy your admiration, which is not in connection with moral worth. Courage, frankness,

---

* See the Rambler, Nos. 56 and 98. The British Essayists, especially the Spectator, Rambler, and Idler, though not always strictly scriptural in their views of human nature and moral obligation, contain an inexhaustible fund of entertainment and instruction, conveyed in a most fascinating style of composition. Who need covet a novel that can converse with Addison and Johnson.

heroism, politeness, intellect, are all valuable; but unless they are united with genuine principle, and true integrity, they only render their possessor more dangerous, and invest him with greater power to do mischief. Suffer not your imagination to be captivated by the dazzling properties of a character, of which the substantial parts are not approved by your judgment; nothing is excellent which is not morally so. The polished rake, the generous profligate, the witty and intelligent sceptic, are to be shunned as serpents, whose variegated and beautiful skin should have no power to reconcile us to their venom. You may be charged with want of taste, or coldness of heart, for withholding your approbation; but it is a far sublimer attainment, and certainly a more difficult one, to have a taste and ardor only in the cause of holiness. Be cautious to examine every character which is presented to you for admiration, to penetrate the varnish of exterior accomplishments; and if you find nothing of genuine integrity beneath, withhold the tribute of your approbation, regardless of the sneers of those shallow minds who have neither the power to try the things that differ, nor the virtue to approve only such as are excellent.

It is a very important hint to give to young people, just setting out in life, to analyze character before they admire it; remembering that, to borrow an allusion from chemistry, a deadly poison may be held in solution by the most beautifully-colored liquid which the eye can behold.

5. An extreme dread of singularity, arising out of a morbid sensibility to shame, is a dangerous disposition of mind, to which young people are very liable.

There are some who are so ambitious to be thought originals, that they affect distinction in folly, or even in vice: they can even bear to be laughed at, if it may be admitted that they are without a prototype; and are content to be persecuted, provided it be for the sake of their originality. These martyrs to strangeness are in one extremity of character, of which the other is that great dread of being ridiculed as singular, which tries a man's attachment, even to the cause of virtue. There are some so acutely, so morbidly sensible to the least sneer, that they are put in dreadful peril of forsaking the cause of righteousness and morality, rather than take up the cross in the face of laughter. I have already in part considered this, and stated it to be one of the obstacles to early piety; but it not only obstructs the entrance, but the subsequent path of piety, and should therefore be most vigorously opposed by all who are subject to its influence. A sense of shame, when felt in reference to what is wrong, is one of the guardians of virtue : in this meaning of the phrase, it can never be too acute, nor can it be too delicately susceptible of impression. When any one has ceased to be ashamed of doing what is wrong, and the last blush with which a tender conscience once suffused the countenance has vanished, the progress of sin is nearly completed, and the sinner may be considered as near the end of his career. But when a person is so morbidly sensible to ridicule, that he shrinks from it, even in the performance of that which is right, he not only lets down his dignity, but endangers his principles.

There is something noble and heroic in that disposition, which can dare to be singular in the cause of religion and morality; which with a mind conscious of doing right, can fight, single-handed, the battles of the Lord, against the host of scorners by which it may be surrounded. It is not a part of virtue to be indifferent to the opinion of others, except that opinion be opposed to the principles of truth and holiness, then it is the very height of virtue to act above it, and against it.

Ridicule is certainly not the test of truth, but it is one of the most fiery ordeals of that courage by which the truth is professed and supported. Many have been vanquished by scorn, who were invulnerable to rage; for men in general would much rather have their hearts reproached than their heads, deeming it less disgraceful to be weak in virtue than deficient in intellect. Strange perversion! the effect of that pride which, being injected into our nature by the venom of the serpent in Paradise, still continues to infect and destroy us. Let us oppose this working of evil within us, and crucify this affection and lust of the flesh. Let no ridicule deter us from doing what is right or avoiding what is wrong. Let us emulate the sublime example of the apostle, who exclaimed, " We are fools for Christ's sake." This is the noblest effort of human courage, the loftiest achievement of virtue to be " faithful found amongst the faithless," and willing to bear any contumely rather than act in opposition to the convictions of our judgment, and the dictates of our conscience.   It is infinitely better to be scorned for doing what is right, than applauded for doing what is wrong.   From the laughter of the wicked you may find a refuge in the approbation of your conscience, and the smile of your God ; but in what a miserable situation is that poor cowardly wretch, whose dread of singularity has led him to sacrifice the convictions of his conscience, and who has nothing to comfort him under the frowns of Deity but the applause of fools.

Neither in little things, nor in great ones, suffer your dread of singularity to turn your feet from the path of integrity.   Arm yourself with this mind, to do what is right, though you can find neither companion nor follower.

XXI.

Redeeming Time.

IT was a very important admonition which St. Paul delivered to the Ephesian church,—" Redeeming the time because the days are evil." The context in which it stands is equally striking : he had just admonished those to whom he wrote, not to walk as fools ; thus implying that a man can give no greater proof of folly, nor more effectually act the part of a fool, than to waste his time : while on the other hand, a just appreciation and right improvement of time are amongst the brightest displays of true wisdom.

Seneca has somewhere observed that we are all of us complaining of the shortness of time, and yet have much more than we know what to do with. We are always mourning that our days are few, and yet acting as though there would be no end of them. This plainly proves that we neither value time correctly, nor improve it diligently. The late Rev. Henry Martyn was known at the University by the designation of " The man who never wasted an hour." Nothing can better explain what I mean by improving time ; it is never wasting it, but always appro-

propriating it to some useful purpose. Many considerations, my children, urge this upon us.

It is the most precious thing in the world. In
the bestowment of it, God differs from the manner
in which he distributes most of his other gifts; in
the latter he is profuse, in the former parsimonious.
He can, of course, give us but a moment at a time, but
that he does without ever promising another ; as if
to teach us highly to value, and diligently to improve the present moment, by the consideration that
for aught we know, it may be the last.

Time, when once gone, never returns. Where is
yesterday ?—" With the ages beyond the Flood," and
we could as soon hope to bring back one as the
other. We talk of fetching up a lost hour, but the
thing is impossible. A moment once lost is lost
forever ; we could as rationally set out to find a
sound that had expired in the air, as to find a lost
moment. We may as well attempt to crowd two
hours into the duration of one, as the employment of
two hours into one ; for, in reality, what we do in any
given portion of time might have been done in it, although we had not wasted the preceding one.

*How much is there of our time which can be ap-
plied to no purpose, except preparing us for improving other portions of our existence.* How much goes
away in sleep, and in all the other demands of nature, for its refreshment and invigoration : this is
not lost, if the subsequent periods be rightly applied,
and diligently employed, any more than the time
spent in oiling the wheels of a carriage impedes the

journey, because the vehicle goes the faster afterwards. But then, if we sleep at night, it is that we might be busy in the day; if we eat and drink, it is that we might be better able to work; and certainly a recollection of the great portion of our time that is necessary for refreshment and repose, should be a stimulus to us to employ the remainder with the greater diligence. We should regard it as an infirmity of nature, that so much sleep and time for eating and drinking is necessary, and endeavor, by diligence in our waking working hours, to improve the surplus.

Then add to this the portions of time which are irresistibly engrossed by the tyranny of custom; all that passes in regulating the superficial decorations of life, or is given up in the reciprocations of civility to the disposal of others; all that is torn from us by the violence of disease, or stolen imperceptibly away by lassitude and langour; that large portion which is spent amidst the toys of childhood, and afterwards amidst the imbecility of old age:* I say, add up these things, and when you have subtracted the amount from the gross sum of man's life, how small is the remainder! Even the active and busy part of mankind apply a very little more than a third part of their existence to any valuable purpose. By this mode of calculation, the old man of eighty has lived but little more than twenty-six years; and the man of forty, but little more than thirteen. A most cogent reason for not wasting an hour.

* See Johnson's Idler.

We should never forget *that our time is amongst the talents for which we must give account at the bar of God.* Time being not the least precious of these, will be required with a strictness proportionate to its value. Let us tremble at this idea, as well we may. We must be tried not only for what we have done, but for what we had time to do, yet neglected to do it: not only for the hours spent in sin, but for those wasted in idleness. Let us beware of that mode of spending time which some call killing it, " for this murder, like others, will not always be concealed: the hours destroyed in secret will appear when we least expect it, to the unspeakable terror and amazement of our souls: they arise from the dead, and fly away to heaven, whither they might have carried better news, and there tell sad tales of us, which we shall be sure to hear of again, when we hold up our hands at the bar, and they shall come as so many swift witnesses against us."

It might stir us up to diligence in the improvement of our time, *to think how much of it has been already misspent.* What days, and weeks, and months, and years, have already been utterly wasted, or exhausted upon trifles totally unworthy of them. They are gone, and nothing remains of them but the guilt of having misimproved them. We cannot call them back if we would ; and all we can do is to let their memorial, like the recollection of any other dead friends whom we treated improperly while they lived, lead us to value more highly, and to use more kindly, those that remain.

How much of our time is already gone, and how little may be yet to come. The sands of our glass may be almost out, without the possibility of having it turned. Death may be at the door. When you begin a day you know not that you shall end it; when you lie down that you shall rise up; when you go from home that you shall ever return. For what is your life? it is even as a vapor that appeareth for a little while and then vanisheth; a bubble that rises, and shines, and bursts. We know not in any one period of our existence, but that it may be the last. Surely, surely, we should then improve our time, when we may be holding, for aught we know, the last portion of it in our hands. With the absolute certainty of a life as long as Methuselah's, not an hour should be wasted; how much less when we know not that there is a day in reversion for us!

But what are the PURPOSES *for which time should be redeemed?*

For the SALVATION OF THE SOUL, the business of religion, the preparation for eternity. You are immortal creatures, my children, and must live forever in torment or in bliss; and certainly you cannot be forming a right estimate of the value of time, nor be rightly employing it, if the soul be forgotten, salvation neglected, and eternity left out of consideration, "For what shall it profit a man if he gain the whole world, and lose his own soul; or what shall a man give in exchange for his soul?" A man may attain to the science of Newton, to the genius of Milton, to the learning of Bentley, to the wealth of

Crœsus, and to the fame of Alexander; but if the salvation of the soul be neglected, he will through eternity confess and curse his folly, in losing his time. Our great business in this world is to pre-prepare for the next; time is capital given us to trade with for eternity; and that man who goes off the stage of life without having attended supremely to the great business of religion, will appear to the inhabitants of the unseen world, as well as to himself, an object of amazement for his unparalleled folly in wasting his time upon matters, which compared with eternal happiness, were utterly insignificant.

We must redeem time *for the pursuits of business,* for it is ordained that men shall gain their bread by the sweat of their brow; *for the improvement of our mind,* so far as circumstances will allow, in all useful knowledge; and *for the exercise of benevolence.* These are the objects which we must ever keep in view, as the claimants who prefer their demands for the years and the days which God hath given us upon earth.

And FROM WHAT is our time to be redeemed?

From *sloth.* How much of it is consumed by this lazy, slumbering, monster! How many golden hours are wasted upon the downy pillow! Late rising is the enemy of piety, of knowledge, of health, of affluence; and the cause of ignorance, irreligion, and poverty. Shall religion, wisdom, benevolence, my dear children, be found knocking at your chamber door morning after morning, exclaiming, "Awake,

thou that sleepest, and arise ;" and receive no other
answer than, " a little more sleep, and a little more
slumber !" A habit of early rising has, in many
cases, been a fortune to the pocket, and in many
more, a fortune to the mind. Reckoning that a day
consists of ten hours' active employment, the difference of life between an individual who rises at six
o'clock, and another who rises at eight o'clock, is, in
the term of sixty years, no less than equal to twelve
years, and those the best years of a man's existence.
There is in this calculation that which proves late
rising not only to be a loss, but a *crime*. It is so
much deducted from a man's existence, and actually
given to his grave.

Many of the most distinguished characters in the
literary world, owe their eminence to early rising.
It is recorded of BUFFON, the celebrated natural
historian, that wishing to acquire the habit of early
rising, both from his love of knowledge and of fame,
he promised his servant half-a-crown for every
morning upon which he should prevail upon him to
leave his bed by a given time. The servant went
most resolutely to work, under a commission that
authorized him to drag BUFFON, if necessary, out of
bed ; and, in spite of threats and ill-usage, which he
often had to endure from his somnolent master, suc-
ceeded in getting him from his chamber by the
stipulated hour. And BUFFON informs us, that to
the unwearied perseverance of his servant, the world
is indebted for his work on Natural History.

It is a most injurious practice to invert the order

of nature, and sit up late instead of rising early. Nocturnal studies rapidly undermine the strongest constitution. Dr. Owen, a name dear to all who love sterling piety and profound theological learning, used to say, when suffering through his excessive application to study, " That he would gladly give up all the knowledge he had acquired after ten o'clock at night, if he could recover all the strength he had lost by studies carried on after that hour."

Let your sleep, then, be necessary and healthful, not idle and expensive of time, beyond the needs and conveniences of nature ; and sometimes be curious to see the preparation which the sun makes, when he is coming forth from his chambers in the east."

Redeem time, *from the vain pursuits of personal decoration and dress.* This applies *chiefly*, though not exclusively, to the softer sex. It is shocking to think how much precious time is wasted at the toilet, in the silly ambition of rivalling the butterfly, the ostrich, and the peacock. What a reproach to a rational creature, is it to neglect the improvement of the mind for the adornings of the body ; this is like painting the outside of a house, and training over it the myrtle, the rose, and the jessamine, while the interior is left to be dark, damp, inconvenient, and filthy.

Unprofitable reading is another consumer of time which must be avoided. *Worldly amusements, and parties of pleasure,* are also injurious. I do not by

this mean to condemn the occasional intercourse of
friends in the social circle, where the civilities of
life are given and received, the ties of friendship
strengthened, and the mind recreated, without any
injury being done to the spiritual or moral interests.
But the theatre, the card-table, the billiard-room,
are all to be avoided as vile thieves, which steal our
time and hurt our souls. Pleasure parties in general are to be watched with care, and resorted to but
seldom, for they seldom pay for the time that is
spent. "There are a multitude of people in the
world, who, being idle themselves, do their best endeavors to make others so : in which work, partly
through a disposition in those others to be made so,
and partly through a fear and false shame, which
hinders them from fraying away such birds of prey,
they are too often suffered to succeed. An assembly
of such persons can be compared only to a slaughter-
house, where the precious hours, and often the characters of all their friends and acquaintance, are
butchered without mercy."

We must redeem time from *the trifling conversation and gossip of idle companions,* "for no man,"
says Jeremy Taylor, " can be provident of his time,
that is not prudent in the choice of his company ; and
if one of the speakers be vain, tedious, and trifling,
he that hears, and he that answers, are equal losers
in their time." The Idler says, " that there are always some drones in society, who make much noise,
but no honey." We should avoid all those who talk
much, but say little, and watch against persons

whose conversation is like the buzz of moths and caterpillars, not only disagreeable, but carrying on a system of spoliation; and who eat into an hour before we are aware that the mischief is commenced. Such persons should consider, that in consuming a man's time, they are committing a felony upon his property, for time is a part of his capital. And all others should retire from such persons, for idleness is contagious.

If you would redeem the time, you should not only avoid absolute idleness, or doing nothing, but a *slow and sauntering habit of doing anything.* To use an old proverb, " We ought not to make greater haste than good speed." There are some persons who are always in a hurry, and all they do bears marks of haste. Everything is half done, or ill done. But there is a wide difference between habits of dispatch, and bustling hurry. A thing is not better done for having twice as much time consumed upon it as it needs. There are individuals who seem always to creep to an engagement, and almost to slumber over it. As it respects general habits, a parent can scarcely teach a child a more valuable art than *despatch without bustle:* nor can any one that values his time, cultivate a more desirable one for himself.

ORDER and PUNCTUALITY are essential to a right improvement of time. I mention these things together, because they are so closely connected, and have such a mutual influence on each other. One, indeed, is the order of place, the other is the order of time. The best, and indeed the only rules, which any man can with propriety preseribe for himself, are these: " A time for everything, and everything in its time: a place for everything, and everything in its place." A habit of order may be fairly said to lengthen a man's life, not by multiplying its hours, but by enabling him more advantageously to employ them. Disorderly habits are perpetually wasting our time. When a person has no one place for any one thing, but lays everything by, just wherever he may happen to be, he is sure to spend his life in confusion. He never knows where to find what he wants. Let such a person conceive what an amount of time would be made up by all the minutes and hours which he has employed during his life in looking for misplaced articles ; to say nothing of the mortification he has endured, and the inconvenience in which others have been involved. In business, order is property, and every tradesman deficient in this virtue, ought, in taking stock, to have this item on the loss side of the balance-sheet, " So much lost for want of order." And, as disorderly habits waste our time, they are not only improper, but *actually sinful*.

PUNCTUALITY is another habit very important to a right improvement of time. Fix your time, and then keep it. Perhaps you know some persons who are always behindhand. The clock is to them an article without use: they do all things as if by whim or impulse. They are thus mischief-makers, without malice; and as far as in them lies, bring a chaos into human affairs. An individual who keeps a company of twelve persons waiting for him but five minutes, wastes an hour. "Punctuality," says an elegant writer, " is a quality which the interest of mankind requires to be diffused through all the ranks of life, but which many seem to consider as a vulgar and ignoble virtue, below the ambition of greatness, or the attention of wit; scarcely requisite among men of gaiety and spirit, and sold at its highest rate when it is sacrificed to a frolic or a jest."*

That a want of order and punctuality should be thought a mark of genius or gentility is astonishing, and I believe *is* rarely thought so, except by those who have nothing of either but the affectation of

---

* Punctuality has another reference besides our time, I mean to our *word*. To promise without intending to perform, is absolute falsehood. But we ought to be very cautious how we bind ourselves by a promise, which is subject to contingencies beyond our foresight, or above our control. Many a man has subjected himself to the reproach of a liar without intending to deceive. Some people make all engagements with their eyes shut, and no sooner open them than they find it impossible to fulfil their word. We should always pause before we issue these verbal promissory notes, and calculate whether we have the means to meet them when they are presented for payment. Nothing can be more unjust or cruel, than a wilful want of punctuality in pecuniary transactions. It is unkind to keep, through our delays, a cook storming over a spoiling dinner in the kitchen, and her mistress fretting in the drawing-room ; but to defeat the expectation of a tradesman, dependent, perhaps, for a settling, important to his credit, upon our punctuality, is a species of cruelty perfectly inhuman.

them.   Many, I have no doubt, have set up for great
wits, and fine ladies, upon no other pretensions to either,
than a sturdy opposition to all order of time and place.

*A good method wisely arranged and punctually
observed in the distribution of our time,* would
materially assist us in rightly employing it.   Religion, business, mental improvement, the exercises of
benevolence, ought all, so far as the ever-varying
circumstances of life will admit of it, to have their proper allotments.   Each hour should know its proper
employment, and receive its proper care in its season.   No man should leave his days to be occupied by whatever accident or chance can seize them;
for then, trifles being more common and clamorous
than other things of greater importance, are likely
to run off with the greatest share.

Have always some work in hand, which may be
going on during the many intervals, for many there
will be both of business and recreation.   PLINY, in
one of his letters, where he gives an account of the
various methods he used, to fill up every vacancy
of time, after several employments which he enu-
merates, says, " Sometimes I hunt; but then I carry
with me a pocket-book, that whilst my servants are
busied in disposing of the nets and other matters, I may
be employed in something that may be useful to me in
my studies ; and that if I miss of my game, I may at
the least bring home some of my own thoughts with
me, and not have the mortification of having caught
nothing all day."   This is the way to excellence and
wisdom ; and it is a road open to all.   Carry about

with you, therefore, some book, or subject, which
shall gather up the fragments, that nothing be
lost ; for these fragments, like chips of diamond,
or fragments of gold, are too precious to be thrown
away. It is with our property as with our time,
when we look at it in the gross, we spend freely because it seems as if it would never be exhausted ;
and when we have hours, half-hours, or quarters, we
squander *them* because they are not worth keeping
There is a proverb which our frugal ancestors have
taught us, " Take care of the shillings, and the
pounds will take care of themselves." So in reference to our time I would say, " Take care of your
hours, and the years will take care of themselves."
A man that is thrifty of his money, will grow rich
upon what another throws away, as not worth saving ; so a man that is thrifty of his time, will grow
wise by those interstitial vacancies which intervene
in the most crowded variety of employment, and
which many are foolish enough to squander upon
trifles, or saunter away in idleness.

Avoid procrastination.—Do at once what at once
ought to be done. Let not the season of action be
spent in the hesitancy of scepticism, or the purpose of
future effort. Do not let *to-morrow* be perpetually
the time when everything is to be done, unmindful
that the present time alone is ours, as the past is
dead, and the future yet unborn.*

Erasmus furnishes one of the most striking in-

* See an admirable story in Miss Edgeworth's Popular
Tales, entitled To-morrow.

stances on record of the fruits of a diligent improvement of time.   " His life was one continual peregri-
nation ; ill supplied with the gifts of fortune, and
led from city to city, and from kingdom to kingdom,
by the hopes of patrons and preferment, hopes which
always flattered and always deceived him ; he yet
found means, by unshaken constancy and a vigilant
employment of those hours, which, in the midst of
the most restless activity, will remain unengaged, to
write more than another, in the same condition,
would have hoped to read.   Compelled by want to
attendance and solicitation, and so much versed in
common life, that he has transmitted to us the most
perfect delineation of the manners of his age ; he
joined to his knowledge of the world, such application to books, that he will stand forever in the first
rank of literary heroes.   How this proficiency was
obtained, he sufficiently discovers by informing us
that the ' *Praise of Folly*,' one of his most celebrated
performances, was composed by him on the road to
Italy, lest the hours which he spent on horseback
should be tattled away without regard to literature."

A right improvement of time, then, my dear children, is the way to knowledge, which does not in
every case require uninterrupted leisure ; only keep
the mind open to receive ideas, and diligently employ every spare moment in collecting them, and it
is astonishing how rapidly the accumulation of mental treasure will go forward.   But it is chiefly in
reference to eternity that I exhort you to redeem

the time. Too many attempt to justify their neglect of religion by pleading a want of opportunity to
attend to its high concerns; but how inadmissible
such a plea is, the subject of this chapter plainly
proves: for, as we have formerly shown, religion is
a right disposition of mind towards the great and
blessed God, and we now see that such a disposition,
besides the more solemn seasons of public and private prayer, will pour its influence over the whole
of a man's life, and fill the interstices which are left
between the most crowded occupations, with ejacu-
latory petitions to heaven, and the aspirations of a
soul panting after God, and the anticipations of a renewed mind looking towards eternity.

Remember then, above all things, that time was
given you to repent of sin, to pray for pardon, to believe in Christ, to work out your salvation, to
lay up treasures in heaven, to prepare for the solemnities of judgment, and secure that happiness
which is not measured by the revolution of years,
but is, in the strictest sense of the word,—ETERNAL.

XXII.

On the Obligation to enter into Fellowship with a Christian Church.

RELIGION is a personal thing, and the gospel first addresses us in our individual and separate existence We must each for himself repent of sin, believe in Christ, obey the law.   Nothing can be a substitute for this; no line of pious ancestry, no connection with living Christians, no communion with the Church of God, will be of any avail to us in the absence of faith and holiness.   Still, however, religion, though personal in its nature, is social in its tendency and exercises ; it is superinduced on a being formed for society, and who carries this propensity of his heart into his every situation.   Hence his piety leads him to seek the companionship of men of " like precious faith."   Christianity acknowledges and hallows this principle of our nature, and exhibits it in her own divine institutions.   The New Testament, therefore, while it insists on the necessity of a personal religion, equally demands a social one.   It knows nothing of that piety which keeps its possessor separate and apart from those who partake with him of the "common salvation" The first thing we read of after the miraculous effusion of the Holy Ghost, is the preaching of the gospel ; the next the conversion of sinners, and then we find that " they that gladly received the word were baptized ; and the same day there were added to them about three thousand souls. And they continued stead-fastly in the apostles' doctrine, and fellowship, and breaking of bread, and prayers. And all that be-lieved were together, and had all things common. And they continuing daily with one accord in the temple, and breaking bread from house to house, did eat their meat with gladness, and singleness of heart, praising God, and having favor with the peo-ple. And the Lord added to the church daily such as should be saved."

Such is the lovely picture which the inspired his-torian gives us of the first effect of the preaching of the gospel, in which we perceive not only that souls were converted, but that immediately upon their conversion, they were drawn to each other by the force of mutual love, and formed a voluntary and blessed fellowship. No one that believed the gos-pel remained separate and apart from the rest, but gave himself up to be one with the church ; and, in-deed, till he did this, was not acknowledged as a Christian. This was always the case in the primi-tive times ; as soon as a man believed, that same day, without being put on his trial for months, he united himself with believers. No such custom then existed, as persons, who were acknowledged to

be Christians, remaining year after in no visible connection with the body of Christ; this is a system of
modern times.

Indulging a hope, which indeed is one of the most
blissful expectations of my heart, that you, my dear
children, will be partakers of the grace of God, the
faith of the gospel, and the love of Christ, I shall
now strongly enjoin upon you an early association
with some Christian society. It is on these suppo-
sitions only that I recommend it. It is intended,
not so much to make men Christians, as to maintain
and improve their Christianity; not as an ordinance
of conversion, as of edification, sanctification, and
consolation. A Christian church is thus described
in the Epistles of Paul: " To all that be in Rome,
beloved of God, called to be saints." " Unto the
church of God which is at Corinth, to them that are
sanctified in Christ Jesus, called to be saints." Unless, therefore you really believe in Jesus Christ,
and are sanctified by the spirit of God, you are not
meet to be partakers of the inheritance of the saints
in light. If you were to join the church in an unconverted state, you would be as an enemy amongst
brethren, a stranger amongst friends, an alien
amongst citizens, a rebel amongst subjects. Taking
it then for granted that you believe in Christ, and
supremely love him, I admonish you to connect yourselves, in his own way, with his own people.

It is your solemn and bounden duty.

Mistake not by supposing that this matter is left
to your choice; it is no more optional than any

other part of religion.   You may just as well imagine that it is optional whether you shall keep the
Sabbath or not.   Strange it is that this part of a
Christian's duty should have been detached by many
persons, from all the rest as an observance which
had no obligation upon the conscience.   Was it not
an invariable practice in the first ages of the church,
for those who were converted to enter immediately
into the fellowship of the faithful?   Our Lord's
language in reference to the sacred supper, is a *command*, not an invitation ; it is the language of *authority*, not of advice : " Do this in remembrance of
me."   Now as the supper is the church ordinance,
this injunction makes it absolutely imperative on all
his disciples to unite themselves to the " household
of faith."

Far be it from me to say that a person cannot be
a Christian unless he be a church member, for I
have already observed, that he ought to be a believer *before* he enters into fellowship ; but I will
say that he who loves Christ, and yet continues unconnected with the church, is living, in that instance,
in direct disobedience to his Lord's commands.
And if one of the primitive Christians were permitted to come from his celestial seat, into our assembly, at the time we were preparing to celebrate the
Supper, he would very certainly and naturally conclude, that all those persons who rose and retired
from the emblems of the Saviour's body and blood,
neither believed in him, loved him, nor obeyed him.
And when informed that amongst that crowd there

were still some of whom we entertained hope, that they did in reality love Jesus Christ, with what surprise and emphasis would he exclaim, " Love Christ ! what, and live in habitual disobedience to his commands ? We have no such love as that in heaven, nor had we when I lived on earth."

IT IS YOUR UNSPEAKABLE HONOR to be early in the church.

It has been the dishonor, and is still the reproach of multitudes, that they neglect this divine ordinance. Admitting that, upon the whole, the man is a Christian, and yet through some mistaken notion is unconnected with a company of believers, what a spot is it upon his character, what a stain upon his garments, to see him, when the company of Christ's disciples are collecting round the table, hurrying away with the multitude of carnal, worldly, sensual, persons ; thus associating in this act of disregard to Christ's authority, with some that are profane, others that are sceptical, others that are immoral. What a disgrace is it to any one who pretends to bear the name of Christ, to be seen thus turning his back on the friends of the Redeemer, and walking away from *the* Christian Institute with the enemies of the cross. But, alas ! this reproach is too common to be felt as it ought to be.

But it is so much the greater honor to observe this duty, by so much the more it is neglected. It is considered delightful to see the head of the youthful senator, whose breast is full of patriotic ardor, lifted amidst the venerable forms of aged statesmen ;

and the juvenile warrior fighting by the side of vete-
ran heroes in his country's cause ; and how much
more delightful is it to see the young Christian, un-
deterred by a false and sinful shame, unrestrained
by the examples of many of his seniors, entering the
fellowship of the faithful, and, in the presence of the
world, exclaiming, " I am not ashamed of Christ, of
his words, before this adulterous and sinful generation. Preserve me, O God, for in thee do I put my
trust. O my soul, thou hast said unto the Lord,
Thou art my Lord, my goodness extendeth not to
thee ; but to the saints that are in the earth, and to
the excellent in whom is all my delight. Their sorrows shall be multiplied that hasten after another
God ; their drink offerings of blood will I not offer,
nor take up their names into my lips. I will take
the cup of salvation, and call upon the name of the
Lord. O Lord, truly I am thy servant, and the son
of thy handmaid ; thou hast loosed my bonds. I
will pay my vows unto the Lord now, in the presence
of all his people, in the courts of the Lord's house,
in the midst of thee, O Jerusalem. Praise ye the
Lord."

Oh, my children, may I see this honor lighting
on you ; may it be granted me to see you sitting
amongst the followers of the Lamb, associated with
the church of the living God ; and I shall not be
very solicitous for you to obtain the wreath of fame,
or any of the distinctions which men can confer upon
each other ; the honor of being an early and consistent member of that fellowship, of which God in

Christ is the head, is, in my eyes, a crown of glory, compared with which the diadems of monarchs are gilded toys.

Church fellowship IS AN INESTIMABLE PRIVILEGE.

It is connected with, and leads to many solemn, delightful, and beneficial observances. It is by joining ourselves to the church, that we have *a right to the Lord's Supper.* This sacred feast is to be observed by the *church ;* not by individuals in their separate condition. In approaching the table of the Lord, we are to go as one of a company. It is intended at once to exhibit our unity, and to preserve it. That bread which is the emblem of the *natural* body of Christ broken for sinners, is at the same time, by its many parts in union with each other, the emblem of his *mystical* body. It is an ordinance which at the same time sets forth both our union to Christ by faith, and to each other by love. It shows one church deriving its salvation from the death of one Redeemer. Hence the object of our partaking of the sacred supper, is to keep up right affections to Christ, and to each other for Christ's sake. Precious, my children, are those hallowed seasons of communion which are spent by the disciples at the table of the Lord. No sensual gratifications will bear any comparison with the sublime delight of those sacred entertainments. What scenes of past wonder, and sorrow, and triumph, are then brought to recollection, even the incarnation, life, sufferings, death, resurrection, and ascension of Jesus Christ ; yes, those apparently insignificant emblems, bring before the mind, so far as the mind can comprehend it, the whole of the vast scheme, devised from eternity in the counsels of Omniscience, for the salvation of a ruined world, and executed by the Son of God upon the cross. What present emotions of wonder, joy, love, gratitude, to him " who loved us, and washed us from our sins in his blood, and made us kings and priests to God and the Lamb," does the Supper produce and cherish! What visions of future glory, connected with the second coming of our Lord, does the institution call up before the eye of hope. How sweetly are the rich blessings of grace, and the eternal blessings of glory, brought home upon the heart. All the virtues of Christianity are strengthened, all its privileges are enjoyed. The soul, by being brought nearer to Christ, is brought nearer to his disciples. The joys of salvation are more rich and full, by being experienced in the company of those who are heirs of the same bliss.

Union with the church gives *a right to attend all the more private meetings of the brethren,* where pastoral exhortation is delivered, brotherly love is cherished, members are admitted, and all the transactions of the household of God are managed.

Church membership is connected with many *pleasant reflections.* In such a situation we have the consciousness of our being where we ought to be; of our obeying the will of Christ; of our being in the midst of the righteous, as one of their number, and an object of their interest.

It is no inconsiderable means of *spiritual safety.* In general it may be argued that the path of duty is the path of safety. Where are we so likely to enjoy the showers of divine grace, as in those gardens of the Lord on which they most generally fall ? " God meeteth him that worketh righteousness." It is connected with *pastoral oversight and watchfulness* with *brotherly inspection, exhortation and reproof;* it secures *an interest in the prayers and sympathy of the disciples ;* and then it leads us *to consider the additional obligations which lie upon us in consequence of our profession,* and the more painful effects which would thus follow an act of inconsistency : in short, it seems to be an additional defence for us against the dangers to which we are exposed in our spiritual warfare. In looking forward to our approach to the table of the Lord, we shall be led to more frequent and serious examination ; in looking back to the vows which we there brought ourselves under, we shall be stirred up to more caution : considering through the month previous, that we are soon to appear amongst the saints at the sacramental board, we shall find this a check to temptation, a stimulus to duty, a .motive to consistency ; and, looking back during the month that follows, upon what then took place, we shall find the restrospect no less salutary than was the prospect. A regard to our own reputation and comfort will join itself with a concern for the honor of Christ, and the prosperity of the church, to operate as a preservative against unholy conformity or sinful indulgence. We are

poor frail creatures, and our spiritual strength is so
feeble as to stand in need of every additional help;
and it is no inconsiderable assistance that is furnished by Christian fellowship.   Companionship is one
of the hot-beds both of sin and holiness.   Trees
grow better, as I have already remarked, in planta-
tions; they shelter each other from the violence of
the wind, and the severity of the cold, and draw
each other into a taller and a straighter growth: so
it is with the trees of righteousness of God's own
right hand planting; and it is by being thus planted in the house of the Lord, that they shall flourish
as the palm-tree, and grow as the cedar in Lebanon.

You may thus *be useful to others.*   Your parents
will rejoice over you with unutterable joy; your
ministers will be encouraged in the work of the
Lord; other young persons, if serious, may be drawn
by you into the church, or, if unconverted, may have
their attention roused, and their conscience awakened; the more aged who have neglected this duty
will be stirred up to shame and repentance: thus
what is so beneficial to you will extend its advantage
to others, and the King of Zion will look upon you
with peculiar and ineffable delight.

Before this chapter closes, however, I must answer
the objections which are but too commonly brought
by young persons, even by those whose hearts are
right with God, against this act of obedience to
Christ.

Some are in doubt about their personal religion.
Where this is the case, let them not remain in doubt

any longer, but examine themselves and bring the matter to an issue. " Examine yourselves," saith the apostle, " whether ye be in faith ; prove your ownselves." This is too important an affair to remain undecided, and in suspense. Nor need you be kept in the dark about it. If you really reflect, you must know whether you believe the gospel or not ; whether you love the Lord Jesus or not; whether you are obeying God or not. Do not doubt your religion under the mistaken apprehension that doubts are proofs of piety, and evidences of humility. Your inquiry is not to be, " Am I a perfect Christian?" but " Am I a *real* one ?" If you can answer the latter question in the affirmative, you ought not to remain out of the communion of the church.

Others are saying, *I am not fit to join the church yet.* Then you are not fit to die. God requires no other pre-requisite to the Lord's table than what he does to heaven ; and all the fitness he requireth for either is to be convinced of sin, to believe the gospel, and to forsake unrighteousness.

I am afraid, say some, *of making a public profession, lest I should dishonor Christ by sinning afterwards.* In some cases, this is nothing more than an excuse for not making a profession at all, as if it were no sin to offend God before a profession is made. Many dread the idea of binding themselves by the acknowledgment that they are Christians ; forgetting that it is their sin not to make a profession, and that they will be condemned for neglecting it, as some others will be for disgracing it. If, however, it be really the mistaken scruple of a timid mind, I would say again, the way of duty is the way of safety ; do your duty, and trust God for preserving grace. For a man to be afraid of doing what is right, lest he shonld afterwards do wrong, is singular caution : he forgets that by his neglect he is already sinning. What reason is there in saying " I am very weak and therefore will neglect this prop—I am liable to start aside, and therefore will not avail myself of this scriptural restraint."

I am too young in years, is the frequent thought of young people. Certainly not, if you are not too young to believe the gospel, to love Christ, and to discern the Lord's body. Is there any age specified in the New Testament, below which no man is to join the Church ? If so, where is it ? There is none. Faith working by love is the qualification for membership, not years. Children of ten years of age, or even younger, if they are believers, ought to be admitted as members. Age has nothing to do with it. If we might make any difference, I was going to say the younger the more welcome. Jesus showed his favor to the young children when he said, " Suffer the little children to come unto me, and forbid them not, for of such is the kingdom of God."

I am too young in the faith, say others. Not if you are sincere. If we make the word of God our guide in this matter, (and what else ought to guide us ?) then we must infer that a sincere belief of the gospel, with a competent knowledge of the ends of church fellowship, is all that ought to be required of a candidate for membership. You may have been converted only a month, but if truly converted, that is no objection. The same *day* that they believed, the three thousand persons converted under the sermon of Peter, were added to the church. The privileges of fellowship are needed if possible, more by the young than by the aged Christian : they are milk for babes, as well as strong meat for them who have attained to riper years.

I see it neglected by others older than myself, even by my own brothers and sisters. Would it be any excuse for *your* neglecting salvation altogether, if *they* were to do so ? Certainly not; for religion is a personal concern, the obligations of which are, in our case, in no degree dependent on the manner in which they are acknowledged by others. The more it is forgotten by others, the more we should feel excited to practise its duties ourselves. Your obedience is not to be withheld, because your friends or relatives neglect theirs. It may be that your decision will have a favorable influence on their minds : if not, and even on the contrary, if you should by such an act incur their displeasure, you are not to let this operate on your heart. Your duty to Christ is paramount to all other considerations, and you must obey him, though it be by taking up your cross.

I do not like the mode of admission to our churches. "I do not like to be examined as to my religious views or experience, nor to submit the

state of my mind to the consideration of the church."
If you mean to say you refuse *all examination*, this
savors of pride or ignorance, and plainly manifests
either that you do not understand the nature of a
Christian church, or understanding it, refuse to submit to its discipline : in the latter case, I do not see
how you can be a Christian : in the former, you
must be better instructed before you associate yourself with the faithful. If you mean only, that you
would rather not either *write*, or deliver *verbally before the church*, your views and feelings on religion,
I reply, that no church ought to insist upon it; all
they ought to do, is to state what is their usual custom, but if you have scruples of a tender conscience,
they ought to be satisfied with the report of the pastor and brethren who have conversed with you.

*I tremble at the denunciation, where it is declared
by the Apostle,* "*He that eateth and drinketh un-
worthily, eateth and drinketh damnation to himself.*" This word had better have been rendered
"*judgment,*" as it refers to those visitations of temporal punishment, with which the members of the
Corinthian church were punished for their profana-
tion of the Lord's Supper. It certainly was not the
Apostle's intention, as some weak and timid minds
seem to think, to teach that sins committed after
this act of Christian communion are unpardonable.
Transgressions committed after a participation of
the eucharist, are, it is confessed, additionally hein-
ous, because committed against increased privileges
and obligations, but they are still pardonable through

31

" the blood of Christ which cleanseth from *all* sin."

I may be a Christian, and get to heaven without being united with the Church.   That there are some in this case, I have no doubt ; but it becomes a question whether any one can really be a Christian, who knows it to be a duty, and yet wilfully neglects it under the pretext just stated.

I do not like the church which is formed in the place where I live.   I am neither pleased with the pastor nor the people.   If the minister is unholy, and erroneous, or the people divided into parties, and destitute of both peace and purity, this excuse may be admitted ; but if the objection apply to the talents of the minister, or to the worldly circumstances of the church, we are discovering a spirit of pride and wordly-mindedness, in thus refusing to obey the command of Christ, which renders our faith very questionable, or proves it to be very weak.

Having thus explained the nature, and stated the advantages of church fellowship, and replied to some of the excuses, by which a neglect of it is attempted to be justified, I must leave the subject to your serious consideration.   It is perfectly obvious to every thinking and observant mind, that the obligations to this act of duty, are not felt, at least as they ought to be, by many who have " tasted that the Lord is gracious."   To such persons I recommend the consideration of those passages in which a profession of our faith *before men* is most imperatively demanded. " Whosoever," saith our Lord, " shall confess my name before men, him will I confess before my Father which is in heaven; and whosoever shall deny me before men, him will I also deny before my Father which is in heaven." These words occur also, with little variation, in the Gospel of Luke. The same sentiment is conveyed by the Apostle Paul: "If thou shalt *confess with thy mouth* the Lord Jesus, and shalt believe in thy heart that God hath raised him from the dead, thou shalt be saved: for with the heart man believeth unto righteousness, and *with the mouth confession* is made unto salvation." In these passagss, and others of a similar meaning, a confession or profession, for the words are nearly the same in signification,* bears a very close connection with the hope of salvation; and how any one can be said to make a confession of Christ, who does not connect himself with a Christian church, I am certainly at a loss to understand.

On this subject I refer, for a more enlarged view, to my treatise on "Christian Fellowship, or the Church Members' Guide."

---

* Perhaps the English words *pro*fession and *con*fession have this difference of signification,—the former means the *unasked* avowal of our faith: the latter, the acknowledgment of our sentiments when *required* to declare them: answerable to which *pro*fessors means Christians in general; *con*fessors, those who in time of persecution acknowledge their sentiments at the demand of their persecutors.

XXIII.

On the Choice of a Companion for Life.

" The first blessing," says Bishop Taylor, " God
gave to man was society ; and that society was a
marriage ; and that marriage was confederated by
God himself, and hallowed by a blessing.   The first
miracle that Jesus Christ ever performed, was to do
honor to a wedding, which he graced with his presence, and supplied with a part of its provision.   Cel-
ibacy, like the fly in the heart of the apple, dwells
in a perpetual sweetness, but sits alone, and is confined and dies in singularity ; but marriage, like the
useful bee, builds a house and gathers sweetness from
every flower, and unites into societies and republics,
and sends out colonies, and feeds the world with
delicacies, and keeps order, and exercises many virtues, and promotes the interests of mankind, and is
that state of good things to which God hath designed
the present constitution of the world.

" But then with how much caution, and extreme
care and sound discretion, and fervent prayer, ought
this union to be formed ; for they who enter into the
state of marriage cast a die of the greatest contin-

gency, and yet of the greatest interest in the world, next to the last throw for eternity. Life or death, felicity or a lasting sorrow, are in the power of marriage. A woman indeed ventures most, for she hath no sanctuary to retire to from an evil husband; she must dwell upon her sorrow which her own folly hath produced; and she is more under it, because her tormentor hath a warrant of prerogative, and the woman may complain to God as subjects do to tyrant princes, but otherwise she hath no appeal in the cause of unkindness And though the man can run from many hours of his sadness, yet he must return to it again; and when he sits among his neighbors he remembers the objection that lies in his bosom, and sighs deeply."

Who then that is wise, would not be slow to decide where so much depends upon the decision; and grow up in a habit of putting the affections and the imagination under the control of the judgment? If it be important to exercise deliberation in reference to those connections which may be dissolved at pleasure, how much more in the case of those, which nothing can terminate but the stroke of death!

The first piece of advice I offer is, *not to think of this all-important affair too soon, nor suppose it necessary that a young person of eighteen or nineteen should begin to pay or receive particular attentions.* Do not court the subject, nor permit your imagination to be forever dwelling upon it. Rather put it from you, than bring it near. Repress that visionary and romantic turn of mind, which considers the whole space that lies between you and the altar, as a dreary waste, all beyond it as a paradise: in innumerable instances the very reverse has been the case, and the exchange of a father's for a husband's house has been like the departure of Adam and Eve from the Garden of Eden to a wide uncultivated wilderness. "The stags in the Greek epigram, whose knees were clogged with frozen snow upon the mountains, came down to the brooks of the valleys, hoping to thaw their joints with the waters of the stream; but the frost overtook them, and bound them fast in the ice, till the young herdsmen took them in their stranger snare. It is the unhappy chance of some persons, finding many inconveniences upon the mountains of single life, they descend into the valleys of marriage to refresh their troubles, and there they enter into fetters, and are bound to sorrow by the cords of a man's or a woman's peevishness; and the worst of the evils is, that they have to thank their own follies, for they fell into the snare by entering an improper way;" and I may be permitted to add, by entering it too early, and too hastily.

It is on this ground that novels, the most pernicious mental poison the press can disseminate, are so much to be depreciated; they inflame the imagination with visionary scenes and adventurous exploits, on a subject which the heart ought never to approach, but under the guidance of a sober judgment. Young people should be cautious in their social intercourse of converting this subject into matter of merriment, much more should they beware of aiding

and abetting each other in the formation of such
connections. Never, never be the confident of individuals who are engaged in an affair of this kind unknown to their parents; nor be the medium of com-
munication between them. Third persons, who have
been ambitious of the honor of match-making, have
often done mischief to others, which, however they
afterwards lamented, they were never able to repair.
I know some whose lives have been embittered, and
ever will be, by seeing the rueful consequences of
those ill-fated unions, of which they were, in great
measure, the authors.

My next admonition is, *Take extreme care of hasty
entanglements.* Neither give nor receive particular
attentions, which cannot be mistaken, till the matter
is well weighed. Keep your affections shut up at
home in your hearts, while your judgment, aided, by
prudence, prepares to make its report.

When the subject comes fairly before your attention, *make it immediately known to your parents.*
Conceal nothing from them. Abhor the very idea
of clandestine connections, as a violation of every
duty you owe to God and man. There is nothing
heroic in a secret correspondence. The silliest girls
and the weakest men can maintain it, and have been
most frequently engaged in it. Spurn the individual
who would come between you and your natural
guardians. Hearken to the opinion of your parents
with all the deference which is due to it. Rare are
the cases in which you should act in opposition to
their wishes.

Be guided in this affair by the dictates of prudence. Never think of forming a connection till there is a rational prospect of temporal provision. I am not quite sure that the present age is in this respect more prudent than the past. It is all very pretty and pleasing for two young people to sing of love in a cottage, and draw picturesque views of two affectionate hearts struggling together amidst the difficulties of life; but these pictures are seldom realized. Connections that begin in imprudence generally end in wretchedness. Young people who marry without the consent of their parents, when that consent is withheld, not from caprice, but discretion, often find that they are not united like two doves, by a silken thread, but like two of Sampson's foxes, with a firebrand between them. I call it little else than wickedness to marry without a rational prospect of temporal support.

Right motives should ever lead to this union. To marry for property only, is most sordid and vile. We are informed that in some parts of the East Indies, it is thought no sin for a woman to sell her virtue at the price of an elephant; and how much more virtuous in reality is *she* who accepts a man for the sake of his fortune? Where there is no affection at the altar of marriage, there must be perjury of the most awful kind; and he who returns from church with this guilt upon his conscience, has brought with him a curse to his habitation, which is likely to make his prize of little worth. When such persons have counted their money and their sorrows

together, how willingly with the price of their slavery would they buy again their liberty ; and so they
could be released from each other, give up all claim
to the golden fetter which had chained them together.

Personal attractions alone are not enough to form
a ground of union.   " It is an ill band of affections
to tie two hearts together by a little thread of red
and white." Few things are more superficial or evanescent than beauty.   The fairest flower often fades
the soonest.   There ought to be personal attachment
I admit, but that attachment should be to the mind
as well as to the body.   Except we discern something lovely that will remain when the color of the
cheek has faded, and the fire of the eye is extinguished, and the symmetry of the form has been destroyed, we are engaging our affections to an object
which we may live to witness only as a sort of ghost
to that beauty which we once loved.   There should
be temper, and qualities of mind which we think
will please us, and satisfy us, when the novelties
and charms of personal attractions have faded forever.

In the case of pious young people, neither personal
nor mental qualifications, nor both together, should
be deemed a sufficient ground of union *in the absence
of religion.* The directions of Scripture on this
head are very explicit.   " Be not unequally yoked together with unbelievers ; for what fellowship hath
righteousness with unrighteousness ; and what communion hath light with darkness ? or what part hath
he that believeth with an infidel?" 2 Cor. vi. 14, 15.
" She is at liberty to marry whom she will, only in

the Lord." 1 Cor. vii. 39. This is a declaration
of the will of God. It is a clear unequivocal annun-
ciation of his mind on the subject. Viewed as advice, it is wise, for it is given by one who is infallible; but it is more than advice, it is the command
of one who has authority to govern, the right to
judge, and the power to punish. He who instituted
marriage, has thus laid down the law, as to the principles on which it is to be conducted. Pious young
persons are here commended to unite themselves
only with those who appear to be partakers of similar dispositions An infraction of this law is followed
with many evils.

It offends others : it discourages ministers, grieves
the church, and is a stumbling block to the weak.
It is a source of inexpressible regret to parents.
"And Esau was forty years old when he took to
wife Judith, the daughter of Beeri the Hittite, and
Bashemath, the daughter of Elon the Hittite, which
were a grief of mind unto Isaac and Rebekah ;" and
Rebekah said to Isaac, " I am weary of my life, because of the daughters of Heth : if Jacob take a
wife of the daughters of Heth, such as these who are
of the daughters of the land, what good shall my
life do me ?" This is deeply affecting, and it is but
the feeling of every truly Christian parent concerning his children when they act as Esau did.

But consider the influence of an unsuitable connection on *yourselves.* We all need helps, not hin-
derances to heaven. Our personal religion requires
props to keep it up, not weights to drag it down. In

this case, not to be helped is to be hindered. The constant companionship of an irreligious husband, or wife, must be most injurious. The example is always near,—it is the example of one we love, and which has on that account the greater power over us. Affection is assimilating : it is easy to imitate, difficult to oppose those we love. Your own religion is put in awful peril daily. But if you should escape *unhurt*, still what *sorrow* will such an association produce. What a dreadful, heart-rending idea, to love and live with those from whom you fear you shall be separated forever; to be moving hourly to a point, when you shall be torn from each other for eternity. How sweet the consciousness which lives in the bosom of a pious couple, that if separated to-morrow, they have an eternity to spend together in heaven; but the reverse of these feelings will be yours, if you marry not " in the Lord."

Besides, how many interruptions to conjugal felicity will you experience. Dissimilarity of taste, even in lesser matters, sometimes proves a great bar to happiness. Between those who are so nearly related, and so constantly together, there should be as great a likeness of disposition as possible. But to be unlike in the most momentous of all concerns, in an affair of perpetual recurrence ! Is this the way to be happy ? Will the strongest affection surmount this obstacle ? or ought the experiment to be made ?

And then, *think on the influence it will have on all your domestic arrangements*, on your servants. and especially on YOUR CHILDREN, should you have

any.   You will be left alone, and perhaps coun-
teracted in the great business of family religion.
Your plans may be thwarted, your instructions neglected, and your influence opposed.   Your offspring,
partaking of the evil nature common to their species,
are much more likely to follow the worldly example
than the spiritual one.

*The Scripture is replete with instances of the evil
resulting from the neglect of religious marriages.*
This was the sin which filled the old world with
wickedness, and prepared it for the deluge.   Some
of Lot's daughters married in Sodom, and perished
in its overthrow.   Ishmael and Esau married irreligious persons, and were both rejected and turned
persecutors.   The first captivity of the Jews, after
their settlement in the Holy Land, is ascribed to
this cause.*   What did David suffer from this evil?
The case of Solomon is a warning to all ages.   This
was the sin that Ezra and Nehemiah so grievously lamented, so sharply reproved.

But I need not go to Scripture for instances of
this nature: they stand thick all around us.   What
misery, what irregularities, what wickedness, have I
seen, or known to exist in some families, where the
parents were divided on the subject of religion.

Young people often attempt to persuade themselves on very insufficient grounds, that the objects
of their regard *are* pious.   They evade the law of
God by considering them as *hopeful, inquiring.*
But are they decided?   In some cases they wish

* Judges, iii.

them to enter into church fellowship, as a kind of proof that they are godly. At other times they believe that, although their friends be not quite decided in their religious character, yet, by being united with *them*, they will become so. But are we to do evil, that good may come ? Is marriage to be considered one of the means of grace ? It is much more probable that such a connection will do injury to the pious party, than good to the unconverted one. I have seen the experiment often tried, but scarcely ever succeed, of marrying an unregenerate person with the hope of converting him. Dr. Doddridge says, he never knew *one* instance in which this end was gained.

I do not mean to say that religion, though indispensable, *is the only pre-requisite* in the individual to whom you should unite yourselves. Temper, age, rank, mind, ability to preside over domestic cares, should all be taken into the account. Many, when expostulated with on their being about to form an unsuitable connection, have replied, " O he is a very good man, and what more would you have ?" Many things ; a good disposition, industrious habits, a prob· ability of supporting a family, a suitableness of age and station, a congeniality of general taste. To marry a person *without* piety, is sinful ; to marry *for* piety *alone*, is foolish.

Again I entreat you to recollect that the marriage union is for life ; and, if it be badly formed, is an evil from which there is no refuge but the grave, no cure but in death. An unsuitable connection, as soon as it is found to be so, throws a gloom, not merely over some particular periods of your time, and portions of your history, but over the whole : it raises a dark and wide-spreading cloud, which extends over the whole horizon of a man's prospect, and behind which he sees the sun of his prosperity go down forever while it is yet noon. It is a subject on which the most delicate reserve, the most prudent caution, and the most fervent prayer, are indispensably necessary. It is not, as it is too frequently thought and treated, a mere sportive topic to enliven discourse with, or an enchanted ground for the imagination to rove in, or an object for a sentimental mind to court and dally with : it is a serious business, inasmuch as the happiness of many is concerned in it ; their happiness not for a part of their lives, but for the whole of it ; not for time only, but for eternity. And, therefore, although I would not surround the altar with scare-crows, nor invest it with shades as deep as those of the sepulchre, which men are more afraid than eager to approach ; so neither would I adorn it with the garlands of folly till I have rendered it as frivolous as the ball-room, where men and women are paired for the dance with no regard to congeniality of mind, with no reference to future happiness, and no object but amusement.*

* I recommend all young persons of true piety, who are in circumstances to need instruction on the subject of this chapter, to read Mr. Jay's Essay on Marriage, to which I am indebted for several remarks. See also Jeremy Taylor's exquisitely beautiful Sermon, entitled, The Marriage Ring.

XXIV.

Keeping in view the great end of Life.

NEVER was there a more rational, or a more important question proposed for the consideration of the human understanding, than that which stands first in the Assembly's Catechism, "What is man's chief end?" This, I say, is a most rational, and a most important inquiry; for every thinking being should certainly ask himself, "What is the great end of my existence? I find myself in a world where innumerable objects present themselves to my notice, each soliciting my heart, and each claiming to be most worthy of its supreme regards. I have faculties of mind capable of high pursuits. I perceive, by universal experience, that my stay in this world will be very short, for I am only a stranger and a sojourner here upon earth, as all my fathers were; and as I am anxious not to go out of the world without answering the end for which I came into it, I would wish to know the chief purpose for which I exist." Such a reflection is what every one *should* make, but which very few do make. Would they fritter away their lives as they do, on the most contemptible trifles, if they seriously inquired for what purpose their lives were given?

What, then, *is* the CHIEF end of man? You will perceive, I lay all the stress of the inquiry on the adjective; for there are many ends to be kept in view, many purposes to be accomplished, many objects to be sought. We must provide for our own sustenance, and the comfort of our family; we should store our mind with useful knowledge; endeavor to be useful, ornamental, and respectable members of society; and there are many other things which may be lawfully pursued; but we are now considering that ONE GREAT OBJECT, *which is paramount to all others, to which all others must be subservient, and the loss of which* will constitute life, whatever else we might have gained, a lost adventure.

There are five claimants for this high distinction, this supreme rank, in the objects of human pursuit, the pretensions of which shall be separately examined.

RICHES, with peculiar boldness, assert their claims to be " *the one thing needful*," and multitudes practically confess the justice of the demand. Hence, there is no deity whose worshippers are more numerous than Mammon. We see many all round us who are obviously making this world the exclusive object of their solicitude. Wealth is with them the main chance. For this they rise early, and sit up late, eat the bread of carefulness, and drink the water of affliction. This is their language, " I care for nothing if I may but succeed in business, and acquire property. I will endure any fatigue, make any sacrifice, suffer any privation, so that I at last may realize a fortune. It is perfectly evident that beyond this they have neither a wish nor an object. Money, money, money, is their chief good, and the highest end of their existence. God, religion, the soul, salvation, heaven, hell, are as much forgotten as if they were mere fables, and all the energies and anxieties of their soul are concentrated in wealth.

Is this *rational*—to say nothing of religion?

Consider *the uncertainty which attends the pursuit of this object.* FORTUNE has been often described as a capricious goddess, not always bestowing her golden gifts on those, who by their prudence and industry seem most to deserve them. " The race is not always to the swift, nor the battle to the strong." The wisest and most plodding worldling sometimes ends in poverty. And shall we seek *that* as the end of life, which after all we may never gain? Shall we deliberately devote existence to secure that which after all we may *never* secure? How many miserable creatures are going down to the grave, confessing that they have spent their lives in courting fortune, and have scarcely obtained a smile, while others, who have hardly asked a favor, have been loaded with them. Poor creatures! they may say in reference to the world, what Cardinal Wolsey did in reference to his king, " Had I served God with half the zeal that I have served Mammon, he would not now have forsaken me in my old age."

But even granting that the end is secured, *do*

riches bring all the pleasures in their train which they promise? It is a very trite remark, that a man's happiness is not in proportion to his wealth. " A man's life," said Christ, " consisteth not in the abundance of things which he hath ;" and yet many act as if they denied the truth of the sentiment. Do you think that all rich men are happy, and that all poor men are miserable ? As to mere animal enjoyment, does the affluent man receive a larger share than his poor neighbor ? Whose head acheth less for the costly plume that waves on the brow ? Whose body enjoys the glow of health more for the rich velvet which enwraps it, or the lace which adorns it ? Whose sleep is sounder because it is enjoyed on down ? Whose palate is more pleased because it is fed with many dishes instead of one, and from silver instead of delf ? Whose rest is more pleasant be-because it is taken upon rose-wood and chintz ? Whose bosom is more free from pain because of the diamond which sparkles there ? Do riches multiply the number of the senses, and give other inlets of sensation to the soul, or increase the power of those we already possess ? Do they add to the just and natural appetites, or afford greater gratifications to those we already feel ? Do they insure health, keep off disease ? Nothing of the kind. Numerous servants, splendid equipages, rich furniture, luxurious living, are in the amount of a man's happiness, but as the small dust of the balance. We may say of these things as Pliny did of the pyramids of Egypt, " They are only proud proclamations of that wealth

and abundance which their possessor knew not how
to use."

Care is the shadow of possession, and the magnitude of the shadow will always be in proportion to
the dimensions of the substance., Great wealth certainly makes a man many anxieties. What shall I
do ? is a question often asked by affluence, as well
as by penury. There is nothing in earthly things
suited as a portion to the desires of the human
mind. The soul of man needs something better for
its provision than wealth. It is on this account,
partly, that our Lord brands the rich man in the
gospel for a fool, who, when he surveyed his treasures, said to his *soul,* " Thou hast goods laid up for
many years in store ; eat, drink, and be merry." " A
fool indeed," said Bishop Hopkins, " to reckon his
soul's goods by barns full. He might as wisely
have boasted that he had provided barns full of
thoughts for his *body,* as barns full of *corn* for his
soul."

Then *how precarious is the continuance of riches.*
They appear to us a sin a dream ; they come and
are gone ; they stand by us in the form of a golden
image, high in stature, and deeply founded on a rock ;
but while we look at them they are tranformed into
an eagle with wings, and when we are preparing to
embrace them, they fly away. What changes have
we witnessed even within our own circles of observation. How many do we know, now suffering want,
who formerly rolled in affluence ! They set out in
life in the full sunshine of prosperity, but the storm

overtook them, and blasted every comfort they had in the world.

But if riches continue to the end of life, *how uncertain is life itself.* How often do we see persons called away by death in the very midst of their prosperity. Just when they have most reasons to desire to live, then they must die. Their industry has been successful, their desires after wealth have been gratified, they build houses, plant gardens, and when preparing for many years of ease and enjoyment, they quit all—for the SEPULCHRE ; and then, whose shall those things be which they have amassed ? " It is recorded of Saladin, the Saracen conqueror, that after he had subdued Egypt, passed the Euphrates, and conquered cities without number; after he had retaken Jerusalem, and performed exploits almost more than human, in those wars which superstition had stirred up for the recovery of the Holy Land ; he finished his life in the performance of an action that ought to be transmitted to the most distant posterity. A moment before he uttered his last sigh, he called the herald who had carried his banners before him in all his battles ; he commanded him to fasten to the top of a lance, the shroud in which the dying prince was soon to be buried. " Go," said he, " carry this lance, unfurl this banner, and while you lift up this standard, proclaim, This, this is all that remains to Saladin the Great, the Conqueror, and the King of the Empire, of all his glory !" Yes, and that piece of crape in which his perishing remains shall be enwrapped, is all that will be left of his wealth to the rich man when he quits the present world. Not one step will his riches go with him beyond the grave. What a sad parting will that be when the soul shall leave all its treasures behind in this world, and enter upon another state of existence, whither it cannot take a farthing, and where it would be useless if it could take it all. Then the miserable spirit, like a shipwrecked merchant, thrown on some strange coast after the loss of all his property, shall be cast on the shore of eternity, without one single comfort to relieve its pressing and everlasting necessities.

Can *riches* then substantiate their claims to be the chief end of man ? What, when it is so doubtful whether, after all our endeavors, we shall possess them; when the possession of them contributes so little to our real felicity ; when their continuance is so uncertain; their duration so short; their influence upon our eternal destiny worse than nothing ? Will any reasonable creature have the folly to assert that the chief end for which God sent him into this world is to amass property, to build a splendid house, and to store it with furniture equally splendid, to wear costly clothes, and feed on rich viands ; to live in affluence, and die rich ?

The next pretender to the distinction of being the supreme good, and man's chief object of pursuit, is PLEASURE. To this many have devoted their lives; some are living for the sports of the field, others for the gratification of the appetites, others for the enjoyment of the round of fashionable amusements.

Pleasure, in one form or other, is the object of pursuit with myriads. As to the gratification of our animal appetites, few will think it necessary to have much to persuade them that to sink to the level of the brute creation, and hold communion with swine, and goats, and cormorants, cannot be the chief end of a rational being. Who would not be ashamed to say, and even deliberately to think, they were sent into the world to consume so much property; to devour the produce of so many men's labor ; to eat and drink away the little residue of wit and reason they have left ; to mingle with this *high* and *distinguished employment*, their impure and scurrilous jests, that they may befriend one another in proving themselves to be yet of human race, by this almost only remaining demonstration of it, that they can laugh as well as eat and drink. Surely, surely, that cannot be the chief end of man which sensualizes, brutalizes his nature ; which drowns his reason, undermines his health, shortens his life, hurries him to the grave. And then, as to what are called *the pleasures of the field*, will any man say that God sent him into the world to ride after dogs, to run after birds, or torture fishes upon a hook ? Are all the high faculties of the soul to be wasted, all the precious moments of life to be consumed, in trying how many foxes, hares, pheasants, and trout, we can kill ; and then to spend all the time we can redeem from this converse *with* brutes, in making ourselves such ?

Fashionable amusements seem to be with many the end of life. Multitudes live for pleasures of this kind. Ball succeeds to concert; the private rout to the public assembly; the card party to the dinner party; and in this busy round of fashionable follies does the life of many pass away. Can it then be the high object of existence to sing, and play, and dress and dance? Do not these things, when we reflect upon them, look more like the pursuits of butterflies and grasshoppers, and canary birds, than of rational creatures? Is it not melancholy to see beings with faculties that fit them, if rightly improved to converse with philosophers, with angels, with God, sinking to the amusements of children; and employing time as if it were given them for nothing but mirth; and using the world as if it were created by God only to be a sort of play-ground or tennis-court for its inhabitants?

Does this kind of life satisfy those who pursue it? Far, very far, from it. Can any person, in reality, be farther from happiness than they who live for pleasure? You shall hear the testimony of a man who will be admitted by all to be no incompetent judge: I mean Lord Chesterfield. The world was the god of his idolatry, he tendered his service to act as high priest for this divinity, published its liturgy, and conducted its ceremonial. What happiness he found in the worship of his deity, and how far he recommends others to the shrine, you shall learn from his own pen; and by the way, this language furnishes the most powerful antidote that was ever published to the poison contained in his trumpery volumes.

" I have run," says the man of the world, " the
silly rounds of business and pleasure, and have done
with them all.   I have enjoyed all the pleasures of
the world, and consequently know their futility, and
do not regret their loss.   I appraise them at their
real value, which is, in truth, very low ; whereas
those that have not experienced, always overrate
them.   They only see their gay outside, and are
dazzled with the glare.   But I have been behind the
scenes.   I have seen all the coarse pullies and dirty
ropes, which exhibit and move the gaudy machines ;
and I have seen and smelt the tallow candles, which
illumine the whole decoration, to the astonishment
and admiration of an ignorant audience.   When I
reflect back upon what I have seen, what I have
heard, and what I have done, I can hardly persuade
myself that all that frivolous hurry, and bustle, and
pleasure of the world, had any reality ; but I look
upon all that has passed as one of those romantic
dreams which opium commonly occasions ; and I do
by no means desire to repeat the nauseous dose for
the sake of the fugitive dream.   Shall I tell you that
I bear this melancholy situation with that merito-
rious constancy and resignation which most people
boast of?   No ; for I really cannot help it.   I bear
it—because I must bear it, whether I will or no.   I
think of nothing but of killing time the best way I
can, now that he is become my enemy.   It is my resolution to sleep in the carriage during the remainder of the journey."

Poor, wretched, forlorn Chesterfield, and was it

thus thou didst close thy career? Is it thus that the worldling, in his last moments, feels and acts, looking back upon the past with disgust, and forward to the future with despair? Then, O God, in thy mercy, " deliver me from the men of this world, who have their portion in this life."

" When a Christian priest," says Bishop Horne, in alluding to the case of this nobleman, " speaks slightingly of the world, he is supposed to do it in the way of his profession, and to decry, through envy, the pleasures he is forbidden to taste. But here I think you have the testimony of a witness every way competent. No one ever knew the world better, or enjoyed more of its favors than this nobleman. Yet you see in how poor, abject, and wretched a condition, at the time when he most wanted help and comfort, the world left him, and he left the world. The sentences above cited from him, compose, in my humble opinion, the most striking and affecting sermon on the subject ever yet preached to mankind. My younger friends, lay them up in your minds, and write them on the tables of your hearts; take them into life with you; they will prove an excellent preservative against temptation. When you have duly considered them, and the character of him by whom they were uttered, you shall compare them, if you please, with the words of another person, who took his leave of the world in a very different manner. ' I am now ready to be offered, and the time of my departure is at hand. I have fought a good fight, I have finished my

course, I have kept the faith; henceforth there is
laid up for me a crown of righteousness, which the
Lord, the righteous Judge, will give me at that day.'
Say, shall your lot be with the Christian, or the
man of the world; with the apostle, or the libertine?
You will not hesitate a moment; but, in reply to
those who may attempt to seduce you into the paths
of vice and error, honestly and boldly exclaim, every
one of you with Joshua, ' Choose you this day whom
you will serve, but as for me and my house, we will
serve the Lord.' "*

You will also call to remembrance, my dear children, that passage in the Life of Colonel Gardiner,
whose history you have read, or should read, in
which he tells us, that when living in all kinds of
dissipation, and when complimented for the external
gaiety of his demeanor, as the " Happy Rake," he
was in reality so perfectly wretched, and so entirely
disgusted with his mode of living, that, on beholding
the gambols of his dog, he wished he could change
places with the unconscious animal.

* Bishop Horne's Sermons.   The works of this author present a beautiful combination of piety, elegance, and pathos.
The introduction of his Commentary on the Psalms is one of
the most delicious morsels of composition in the English language; and if the Commentary itself be too systematically
conducted, on the principles of a typical reference to Christ,
which I certainly think it is, yet who is not disposed to consider as venial the sin of being too evangelical?   The man
who wishes to keep alive the flame of piety in his soul, will
find no inconsiderable help from Horne on the Psalms, and
Leighton on Peter.

Is *pleasure* then the chief end of life? Yes, in Dr. Doddridge's explanation of it, in his beautiful epigram on his own motto—" Dum vivimus vivamus."

> "Live while you live, the epicure will say,
> And take the pleasure of the present day:
> Live while you live, the sacred preacher cries,
> And give to God each moment as it flies.
> Lord, in my view, let both united be—
> I live in pleasure when I live to thee."

FAME is with some the great end of life. This is an object which comparatively few can hope to obtain, and therefore for which few contend. Still there are some; and if they were honest, they would tell you that vanity, which is another name for the love of fame, is a passion, which, like the venom of a serpent injected into its own body, tortures itself. The pursuit of fame is attended with a state of mind the most remote from happiness. " When it succeeds, it degenerates into arrogance; when it is disappointed, (and it is often disappointed,) it is exasperated into malignity, and corrupted into envy. In this stage, the vain man commences a determined misanthropist. He detests that excellence which he cannot reach. He lives upon the calamities of the world; the vices and miseries of mankind are his element and his food. Virtue, talents, and genius are his natural enemies, which he persecutes with instinctive eagerness and unremitting hostility. There are, who doubt the existence of such a disposition; but it

certainly issues out of the dregs of disappointed
vanity; a disease which taints and vitiates the whole
character, wherever it prevails. It forms the heart
to such a profound indifference to the welfare of
others, that whatever appearance he may assume, or
however wide the circles of his seeming virtues may
extend, you will infallibly find the vain man in his
own centre. Attentive only to himself, absorbed in
the contemplations of his own perfections, instead of
feeling tenderness for his fellow-creatures, as members of the same family, as beings with whom he is
destined to act, to suffer, and to sympathize; he considers life as a stage on which he is acting a part,
and mankind in no other light than spectators.
Whether he smiles or frowns; whether his path is
adorned with the rays of beneficence, or his steps are
dyed in blood; an attention to self is the spring of
every movement, and the motive to which every action is referred."*   When therefore we consider that
perpetual restlessness of mind, that mortification,
arising from disappointed hopes; that envy, which
is granted by the success of competitors, that feverish
excitement, which is kept up by the intense desire
of victory; the love of fame will appear too torturing a state of mind to be the end of man's existence;
it is plunging into a kind of purgatory for the *mere
chance* of reaching a celestial summit.

Should the effort to gain distinction *be successful,*

* Mr. Hall's Sermon on Modern Infidelity; one of the most
eloquent and conclusive pieces of argumentation in the English language.

will it then *reward the pains that have been expended
to gain it ?* We have a striking illustration of the
emptiness of the rewards of fame, in the memoirs
of HENRY MARTYN. He tells us that after a severe
contest with many distinguished competitors, for the
prize of being Senior Wrangler, the highest mathe-
matical honor which the University of Cambridge
can bestow upon its students, the palm was awarded
to *him ;* and having received it, he exclaims, " *I was
astonished to find what a shadow I had grasped.*"
Perhaps there never yet was a candidate for fame,
whatever was the particular object for which he contended, who did not feel the same disappointment.
The reward of FAME may be compared to the garlands in the Olympic games, which began to wither
the moment they were grasped by the hand, or worn
upon the brow, of the victor.

How often do we see the aspirants to a place in
the Temple of Fame cut off by death; some, just
when they have begun the difficult ascent, others
when half way up the hill, and a few when they have
gained the summit, and tread upon the threshold of
the sacred fane. A traveller thinks to gain immortal renown by tracing the unknown course of a river,
laying open a new continent, discovering a new
island, or describing the remains of ancient States;
but dies like Cook, or Mungo Park, or Tweddle, or
Bowditch, in the very midst of his discoveries. A
warrior enters upon a military or naval life, and
hopes to gather his laurels on the ensanguined field
of conflict ; and falling, like Wolfe or Nelson, in the

33*

hour of victory, receives the crown upon his bier,
instead of his brow; and leaves his monument, in
lieu of himself, to receive the tribute of his country's
praise.   The scholar and the philosopher pursue
some new object of science or literature, and hope,
by their success, to gain a niche for their shrine in
the Temple of Fame: just as they have established
their theory, and are about to receive their honor,
they are removed, by death, to a world where the
rewards of talent have no place, and where virtue
constitutes the sole distinction.

Those distinctions which now excite the desires,
and inflame the ambition of so many ardent minds;
which absorb the time, the energies, the interest, the
health of their impassioned admirers and eager pur-
suers, are all of the earth, earthly : all terminate with
the present world, and in reference to the eternal
destiny of their possessors, have not the place of an
atom, nor the weight of a feather.   In the admiration and gratitude and applause of their fellow-creatures; in the records of the journalist, the biogra-
pher, and the historian; in the acknowledgments of
the present generation, and the remembrance of posterity, the envied individuals have their reward; but
if they possessed not true piety, in these things alone
their object terminates.   "Verily, verily I say unto
you, they have their reward;" but the smile of an
approving God, the hope of eternal life, the possession of everlasting happiness, is no part of it.   The
star of their glory is amongst the number, which, at
the last day, shall fall from the heavens, and set in

the blackness of darkness forever. The astonishing
works of SHAKSPEARE, BACON, NEWTON, MILTON,
LOCKE, which have surrounded their authors with
such a radiant crown on earth, will not be mentioned
in the judgment; nor procure so much consideration
as a cup of cold water, that was given to a disciple
of Christ out of love to his Master.

What is earthly renown to a man that is in eternity? if he is in heaven, the praises of the whole
globe cannot add one jot to his felicity; if he be in
hell, they lessen not one pang of his misery: he is
in either case unconscious of all—inaccessible to all.
To a lost soul in prison, who had sunk to perdition
under a weight of earthly honors, what a dreadful
sting must such a reflection as this give to all his
sufferings! " Alas! Alas! while my memory is
almost idolized on earth, I am tormented in this
flame."

KNOWLEDGE presents itself to some as the end of
life. To store up ideas, to amass intellectual treasures is the end and delight of their existence; they
are never satisfied with what they know, and are
always seeking for something which they do not
know. They are literary misers. They labor in
the world of mind. These, I admit, are far more
rational than the others, in selecting *their* chief end
of existence. But still *they* are far from wisdom.
The wisest of men has told us, " I gave my heart to
seek and search out by wisdom, concerning all things
that are done under the sun. I communed with
mine own heart; lo, I have gotten more wisdom

than all they that have been before me in Jerusalem : yea, my heart had great experience of wisdom
and knowledge.   I perceive that this also is vexation of spirit : for in much wisdom is much grief ;
and he that increaseth knowledge increaseth sorrow.
Of making many books there is no end ; and much
study is a weariness of the flesh." Will knowledge
comfort its possessors amidst the ills of life ?   Will
it soothe them in the agonies of death ?   Will it
avail them at the day of judgment ?   However it
may dignify and delight them on earth, will it entitle
them to heaven, or prepare them for its bliss ?   No,
no.   Knowledge alone will raise no man to the celestial city in which God dwells.   It may elevate
them to earth's pinnacle, but will leave them at an
infinite distance from heaven's threshold.   It may lift
them high above the scorn and contempt of men below, but still leave them all exposed to the wrath
and curse of God from above   There is something
ineffably dreadful in anticipating the loss of *any*
human soul ; but the sense of agony is increased,
when we think of the eternal ruin of a mind, which
had accumulated all the stores of the most varied
knowledge ; it is painful to see the least and lowest
spark of intelligence fluttering to extinction over the
marshes of sensuality ; but it is most painful to see
one of the highest order of intelligences, darting,
like a falling star, into the blackness and darkness
of eternal night.   It is dreadful to follow such a
spirit into the unseen world, and to behold, in imagination, the meaner damned, whom he spurned on

earth as a vulgar herd, taking up against him the ancient taunt, " Art thou also become like unto us ?" " How art thou fallen, O Lucifer, son of the morning."

DOMESTIC COMFORT is with many the chief, the only end of life. They aspire not to riches, they pace not the giddy round of pleasure, they have no ambition for fame, they have no taste for science or learning ; to marry happily and live comfortably, in moderate competency, is the limit of their prospects and pursuits. And is this all ? *This* the *chief* end of life ! Consider, much that has been said of riches will apply to this Although you seek it, it is uncertain whether you will succeed. Should you gain your object, how soon it may be taken from you again. Your trade may be ruined, the partner of your joys and sorrows may be removed by death, your health may be impaired ; if none of these things happen, you yourself may be removed to another world, when the one you now inhabit may appear most enchanting ; or if spared to old age in undiminished enjoyment, how dreadful is the thought of going from a state of such comfort, to another, in which not a ray of peace will ever fall upon the spirit through everlasting ages.

None of these things which I have mentioned, therefore, are worthy to be the objects of our *supreme solicitude*, or *ultimate pursuit*. They may be all taken up as inferior and subordinate objects. We may in moderation, and by honest industry, not only endeavor to obtain a competency, but even affluence; we are allowed to desire to seek a comfortable settlement in the world: we may enjoy, in measure, the lawful pleasures of life; we may endeavor, if our motives are right, to establish our reputation, not only for virtue, but for talents: we may, to the widest extent, pursue our researches after knowledge: all this is allowed not only by reason, but by revelation. Religion is not the enemy of one single excellence of the human character, nor opposed to any of the lawful possessions of the present world.

But the question to be decided is, *What is the* CHIEF *end of man?* Now the definition which I would give of this is as follows: " It must be an object suited to the nature of man as a rational creature; an object which, if sought in a right manner, shall with absolute certainty be obtained; which shall not interfere with any of the necessary duties of the present state; which, when obtained, shall not only please but satisfy the mind; which shall prepare us for our eternal state of existence, and accompany us to the unseen world as our portion forever." All these things must enter into the chief good, the great end of life, the ultimate object of pursuit. There is but one thing in the universe to which this will apply, and to that one, it will in all parts of the definition most strictly apply, and this is THE SALVATION OF THE SOUL.

You are immortal creatures, lost sinners, capable of enjoying eternal happiness, yet exposed to the sufferings of eternal death; and what can be the

chief end of an immortal being short of ETERNAL
LIFE? Once admit that you are going on to eternity, and it would be idiotism to deny that anything
less than eternal happiness should be your great aim.
The Assembly's Catechism has defined the chief end
of man to be, " *To glorify God and enjoy him forever.*" This is strictly true, and accords with what
I have said ; for to glorify God is to believe in Jesus
Christ for the salvation of the soul ; and under the
influence of this faith, to live soberly, righteously,
and godly, in this present evil world ; and thus glorifying God on earth, we shall be taken to enjoy him
forever in that state of ineffable felicity which he hath
prepared for them that love him. The salvation of
the soul is a good which suits our rational nature ;
it is absolutely certain to those who seek it in the
right way : it rather insures than interrupts all the
other duties of life : it satisfies and delights the mind,
giving consolation under its troubles, and content-
ment to its desires ; it fits us for our eternal state,
and goes with us to glory as our portion forever.

But there are few who deny this in theory, although they neglect it in practice, and therefore I
must now exhort you *to keep this end of life constantly in view.* Every man, when he sets out on
a journey or pursuit, should have a definite object,
and constantly keep it in view. My dear children,
you are setting out on the journey of life, you know
the chief object of that journey, and now, ever keep it
before your mind. Let this conviction not only be
written on your understanding, like a picture delin-

eated on ice, or an impression produced on the snow, which thaws beneath the next sun; but be engraven on your heart, like characters on a rock, which nothing can efface,—that YOUR MAIN BUSINESS ON EARTH IS TO OBTAIN THE SALVATION OF YOUR IMMORTAL SOUL. Let this conviction lie at the bottom of your whole character let it be thoroughly wrought into the contexture of all your mental habits,—let it be the main wheel·in the whole machinery of your conduct.　It is recorded of a pilgrim on his way to Jerusalem, that in passing through Constantinople, when that city was in its glory, he met with a friend, who, wishing to detain him in the eastern metropolis, took him about to see the beauties of that celebrated place. "Very splendid," exclaimed the pilgrim, "but this is not the holy city." So should we say to everything which would limit and detain our hearts on earth, "Very good in its place, but it is not salvation."

Often inquire of yourselves, and examine your hearts, whether you are keeping in mind this one thing needful.　At the close of every division of your time, of your years, your months, your weeks, ask yourselves the question, "Is my eye upon the supreme summit of Christian desire and expectation, or am I beginning to lower my aim, and sink my pursuit ?"

Regulate all your feelings of admiration and pity, in reference to the conduct and situations of others by this object.　If you see the rich man accumulating wealth, the scholar increasing the stores of learning, the philosopher adding to the discoveries of science, the man of martial or literary renown gathering laurels to decorate his brow, but, at the same time, neglecting the claims, and despising the blessings of religion, view them rather as objects of pity, than of envy ; and rank them among the individuals who are losing sight of the great end of a rational creature's existence. On the other hand, wherever you perceive an individual, however obscure in station, limited in acquirements, or afflicted in his circumstances, but who is yet glorifying God, and preparing to enjoy him forever, there realize a character who is keeping before him the great end for which God sent him into this world, and who is fairly entitled to your warmest congratulations.

Keep this in view in the selection of situations and the formation of connections. Are you going out into life ?—accept of no situation, however advantageous in a worldly point of view it may appear, where you are likely to be cut off from the means of grace, and the helps to a life of faith and holiness ; bring the rule of life to it, and ask, Will it help or hinder me in the pursuit of salvation ? Let this direct you in choosing the place of worship you attend, and the minister you hear. Inquire not where the people of fashion go, or who is the most eloquent preacher, but where the most instructive, awakening, and improving ministry of the word is to be enjoyed ; and where you are likely to be kept most steadily in the pursuit of eternal life. In the profession of your religion, dwell most on the plain, and obvious, and important truths of the gospel, such as are most intimately connected with the life of piety in the heart; and turn not aside to novelties, speculations, and religious curiosities. In selecting your avocation in life, keep this in mind, and if there be any calling which, in your judgment, necessarily takes off the mind from religion, choose another in preference. In accepting or selecting a companion for life, let not this subject be put out of view, but consider how much you will be assisted or opposed in seeking eternal salvation, according as your nearest earthly friend shall be one with you in Christ. In pitching your tabernacle, inquire not only what is the air, the prospect, the facilities for trade or pleasure; but what are the means of grace, the helps to religion, the ministry of the word, the company, in the neighborhood. In short, let it appear in all you do, that *the salvation of your soul is* THE ONE THING NEEDFUL, THE CHIEF BUSINESS OF LIFE.

Act, in reference to eternal salvation and the affairs of this life, as a man, who most tenderly loves and ardently longs for his home, does upon his journey, in reference to that home; he provides as comfortable an inn as he can honestly obtain, he enjoys the prospects which present themselves to his eye, he is pleased with the company he meets with on the road, he gains as much knowledge as he can accumulate by the way, he performs the duties of his calling as diligently, and secures as much profit as he equitably can, but still his eye and his heart are at home; for his comfort there, and not his

pleasure abroad, he is *supremely* anxious ; so far as he
can promote, or not hinder his prosperity at home,
he is willing to gain knowledge, to take pleasure, to
secure respect abroad ; but HOME is his great object; to reach that and prepare for its increasing
comfort, is his aim and his hope.

So act, my children, towards *the salvation of the
soul.* THIS, THIS is the end of life ; keep it constantly in mind; never lose sight of it. Gain all
the knowledge, all the comfort, all the fame, all the
wealth, you can, in subordination to this *one great
business ;* but remember that whatever subordinate
ends you *may* pursue, the paramount object which
you *must* seek, is to GLORIFY GOD AND ENJOY HIM
FOREVER.

XXV.

The Meeting of a Pious Family in Heaven.

THE strength of our social feelings, and the pleasure which we derive from the indulgence of them, have very naturally originated the question, "Will those who were known to each other on earth, renew their acquaintance in heaven?" The feelings which prompted the question, have led us to answer it in the affirmative. It might, indeed, be enough to satisfy our hopes in reference to eternal happiness, to be assured that nothing shall be present which could operate as an alloy, nothing be absent that shall be felt as a defect. We know that the manifold wisdom of God is employed under the impulse of infinite love, in *preparing* a place for us; and we are also assured that God " is not ashamed to be called our God, because he hath prepared for us a city." All that is most essential to a state of perfect and everlasting felicity is exhibited and promised in the word of God, the beatific vision of God and the Lamb; complete resemblance in body and soul to the Lord Jesus, the light of perfect knowledge; the purity of perfect holiness; the glow

of perfect love; the external exclusion of sin and of
the sinner; the company and converse of the spirits
of just men made perfect, and the myriads of holy
angels; the absence of pain and sickness, care and
labor, sorrow and sighing, death and the curse; all of
which are explicitly assured to the believer in the
gospel of Christ; these form a heaven which might
entirely satisfy us, as a state of felicity seemingly
incapable of addition. This is glory, honor, immortality, and eternal life. And, yet, in view of all this, our
social nature often prompts that one me question,
"Shall we know each other in the celestial world?"

The scripture, I admit, has not, in so many words,
replied to the question, nor relieved the solicitude
which asks it; and in this very reserve, we see a proof
of the wisdom of God. Had the scriptures been explicit and diffuse on such topics; had they said much
about the social intercourse of the unseen world;
had they represented its felicity as arising in a great
degree from the renewal of those friendships which
were formed on earth but suspended by death, how
many would have concluded, in the total absence
of all religious feeling from their hearts, that *they*
were meet for such an inheritance as this. Whereas,
the Bible, by representing no part of the happiness
of heaven but that which arises from sources
strictly devotional, has given no countenance to
delusion, nor furnished occasion for self-deception.
None of the splendid visions which lie behind
the veil are manifested, but such as tend to impress

us with the conviction that, in order to behold and enjoy them, we must be holy even as God is holy.

These considerations, while they account for the reserve which is maintained by the Scripture on this subject, do not, by any means, disprove the sentiment. Though I would not say with Iraenaeus, one of the earliest fathers of the church, that separate souls retain the likeness and figure of their bodies, so that they may still be known thereby in the other world, though I by no means pretend even to speculate on the precise manner or means whereby glorified immortals will attain a knowledge of each other, whether by revelation or information, by any resemblance being left one newly raised body, to what they formerly were, or by that intuition which will, no doubt, be the way in which many things will be known, yet still I think that , in some way or other, this knowledge will be obtained.

1. The enjoyments and occupations of heaven are uniformly represented as social; but where is the charm of society without mutual knowledge.

2. Heaven is uniformly represented as perfecting all our faculties; is it then probable that it will diminish *memory*, one of the most important of them? And if memory be still retained in full vigor, and if it be perpetually employed, as it inevitably must be, on the past scenes of our earthly existence, is it likely that the friends and companions of that existence, inhaling then the same celestial world with us, will be unknown to us?

3. The chief grace that will be increased in the

regions of the blest, next to love to God, will be
love to our companions in glory. But will not one
of the most pure, elevated, and delightful exercises of this holy passion be wanting, if we are ignorant of our glorified relatives ?

4. In the general judgment, which is appointed to
vindicate the ways of God to man, it is nearly certain that individuals will be known to each other ;
and if this be the case, is it likely that their mutual
knowledge will be immediately obliterated ?

5. Is it likely that individuals, whose names and
labors bear such a close and extensive connection
with the redemption and history of the church, as
those of the prophets and apostles, will be unknown ?
And if *they* are known, may it not be inferred that
others will be?

6. During our Saviour's abode upon earth, he af-
forded to the three favored disciples a glimpse of
the heavenly glory ; he himself was transfigured, and
Moses and *Elias* descended in celestial brilliancy.
These two eminent servants of God were known by
the astonished apostles ; and if known on Mount
Tabor, is it not likely they will be known in the
New Jerusalem ?

7. Our Saviour, in one of the most impressive of
his parables, represents the rich man in torments, as
knowing Lazarus and Abraham in glory ; now
though it be a parable, and though the *whole* scenery
of a parable is not to be considered as conveying
some moral sentiment, yet certainly nothing materially and obviously at variance with the truth is ever

taught by even the appendages of the chief parabolic idea.

8. We find the apostle Paul very frequently consoling himself under the sufferings and persecutions which he had to endure, by the prospect of meeting in heaven those who had been converted by his ministry on earth. His address to the believing Thessalonians is especially in point. "What is our hope, or joy, or crown of rejoicing? Are not even ye in the presence of our Lord Jesus Christ, at his coming?" I do not see how these Christians could be Paul's crown of rejoicing in that day, if they were not known to him.

These are some of the reasons which led me to suppose, that in heaven the saints will know each other.

I am aware that it is felt by some as an objection to this sentiment, that if we shall know those of our friends who were present in glory, we shall, of course, know if any of our relatives are absent; and that, if we derive pleasure from the former consideration, we shall experience as much distress from the latter. The only way of solving this difficulty is, to suppose that as a perfect knowledge of the Divine Being, and of the wisdom of all his schemes and operations, will constitute a chief part of the happiness of heaven, we shall be so convinced of the equity of his dealings towards the wicked, so divested of all the weakness of the passions, so absorbed in the love of what is right to be done, that our bliss will experience no interruption in the absence of our relatives from the world of glory. This, I acknowledge, is now hard to conceive. The day shall declare it.

Assuming then the fact, that saints will know each other in the celestial state, let us imagine, my dear children, if indeed the imagination is equal to the effort, what must be the joy attendant on the final meeting of a pious family in heaven. One of the most exquisite delights which we ever experience on earth, is the enjoyment which springs from the first interview with a friend, from whom we have been separated ; and this delight is in proportion to the length of time, and greatness of distance, and magnitude of danger, which have intervened between the separation and the meeting. What language can describe the thrill of transport, the almost agony of rapture which the wife experiences in that moment, when she receives a husband back again to her arms who has been away from home for months, who has been separated from her by half the circumference of the globe, and threatened to be torn away from her forever, by the dangers of shipwreck or of battle ? Or who shall set forth that scene of domestic bliss, which is exhibited when the sailor boy, after having been absent for years, returns from the dangers of the sea, and the horrors of captivity, to the bosom of his family, and exchanges ecstatic greetings with his parents, and his sisters, and his brothers, till all seem ready to dissolve with excess of joy ? What then must be the meeting of these same relatives in heaven, after having been separated by worlds and ages; that meeting, when the mother receives her children to the skies, from this degenerate earth; and the father hails his offspring from the world of death, to the region of life and immortality! Here imagination confesses its weakness. It is a scene we have never witnessed ourselves; nor have we ever conversed with one who has. My heart, while I write, seems to beat quicker at the thought; and the very anticipation, my dear children, raises a commotion of pleasurable feelings in my bosom, which no words could enable me to express

Then remember this meeting is not for a *mere transient interview*, but for an eternal association. It is to take place in a world, where adieus and farewells are a sound unknown. What an interruption does it now form to the enjoyment of domestic intercourse, that the different branches of the family cannot always live beneath the same roof, or in the vicinity of their parents. One member after another goes from the paternal abode, and settles at a distance, till counties and perhaps kingdoms separate them from each other. Rarely does it happen, where the children are numerous, and grown to maturity, that they can all meet together. Occasionally this does happen, perhaps on a parent's birth-day, or at the festive season of the year, and then home puts puts forth all its charms, and pours out in copious streams its pure and precious joys; such a circle is the resort of peace and love, where friends and near relations mingle into bliss. The parents look with ineffable delight upon their children, and their children's children, and see their smiles of love reflected from the faces of the happy group. Piety gives the finishing touch to the picture, when, ere they part, they assemble round the domestic altar, and after reading in that Book, which speaks of the many mansions in our Father's house above, where the families of the righteous meet to part no more ; and after blending their voices in a sacred song of praise to Him, who hath united them, both by ties of nature and of grace, they receive the benedictions, and join in the prayers of their saintly and patriarchal father, who over the scene that surrounds him feels a divided heart, one moment thinking he has lived long enough in that he has been permitted to witness it, but the next breathing an aspiration to heaven for permission to witness it a few years longer.

This scene, and it is not an uncommon one, is one of the purest to be found on earth. It is, as nearly as it can be, paradise restored ! or if it be, as it certainly is, still without the gates of Eden, it is near enough to the sacred enclosure, to receive some of the fruits which drop over the wall. What is wanting here ? I answer, Continuance. It is bliss only for a season. It is a day that will be followed with a night. And the heart is often checked in the full tide of enjoyment, in the very meridian of its delights, by looking at the clock, and counting how rapidly the hours of felicity are rolling away, and how soon the signal of parting will be struck. But the meeting in heaven shall be eternal. The family shall go no more out forever from the mansion of their Father above. Their interview shall not be measured nor limited by time. They shall meet for one day, but then that day will be everlasting, for " there is no night there." They shall spend eternal ages together. Neither the fear nor the thought of parting, shall ever pass like a cloud over the orb of their felicity, nor let fall a passing shadow to disturb the sunshine of their breast. " We are met," shall they say one to another, " and we shall part no more. Around us is glory, within us is rapture, before us is eternity."

Then add to this, *the happy circumstances under which they meet,* and in which they will dwell together forever.

They will meet as *spirits of just men made perfect.* The best-regulated families on earth will sometimes experience little interruptions of their domestic enjoyment. We all have some imperfection or other, some infirmity of temper, or some impropriety of manner, from which, through want of caution on one part, or want of forbearance on the other, occasional discords will be heard to disturb the harmony of the whole. We *see* that others are not altogether perfect, and we *feel* that we are not so We lament the failings of the rest, and still more lament our own. This prevents perfect domestic bliss, but in heaven we shall all be perfect. We shall see nothing in others to censure : feel nothing in ourselves to lament. We shall have all that veneration and love for each other, which shall arise from the mutual perception of unsinning holiness. We shall mutually see reflected the image of God from our character. There will be everything lovely to attract esteem, and the most perfect love to show it. Every one will possess the virtue which is loved, and the complacency by which it is beloved. Every one, conscious of unmingled purity within, approves and loves himself for that divine image, which in complete perfection, and with untarnished resemblance, is stamped upon his character. Each, in every view which he casts around him, beholds the same glory shining and brightening in the circle of his parents, his brothers, and his sisters. Out of this character grows a series ever varying, ever improving, of all the possible communications of beneficence, fitted in every instance only to interchange and increase the happiness of all. In the sunshine of infinite complacence, the light of the New Jerusalem, the original source of all their own beauty, life, and joy, this happy family will walk forever.*

The joy of that meeting will arise from seeing each other in the possession of all that happiness which God hath prepared for them that love him. In a family where genuine affection prevails, the happiness of one branch is the happiness of the rest and each has his felicity multiplied by as many times as there are happy members in the circle. In heaven, where love is perfect, how exquisite will be the bliss of each, arising from being the constant witness of the bliss of all: where the parents will

* See Dwight's Sermon on Brotherly Love.

see the children basking in the sunshine of divine
love; receiving the warmest expressions of the favor of Christ: shining in the beauties of unsullied
holiness; and bounding in the fields of uncreated
light; and where the children shall see the parents,
and each other, in the same happy circumstances;
where each shall see all the rest in the full possession
of the inheritance incorruptible, undefiled, and that
fadeth not away: the exceeding great and eternal
weight of glory.

How, amidst all this unrevealed and inconceivable
splendor, will the joy be increased *by a recollection
and enumeration of the benefits-conferred by one
party, and the obligations incurred by the other.*
What must be the delight of parents in thus seeing
the fruit of their prayers, instructions and anxieties,
constantly before their eyes, in the honor and felicity of their glorified children. How happy and
grateful will they feel, that their solicitude on earth
was chiefly exercised in reference to the spiritual
and eternal welfare of their offspring, and not wasted
upon trifles which had no connection with piety and
immortality!

With what thrilling emotions of delight will they
hear these children ascribing all their salvation, so
far as instruments are concerned, to them; and giving a high place in their anthems of praise, to the
names of their father and mother. While, on the
other hand, it will raise the felicity of the children
to the highest pitch, to see those parents near them,
to whom they owe, under God, their possession of

heaven. With what mutual interest will both parties retrace the winding ways of Providence, which
led to such a termination of the journey of life. How
will they pause and wonder at those mysterious
links, now invisible, but then plainly seen, which
connected the events of their history, and united
them into one perfect whole. Especially, with what
intense excitement will they mark each effort of parental anxiety for the salvation of the children, and
see the individual and collective results of all. The
revolutions of empires, the fate of armies, will then
have less to engage and charm the attention, than
the influence of any one piece of advice which was
ever delivered on earth, and which had the smallest
influence in impressing the heart, awakening the
conscience, converting the soul, or forming the character.

What felicity will arise from the *sublime converse
and employment of such a state.* Conceive of a
family even on earth, where of all the numerous
branches of which it is composed, each one for dignity was a prince, for science a philosopher, for affection a brother, for purity a saint, for meekness a
child, all meeting in sublime and affectionate discourse; all employed in exploring together the secrets of nature, and tracing the streams of knowledge; blending, as they proceeded, the ardor of love
with the light of truth. But this, what is it, to the
heavenly state, where with minds inconceivably more
capacious than that of NEWTON's, when he weighed
the gravity, and measured the distance of the stars;

with hearts perfect in holiness ; and ages endless as eternity ; we shall converse on all the highest themes which the universe can supply. Think of studying together the laws of creation, the history of all God's providential dealings with mankind, the wonderful scheme of human redemption, the character of the great Jehovah, the person of Jesus Christ, with all that stands connected with the whole range of universal being, and the manifestation of the First Cause. What a view does it give us of the felicity of heaven, to think of parents and children engaged with millions all around them, in sounding the depth of that ocean of eternal truth, which is as clear as it is deep ; and eternally employed in acts of worship, exercises of benevolence, and other pleasurable pursuits, now unknown, because unrevealed ; and perhaps unrevealed, because not comprehensible by our present limited faculties.

But after all, my dear children, I seem as if I were guilty of presumption in thus attempting to describe that which is quite inconceivable. It doth not yet appear what we shall be. We now see through a glass darkly. The Scriptures tell us much of the heavenly state ; but they leave much untold. They give us enough to employ our faith, raise our most lively hopes, and produce a joy unspeakable, and full of glory ; but they offer nothing to satisfy our curiosity. " They bring before us a dim transparency, on the other side of which the images of an obscure magnificence dazzle indistinctly upon the eye ; and tell us, that in the economy of redemption, and the provisions of immortality, there is a grandeur commensurate to all that is known of the other works and purposes of the Eternal. They offer us no details, and man, who ought not to attempt a wisdom above that which is written, should be cautious how he puts forth his hand to the drapery of the impenetrable curtain which God, in his mysterious wisdom, has spread over that region, of which it is but a very small portion that can be known to us."

In this state, amidst all this glory, honor, and felicity, it is my sincere desire, my ardent prayer, my constant endeavor, my supreme pursuit, that your journey, my dear children, and my own, should terminate. Everything else appears, in comparison of this, as nothing. In the view of this, thrones lose their elevation, crowns their splendor, riches their value, and fame its glory ; before the effulgence and magnitude of celestial objects, *their* grandeur dwindles to an invisible point, and their brightness is but as the shadow of death. Did we not know the depravity of our nature, and that the natural man knoweth not these things, because they are spiritually discerned, we must indeed wonder, and inquire what bewildering influence it is, that is exerted on the human mind, by which its attention is so fatally diverted from things unseen and eternal to the shadowy and evanescent forms of things seen and temporal. It is only on this ground that we can account for the folly, the madness, of neglecting the great salvation, and seeking anything in preference to

35*

eternal glory. Dreadful madness ! which, though it
indulges in the miscalculations of insanity, has none
of its excuses. What but this moral insanity could
lead men for any object upon earth, to neglect the
pursuit, and resign the hope of eternal life?

My children! my children! whom I love with
an affection which can be equalled only by that solicitude for your welfare to which it has given rise,
and which never sleeps nor rests, receive my admonition, and make eternal happiness the end of your
existence. Look at that heaven, which, though but
partially revealed, is revealed with such pure brightness on the page of eternal truth, and " on the description of which, so to speak, the Holy Ghost employs
and exhausts the whole force and splendor of inspi-
ration ;" look at it, that state of inconceivable, infinite, eternal honor, and bliss, and is there aught on
earth, aught of pleasure or of gain, for which you
will deliberately resign that crown of unfading
glory.

I am anxious, as I have already informed you,
that you may live in comfort and respectability on
earth. I would have your mind cultivated by learning and science ; your manners polished by complaisance ; your industry crowned with success ; in
short, I should be thankful to see you living in comfort, respected, and respectable ; but above everything else, I pray, I desire, I long that you may
partake of " that faith, without which it is impossible to please God ;" and that " holiness, without

which no man shall see the Lord." I have fixed my aim for you, high as heaven; and covet for you everlasting life. I love your society on earth, and wish to enjoy it through eternity in the presence of God. I hope I am travelling to that goodly land, of which God hath said, he will give it to us for an inheritance, and I want you to accompany me thither. Reduce me not to the mere consolation of David, who said, " Although *my house* be not so with God, yet hath he made with *me* an everlasting covenant, which is ordered in all things and sure." Rather let me have to say with Joshua, " As for me, *and my house*, we will serve the Lord."

May it be granted me to see you choosing the way of wisdom and piety, and remembering your Creator in the days of your youth : giving to all your virtues that stability and beauty which can be derived only from religion ; first receiving by faith, and then adorning by holiness, the doctrine of God your Saviour.—Then will my highest ambition, as a parent, be gratified, my most painful solicitude relieved. I shall watch your progress amidst the vicissitudes of life, with a calm and tranquil mind, assured that your piety will be your protector amidst the dangers of prosperity ; or your comforter amidst the ills of adversity. If called to follow your bier, and weep upon your sepulchre, I shall only consider you as sent forward on the road, to await my arrival at our Father's house, or if called, according to the order of nature, to go down first into the dark valley of the shadow of death, I shall find the agonies of separation assuaged, and the gloom of the dying chamber irradiated by those bright visions of glory, which connect themselves with the prospect OF THE MEETING OF A PIOUS FAMILY IN THE HEAVENLY WORLD.

THE END.